From Medieval Pilgrimage
to Religious Tourism

Recent Titles in
Religion in the Age of Transformation

From Medieval Pilgrimage
to Religious Tourism

The Social and
Cultural Economics of Piety

*Edited by William H. Swatos, Jr.
and Luigi Tomasi*

Religion in the Age of Transformation
Anson Shupe, Series Adviser

Westport, Connecticut
London

Library of Congress Cataloging-in-Publication Data

From medieval pilgrimage to religious tourism : the social and cultural economics of
   piety / edited by William H. Swatos, Jr. and Luigi Tomasi.
      p. cm.—(Religion in the age of transformation, ISSN 1087–2388)
   Includes bibliographical references and index.
   ISBN 0–275–97384–0 (alk. paper)
   1. Pilgrims and pilgrimages—Congresses. I. Swatos, William H. II. Tomasi,
Luigi. III. Series.
BL619.P5F76 2002
291.3'51—dc21   2001051170

British Library Cataloguing in Publication Data is available.

Library of Congress Catalog Card Number: 2001051170
ISBN: 0–275–97384–0
ISSN: 1087–2388

First published in 2002

Praeger Publishers, 88 Post Road West, Westport, CT 06881
An imprint of Greenwood Publishing Group, Inc.
www.praeger.com

Printed in the United States of America

The paper used in this book complies with the
Permanent Paper Standard issued by the National
Information Standards Organization (Z39.48–1984).

10 9 8 7 6 5 4 3 2 1

For Monica as she begins life's pilgrimage

Contents

Illustrations

Preface

This book has its origins in a conference entitled "From Medieval Pilgrimage to the Religious Tourism of the Twentieth Century" hosted by the Center for Euroasian Studies (ACSA), held at the University of Trento, under the direction of Luigi Tomasi, in October 1999, after which it seemed worthwhile to bring together some of the presentations that were made there for publication. We also wanted to invite other scholars to make contributions that would broaden the focus of the volume. Happily for us at least some of those to whom we turned were able to add significantly to the kernel that we had extracted from the conference.

Thanks to Judith Adler's work—which has already had something of a *samizdat* existence among students of pilgrimage—we have been able to reach "behind" the medieval period, widely thought and taught in the West to be the "beginning" of pilgrimage, to a Christian heritage that preceded it. Her work provides a scholarly complement to the fine work of William Dalrymple, *From the Holy Mountain*, which retraces the journey of John Moschos at the turn of the seventh century among the monasteries of the fast-fading Christian East. At the other end of the spectrum, Richard Quinney's reflections upon his own pilgrimage attempt to Nepal, on the one hand, and changes going on in his own life, on the other hand, help to raise to our consciousness the deeply personal and multifaceted character of all decisions to search for something we have not yet experienced.

Through the chapters as a whole, we have tried to lift up and critique facile assumptions about both "pilgrimage" and "tourism." It is certainly not our contention that "nothing has changed" across the last fifteen hundred or more years, but at the same time, we want to suggest that there are constants and variables that continue to work back and forth between each other, creating new forms of expression and experience that we must engage reflectively. When people say they are "making a pilgrimage to Graceland," for example, we need to seek to understand what they mean and what that means for them. Similarly, when someone in, for example, Chartres cathedral says, "Oh, I'm just a tourist," what does that mean? The word "tourist" is obviously new. It would not have been said, in 1400. But might it not have had an equivalent—"Oh, I'm just a workman" or "I'm just a washerwoman"—that would have had its own impact on "pilgrimage sites" and times that we now have a tendency to romanticize into a golden Age of Faith, when "everyone" was deeply religious? What has changed and what has stayed the same? Why? What difference does it make? These are some of the things upon which we hope you will reflect as you assess these chapters.

Regrettably, serious illness prevented Professor Tomasi from working on this volume in its final stages. Hence I have had to take responsibility not only for this preface but for organizing the final collection of chapters, making various technical decisions, and so on. I am grateful to our editor, Suzanne Staszak-Silva, for her tolerance as the process has ground along and to our contributors for their patience. The weeks I spent in Trentino over the past year I will never forget as they were among the most pleasant in my own pilgrimage. I hope that what I have done to complete this work is fitting return on the initial investment that was his.

William H. Swatos, Jr.

Chapter 1

Homo Viator: *From Pilgrimage to Religious Tourism via the Journey*

Luigi Tomasi

It is the intention of this chapter to examine a topic hitherto neglected by sociology: namely, the journey as part of an ideal trajectory between pilgrimage and religious tourism. This is a theme, both old and new, which today lends itself to objective and detailed analysis.

The *homo viator*—a figure who features in all cultures and civilizations—is a person constantly on a journey in search of what was the *supernatural* in the past and is now the *cultural-exotic*, but also the *sacred*. The desire to travel in order to satisfy the need to know both mundane reality and celestial mystery is an impulse that has constantly driven humankind. As Victor and Edith Turner point out: "pilgrimages are probably of ancient origin and they were to be found even among populations that anthropologists call 'tribal,' like the Huicol, the Lunda, and the Shona. But institutionalized pilgrimage became of real importance with the advent of the great religions: Hinduism, Buddhism, Judaism, Christianity, and Islam."[1] Pilgrimage therefore originated in a desire to travel that was already manifest, albeit in noninstitutional forms, in primitive societies, subsequently in ancient ones, then in modern ones, and finally in the current societal condition of late modernity.[2]

The members of all societies have interrogated nature and sought to communicate with the divinity manifest therein. This interrogation is not easy, nor can it be taken for granted; on the contrary, it is a laborious endeavor because it is a search for knowledge, and the acquisition of knowledge re-

Photo 1. Sanctuary of San Romedio, Val di Non, Trentino, Italy. *Luigi Tomasi.*

quires sacrifice. And it is an interrogation whose features and form have changed with the passage of time.

This chapter will seek to demonstrate the importance of pilgrimage, and the evolution that it has undergone in the course of the centuries. It is not a historical survey; rather, its purpose is to show how human travel and its approach to the sacred have changed with the social context, and how the latter is today profoundly different from what it used to be when the first traveling societies arose.

PILGRIMAGE

Pilgrimage can be defined as a journey undertaken for religious purposes that culminates in a visit to a place considered to be the site or manifestation of the supernatural—a place where it is easier to obtain divine help. In the past especially (but also to some extent today), pilgrimage was an option available to all members of society: it could be undertaken because it was not constrained by culture or wealth, although this is not to imply that pilgrims were not people of learning and substantial economic means; the typical image of the pilgrim, however, is that of "a poor wayfarer who travels on foot."[3]

Pilgrimage has also been validly described as "an individual, but more frequently collective, journey toward an 'elsewhere' sometimes more desired than known, and which in certain respects may assume utopian features in the imaginations of those about to undertake it."[4] This definition centers on the pilgrim's desire for salvation and a relationship with the divinity. The pilgrim, in fact, feels compelled to travel to the places most imbued with mystery, those where the meaning of religion is most evident. These are usually the sites of prodigies or places where the sense of the sacred can be replenished, and where the pilgrim may seek blessing, forgiveness or healing—as evinced by the *ex-votos* testifying to graces bestowed. The Crusades, too, can be considered a form of pilgrimage, albeit a peculiar one: a form of *armed pilgrimage* undertaken to protect the holy places of the East.[5]

There are places of pilgrimage frequented by believers who belong to a single religion, just as there are ones visited by pilgrims belonging to a variety of religions. Perhaps the most exemplary case is Jerusalem, which in tiquity was already a celebrated site of Jewish pilgrimage and co (as it still does today) the spiritual center of the people of Isr᾽ amples are the tomb of St. Francis Xavier in Goa or A᷂ Lanka, both of which attract Christian, Hindu, and Musli᷑

While different forms of pilgrimage are to be found in all religions, both ancient and recent, centers of pilgrimage have been known since antiquity. They existed, for example, in the Hellenic civilizations. Delphi, where the Pythia issued her oracles, was the holiest place in Greece, and was visited by numerous pilgrims seeking to approach the sacred.[6] But there were other, minor shrines to which pilgrims traveled to propitiate the gods or to ask for grace or healing, most notably Delos, Pergamum, and Epidaurus, as well as the centers of mystery cults: the rites celebrated at Eleusias in Attica, for example, were attended by huge numbers of people from Athens and other Hellenic cities. Nor should one forget the sacred cosmology of ancient Egypt.[7]

Pilgrimage in Western Christendom

But when one speaks of pilgrimage, it is mainly the Middle Ages that one has in mind, with its religious atmosphere of *sic transit gloria mundi* and the man who "never attributed capital importance to his pleasures."[8] This concept, which obviously belongs to the past, induces us to reflect on a time profoundly different from our own, a time when the sacred was more widespread in society. The Middle Ages was a period pervaded by a profound sense of the religious and one in which the pilgrim had his own particular status, "a sort of privileged, almost ecclesiastical, status."[9]

The Middle Ages saw the creation of a system of itineraries followed by pilgrims as they traveled to the most important of the sanctuaries: the holy places of Jerusalem, the tombs of Peter and Paul in Rome, Santiago de Compostela, and others.[10] Pilgrimage constituted a form of *itinerant devotion* that began in Western Christendom in the seventh century and reached its apogee in the twelfth and thirteenth centuries with the formation of a *sanctuarial network* that gave rise to a "new, more concrete and geographically more variegated European sacredness."[11] This also came about because salvation was an obsession during the Middle Ages, and the undertaking of a pilgrimage was to make a major investment in eternal life.

However, to complete the panorama and to contextualize the phenomenon of pilgrimage, it should be noted that, as early as the third century, numerous Christians were convinced that living in the world and evangelical ideals were incompatible: thus, "at the beginning of the fifth century there were around seven hundred monasteries established in the area between Jerusalem and the southern frontier of the Byzantine empire."[12] Cenobites and anchorites constituted a network of prayer and sanctity; the desert had become an *inhabited* desert. Oursel writes that "examination of Merovingian and Carolingian maps . . . shows a network much more extensive than one might suppose, a tight and surprising crisscrossing of *viae publicae*, many of which could not have been much more than beaten earth . . . but which marked the boundaries of lands and fields and were censused as such in the deeds."[13] The extent to which the sanctuary network, European and Roman, had developed is described by Genoveffa Palumbo and Thomas Szabò in two significant works.[14]

It should be added that the period following the year 1000 saw a rural renewal, a revival of commerce, and a certain stabilization of society that had positive repercussions on religious life—which became more organized—and they were accompanied by renewed intellectual ferment. It was in this context that once again impetus was given to the *spirituality of the journey*, the most classic instance of which was indubitably the one to Compostela. As Oursel observes: "thus forged was a true spirituality of the journey, constituted of denial and resignation, and indifference to the enticements of the journey, where the pilgrim sought and found the sacred itinerary of the dolorous *via crucis* made also by the solidarity which united under the same burden and with the same needs all the pilgrims bound for infinite horizons."[15]

The journey was hard and dangerous, and the pilgrim was subject to the canonical discipline of the Church, though protected as a person of moral worth. One may rightly affirm that the road system of the age largely served to link sanctuaries, hospices, and hospitals—which also provided the pilgrim with a certain degree of safety during the journey. Testifying to this endeavor are the numerous small sanctuaries and chapels still found along many of Europe's roadsides. These places are a sign of the past, the mark of those who passed by, in groups or singly, those who sought to become "new men"—those, in short, who had set off in search of sanctity:

In the Middle Ages, as testified by the narratives of Felix Fabri and Pietro Casale, it was the usual practice for pilgrims to travel in organized groups in caravans or ships. Pilgrimages were part of the Church's system of salvation, which was willing to absolve impenitent sinners as long as they visited a distant holy shrine. Kings and important personages developed a taste for pilgrimage and traveled the pilgrim routes with vast retinues.[16]

From the eleventh century onward, the Christian reconquest of Spain, urged by the Cluniac monks, gave origin to the pilgrimage to Santiago de Compostela: famous in this regard is the *Guide du Pélerin de Saint-Jacques de Compostelle*.[17] "The true golden age of Galician pilgrimage," write Pierre Barret and Jean-Noel Gurgand, "was between the 1110s and the 1140s. Departing from every part of Europe, where they left their hovels behind, thousands of pilgrims abandoned everything to take the road to Santiago.

Many of them returned invigorated and purified by the experience; but many died, for the journey was long and perilous."[18] A pilgrimage was equivalent to a "civil death"—for some temporary, for others permanent. For this reason medieval law stated that the pilgrim, God's wayfarer, should be considered dead when a year and a day had passed since news had last been had of him—which is indicative of how dangerous pilgrimage was at the time. The flow of pilgrims, however, began to dwindle in the sixteenth century. Compostela was not to take the place of Rome and Jerusalem; rather, it flanked them, constituting a further pole of attraction to the sacred, while in the course of time other places of pilgrimage of lesser importance sprang up around holy relics or places of supernatural apparitions. Numerous localities grew famous from the mercies, healings, and miracles attributed to them, and this development prompted a flow of pilgrims to such places: "the sanctuary became at once a source of spiritual energies and a pole of miraculous potentialities."[19] At the same time, piety began to shift from the tomb of the saint to the place in which his or her relics were kept.

A distinction gradually emerged between small and large pilgrimages; the former were local and the latter were international in character. Minor places of pilgrimage appeared along the itineraries connecting the most important, and by now famous, centers: these were sanctuaries dedicated to the Virgin Mary—Pompeii in Italy, for example—or to the Archangel Gabriel, like Mont-Saint-Michel in Normandy.[20] The geographical spread of sanctuaries was matched by an increase in the number of pilgrims, and places of worship proliferated in concomitance. In this regard, Turner and Turner write: "The pilgrim's way crossed the boundaries of provinces, kingdoms and even empires. . . . In every nascent nation, certain shrines became the pre-eminent centers of legitimate worship. With the Church's aspiration to universality, pilgrims were encouraged to pick up their staves and knapsacks and set off for the great sanctuaries in other Christian lands."[21]

The traffic of pilgrims intensified to such an extent that in Venice,

in June 1392 . . . the *Maggior Consiglio* intervened to ensure the seaworthiness of the ships used to transport them. It had happened that certain unscrupulous shipowners had adapted antiquated vessels without observing the minimum standards of safety. As a consequence, the authorities ordered that ships used to transport pilgrims should be inspected by public officials who could authorize, or otherwise, their departure.[22]

With time, however, the routes to the East were rendered dangerous by invasions, and the flow of pilgrims shifted toward safer destinations, one of which was Rome. A close relationship consequently developed between the *places* of faith and the *ways* of faith. It was in this context that the Catholic church, on behalf of Pope Boniface VIII, institutionalized pilgrimage by proclaiming the Jubilee and organizing it with the intention of reviving pilgrimage to Rome, thereby redirecting a significant quantity of pilgrims who had previously traveled elsewhere. Simultaneously, because the Church regarded itself to be the legitimate dispenser of the spiritual and ethical capital accumulated by Christ, it distributed that capital in the form of indulgences to the repentant faithful, who were absolved of their sins by the sacrament of confession. This was to be a constant feature of all subsequent Jubilees.[23]

The pilgrim of the Middle Ages had been legitimated by the social context of the time, a society in which the sacred was forcefully present and exerted its own fascination. The search for salvation was indubitably more widespread than it is today. It sprang from the individual, although it was at the same time a social event.

The decision to take part in a pilgrimage was an individual one, but it joined the pilgrim with kindred souls driven by the same impulse whom he met on the road and at the sanctuary. The social dimension was generated by individual choice, which multiplied many times. During the pilgrimage, social interaction was not governed by the old rules of the social structure. When a system of pilgrimage was instituted, however, it worked together with the other social institutions. Society took precedence over the individual at all levels. The group prepared the journey; prayers at the sanctuary were collective and followed a well-defined program. But the pilgrimage was an individual good work, not a social initiative. Ideally, pilgrimage was charismatic, in the sense that the pilgrim's decision to undertake it was a response to a charism, to a grace, while at the same time he received grace when he said his prayers.[24]

This custom of visiting holy places is also found in non-Christian societies. For example, the Australian aborigines regard as sacred the places where the heads of the clans have accomplished heroic feats, which are subsequently re-evoked by visitors to those places. In other cultures, for example those of the nomadic peoples of Afghanistan, "seasonal migrations follow ancient routes scattered with tombs at which the nomads halt to pray: these are the tombs of the pious, venerated and sanctified men to whom the nomad addresses a prayer or an invocation, leaving a rag or a stone as a sign of homage and prayer."[25]

One reason for pilgrimage resided in the societal model of the time: "In a society which offered scant economic opportunities to leave one's close circle of friends, neighbors and local authorities tied to the land, the only possible journey for those who were not merchants, peddlers, minstrels, jugglers, acrobats, wandering friars or outlaws was a holy journey, a pilgrimage or a crusade."[26]

This desire for pilgrimage was also prompted by the haunting presence of *death* in the medieval age, a presence as certain as its hour of coming was unpredictable. This desire proceeded *pari passu* with the yearning for salvation: "in the Middle Ages, pilgrims did not form groups solely for reasons of safety or for pleasure: at that time, the collective soul seems to have been even stronger than the individual one."[27]

The medieval pilgrim was less terrified by the death of the body, with its constant possibility in epidemics, famine, the devastations of war, and the brevity itself of life, than by spiritual death, and specifically by the threat of hellfire—a reality ever present in the medieval age. The extent to which the death of the body was a constant reality is evinced by St. Francis of Assisi in the *Canticle of the Sun*: "Praised be the Lord for this, the death of our body from which no man may escape."

It was undoubtedly thought in the Middle Ages, as it is today among Catholic peasants, that illness was a temporal punishment and that recovery from illness was an indicator of the remission of sins. For this reason, pilgrimage to a holy shrine, where a plenary indulgence could be obtained, was considered to be a journey toward a source of healing, like a therapeutic journey. Illness was something more than a medical problem, it was a moral problem. The sanctuaries of pilgrimage were, and are, the doctors of the poor.[28]

Of the various types of pilgrimage, the penitential form—including the "tariff-based" pilgrimage that established an expiation for every sin—assumed particular importance.[29]

As early as the eighth century, the Irish monastic authors had prescribed that pilgrimage should be both a spiritual exercise and a penitence—the *peregrinatio penitentialis*—in the conviction that penitence in this life reduced punishment in the next world. In the eleventh century, European civil law, under the influence of the Church in the form of the Inquisition, established a range of destinations for pilgrims according to the sins to be expiated. Pilgrimage was deemed able to revitalize faith in those suspected of heresy, and it was made more painful by the attachment of chains to the pilgrim's arms or legs according to the gravity of the offence committed. In the case of murderers, indeed, the weapon used for their crime was hung round their necks as a public admission of guilt. These types of pilgrims rarely found hospitality, and they very soon came to constitute a threat to the safety of citizens. The practice was discontinued in the fourteenth century in order to prevent the roads from being overrun by criminals in the guise of penitents.[30]

The attribution of penitential value to pilgrimage has been pointed out by Franco Ferrarotti: "The religious pilgrimages that constelled the Middle Ages can be viewed as techniques of penitence intended to re-enchant the world. They were ways to live everyday experience in the light of a higher spiritual tension, in an age still very distant from the rationalization of life and in which religious meanings permeated quotidian reality."[31]

Pilgrims also found support from the great abbeys, most notably Cluny. As Barret and Gurgand observe, they constituted a heterogeneous group of travelers: "mingled with the penitents were the maniacs, the deranged, the frenetics. In the thirteenth century the latter were recognizable by their harsh laughter, their gnashing teeth and, when they were examined, 'by the pounding of their pulse, the clarity of their urine.' They should not be confused with the victims of demoniac possession, who sometimes behaved in the same way."[32] Pilgrims exerted great impact on medieval society, and at the same time they played an important role in determining the opening of roads, the building of hospitals, the promotion of markets, and the development of society in general.

On the other hand, however, the interweaving of the sacred and the profane, which was typical of the Middle Ages, meant that roads and maritime routes were also populated with pilgrims by proxy, false pilgrims, and people who traveled for the purposes of folklore. In these cases, the motives for pilgrimage were not properly spiritual, and behavior tended to diversify as a consequence. The material aspects of pilgrimage, in fact, were very apparent in the devotion and religiosity of the age, over which there loomed the popular universe with its now remote but profound pagan roots.

There were, in fact, forms of pilgrimage that we would today call questionable: "pilgrimage by proxy, although quite understandable in certain cases of impediment, very soon became a commodious form of devotion for those who lacked the means."[33] Penitential practices, which inculcated in the pilgrim the idea that earthly life is a journey to the Home of the Father, were not always taken seriously. In certain circumstances, the *status viatoris* could turn into deliberate flight, prompted by other motives. Thus, I fail to agree with Stopani when he writes "one cannot evade the suspicion that in many pilgrims a desire for inner renewal overlapped with other reasons for traveling, ones similar to those that motivate the modern tourist."[34] Seeking to compare the nonreligious mode of travel in the Middle Ages with that typical of the modern tourist is entirely improper because it is difficult to support empirically. As Turner and Turner point out, the religious fervor of the Middle Ages, especially with the Marian pilgrimages, was never transformed into "pure tourism," because the pilgrimage was an instrument of penitence, a prolongation of the sacrament of penance.[35]

In any event, pilgrimage had a series of repercussions on the social system, as Turner and Turner rightly emphasize:

If the Protestant ethic, with its emphasis on hard work, thrift, virtue and moral pro-
bity in the secular vocation of everyone, and with its conviction that one's place in
the world was a sign of faith and of election by God, was really, as Max Weber
thought, a "precondition" (a necessary but not sufficient cause) for capitalism, then
the "pilgrimage ethic," with its emphasis on the "holy journey" and the benefits de-
riving from it, helped to create the networks of communications which subsequently made mercantile and industrial capitalism a vital system at the national and
international level.[36]

Nor should one underestimate the invention of the printing press, which fos-
tered pilgrimage with publication of the travelers' instructions and guidebooks to Rome entitled *Mirabilia*.

This intense flow of pilgrimage dwindled after the sixteenth century,
with the advent of the Reformation, on the one hand, and secular social
problems, on the other, which undermined both the experience of the sacred
and the relationship between the individual and religion.

Pilgrimage and Nature

Any thorough discussion of pilgrimage cannot ignore the role of nature,
and the special importance of mountains—whose peaks, in particular, assumed the significance of nouminous points that were charged with the
meaning of the sacred. Climbing to the summit of a mountain became a pilgrimage, an act of expiation and redemption. "Many rock carvings and
other documents . . . attest to the relatively assiduous frequenting of mountain slopes, when man was still engaged in developing a cultural language
with which to establish contact with the divine, the absolute master of nature and its multiple forces."[37]

The bond between the sacred and nature is a recurrent theme:

Hindu and Buddhist pilgrims travel to the sources of the Ganges and the
Brahmaputra rivers at the foot of Mount Kailasa, the holy mountain, the roof of the
world, whence flow the pure waters that cleanse the men of the lowland floodplains
from their filth and sins. . . . Every year, the Peruvian *indios* undertake long and ex-
hausting pilgrimages to the peaks and glaciers of the Sierra de Vilcanota, carrying a
cross in procession. And in Japan fully three million people every year set off to
climb to the summit of Fujiyama, the holy mountain, the highest peak in the Japanese archipelago. . . . In Nepal, the geography of pilgrimages corresponds to the geography of the country's rivers: the broad valleys that extend into the high
Himalayas are highways which lead directly to important shrines or monasteries.[38]

Another important center of pilgrimage is the Potala in Lhasa, which attracts (or used to attract, before the Chinese invasion) thousands of Tibetans

from every part of the country. There are also other mountain pilgrimage sites: Mount Kailasa, the Himalayas, the Karakoram, Mount Albanus on which stands a shrine to Jupiter, Mount Olympus, and Kun Lun in China. Nor should we forget the role that mountains played at the time of Christ and in the Old Testament.

Mountains have always been places of holiness, and in every age taking to the mountains has been an act replete with religious or mystical-esoteric significance.[39] Humanity has also externalized the sacred character of mountains by placing icons and the statues of gods on their summits. This can be linked

with the theme of elevation reflected in religious architecture. From the menhir to the pyramid, from the ziggurat to the stupa, to the steeples of our churches, the desire to erect a structure able to form a "connection" between earth and heaven is striking. It marks the continuation of an iconographic tradition which makes no concession to symbolism but has instead maintained its profundity since ancient times.[40]

Warranting specific discussion is the role attributed to mountains in Europe, and to the Alps in particular. Still today, on traveling through Europe's mountains, one perceives the signs left by the age of pilgrimages. Traveling as a tourist and no longer as a pilgrim, one still sees the hospices built in the past on the high mountain passes, mainly in the Middle Ages, to accommodate pilgrims crossing the Alps with simple means and scant equipment. "The pilgrims traveled with very little baggage, and any unexpected change of temperature, a thunderstorm or a blizzard could be fatal for those without warm and dry clothing. Added to this was the fact that many pilgrims walked barefoot, either because of poverty or to give greater value to their pilgrimage."[41] Closer examination shows that these hospices have been built on sites where others existed before. Many of them date back to the Roman empire, when "the roads were designed mainly to meet the military and therefore administrative needs of the Empire; they had to ensure the rapidity and safety of communications, of supplies to the armies, and of the collection of taxes."[42]

The historical literature tells us that as early as Roman times there existed places where travelers halted for religious purposes to make offerings, to thank the gods, and so on. Tenderini provides two examples: "On the Great Saint Bernard Pass stands the highest temple enclosure in the entire Empire. The bronze *ex-voto* tablets with their dedications to *Iuppiter Poeninius* indicate the type of traveler who passed that way: soldiers of every rank, merchants, state secretaries and even a slave trader, Helvetius, with his precious wares." Even more significant is the second example:

On the Giulio Pass along the road to Coira, offerings to the gods took the form of coins. . . . The practice of oblation was a common one on all routes, but in particular when the road traversed the mountains. Vows were made before setting off for the pass and then fulfilled when the traveler had surmounted the obstacle and descended to the lowlands again. If the traveler went and returned by the same road, the offering *pro itu et reditu* was made on departure. However, if the pass had a sanctuary, a temple enclosure or an altar, it was there that the traveler thanked the god for the successful ascent and prayed for a clement descent.[43]

The situation under the Roman empire, therefore, was not greatly different from that in the Middle Ages. The only difference consisted in the fact that the holy places along the route were dedicated to pagan divinities, while in the Middle Ages they were places of Christian worship. As Christianity asserted itself, and with its legalization in 313, it gradually superimposed itself on the pagan cults—in some cases becoming hegemonic, in others coexisting with them. There thus came about the same process as when Roman society sought to eliminate the mythic heritage of Etruscan and Mediterranean origin. The Alps became Christian in the fourth and fifth centuries. With the spread of sanctuaries and the proliferation of places of worship in the mountains comprising a variety of shrines, lists of sanctuaries—the *itineraria*—were produced to guide pilgrims, whose numbers had grown to considerable proportions by the fourth century.

The gradual spread of Christianity in the Alps led to the founding of monasteries. From the eighth century onward the most significant of those offering hospitality to wayfarers were the monasteries of Pfafers, St. Gallen, Klais, Mustair, and Mistali and the Abbey of Novalese. The principal alpine passes crossed by pilgrims were Saint Gotthard, Great Saint Bernard, Mont Cenis, Simplon, Gries, and the Grisons, and they were the routes used for pilgrimages for the centuries thereafter. Significant evidence of the religious revival in the alpine valleys is provided by Tenderini: "In 784, Pope Adrian I asked Charlemagne to attend to the restoration of the hospices on the alpine passes in view of the growing number of pilgrims bound for Rome from every part of Europe."[44]

Being of service to pilgrims was regarded as a duty, and as a way to give praise to God. According to the rule of St. Benedict, "hospitality was provided for a maximum of three days, to alleviate the burden on the monasteries, and the guest lodgings were to be separate from the main body of the monastery so that prayers might not be disturbed."[45] When later, in the ninth century, the Benedictine Order split between Cluniac and Cistercian, one issue of dispute was defining the rules on hospitality for pilgrims.

The alpine hospices were generally of small size—as one sees still today—and their services were rudimentary. They took care of the pilgrim and helped him during his stay. The conviction at the time, in fact, was that the more difficult the journey, the more devout one appeared in the eyes of the Lord, and consequently the closer one came to eternal salvation.

Toward the end of the year 1000, the constant expansion of Christianity in the alpine region led (also under the impetus of the millennium) to the founding of numerous new monasteries and hospices along the now customary routes leading to Rome and Santiago de Compostela. It was in this period that the pilgrims were differentiated, externally as well, by the two distinctive symbols of the *cape* and the *staff*.

Medieval pilgrimage—as an individual and social phenomenon typical of a particular historical period and the expression of an equally typical vision of earthly life—reached its apogee in the fourteenth and fifteenth centuries. Thereafter a new age arose—that of the *journey*—which acted as the transitional link between the classical medieval pilgrimage and religious tourism in the modern age.

FROM THE CULTURE OF THE PILGRIMAGE TO THE CULTURE OF THE JOURNEY

Unlike in the Middle Ages, when pilgrimage was conceived mainly in terms of penitence, expiation, purification and redemption, during the postmedieval period the emphasis was on the changes that took place in the person during the journey. While the *destination and faith* were central to the pilgrimage, in the case of the journey it was the *experience* of traveling itself that mattered. One notes the increasingly close interweaving of the culture of the pilgrimage with that of the journey undertaken for other purposes. The great resurgence of mobility in Europe was an indispensable precondition for what subsequently came to be called "religious tourism." The culture of pilgrimage, so dense with values and so intensely experienced, slowly changed in the new social context now emerging.

Eric J. Leed, one of the most outstanding scholars of the journey, writes as follows in the introduction to his well-known study: "This book seeks to answer [this question] . . . by examining the manner in which the journey acted—and continues to act—as a force which transforms individual personalities, mentalities, and social relationships."[46] It should be pointed out in this regard that the journey acquired a rationale in the postmedieval period that would subsequently become that of modernity itself, and that in a certain sense focused on the fulfillment of the person "down here," and on the expression of *personal freedom*. Leed defines its conception as follows: "For the ancients the journey had value in that it explained human fate and necessity, while the moderns extolled it as a manifestation of freedom and as an escape from necessity and purposiveness. The ancients saw the journey as suffering, even as punishment, while for the moderns it was a pleasure and a means to obtain it."[47]

This view takes us a long way from the idea of purification that was typical of the pilgrimage. The journey as a demonstration of freedom and of personal independence became, as Leed points out, the modern *topos*, the meaning itself of modernity. From approximately the beginning of the fifteenth century onward, concomitant rights and desires to travel gradually spread, accompanied by the increasing *pleasure* of the journey, a pleasure unconstrained by the search for salvation, or indeed by any religious purpose.

This change was not sudden; instead it came about very gradually. Yet it was already evident toward the end of the fifteenth century and the beginning of the sixteenth century, when the journey *qua* pilgrimage yielded to the inexorable advance of modern culture. Tenderini makes the same point:

The travelers of the sixteenth century were keen observers of their surroundings. During the Middle Ages, travelers had concentrated on describing the dangers and hardships that they faced, and on the ultimate purpose of the journey, namely reaching the destination, expiating a sin, and demonstrating courage. After the fifteenth century, but in some cases even earlier, travelers began not only to observe the landscape or the customs of the local inhabitants but also to consider the journey as a diversion, so that they would travel purely for the pleasure of traveling.[48]

Other changes took place as well: "Hotels sprang up along the main roads, and thus came to play an ambiguous role in pilgrimage: as places of privileged comfort, mirages to exhausted wayfarers, but also as places of the profane *par excellence*, where there were no lack of temptations and where, above all, nothing was done out of charity."[49]

The cause of this change was a shift in the social climate, the fading of the notion of *sic transit gloria mundi*, and the birth of the "new man," different from his or her predecessor and more inclined to set value on the mundane—the person, in short, who would subsequently be called "modern." Thus born was the *journey* that transformed social identities, a journey that was the fruit of an increasingly mobile society, a journey untrammeled by purely penitential or expiatory ends and oriented to the enhancement of knowledge.

The sixteenth century was a period marked by the large-scale movement of peoples across Europe. There was, moreover, pronounced mobility in the ecclesiastical world, as well as greater rationality among the population. It was this context that bred the Reformation and the assault by Martin Luther on the praxis of indulgences, vows, pilgrimages and fasts. Luther assailed the Catholic church and thereby gave rise to a new form of religiosity.[50] "In that period . . . on the one hand pilgrims became more closely aware of the various holy places passed on their travels; on the other, they were more 'secularly' interested in discovering the world."[51]

This process was part of the new individualism concerned with mundane reality that was so typical of the Renaissance. This was a "new person," with greater self-consciousness, greater confidence in his or her abilities, and a person who traveled. Ideas were exchanged by travelers, so that new religious opinions and political notions circulated.

Those who traveled were no longer the pilgrims blinded by faith, or the merchants with their oriental spices, but scholars, the preachers of the new Protestant religions, the erudites of the newly founded universities. Now the roads were traveled by impressive quantities of goods, less precious than those of previous centuries but more varied, by armies consisting not of knights in shining armor with multi-colored plumes, but of footsoldiers, painters, men of letters, messengers, bankers, women, ambassadors, and functionaries.[52]

In Europe this phenomenon marked the beginning of the Grand Tour—which covered roughly three centuries, from the sixteenth to the eighteenth, and was characterized by pronounced mobility accompanied by an equally marked desire to travel, initially restricted to the wealthier classes but which subsequently spread to the poorer ones as well.[53]

The beginning of the seventeenth century not coincidentally saw publication of the first comprehensive guidebook for those undertaking the continental tour for the purpose of study or pleasure: Fynes Moryson's *Itinerary*, compiled in around 1593 and published in 1618, which interrupted the long series of *libri indulgentiarum*, or guidebooks for pilgrims traveling to the great European sanctuaries or the Holy Land.[54]

During this period, the journey became a course of instruction and education, centered on constant comparison of the known with the unknown, of the familiar with the strange. Travel was now conceived as exploration and research, and travelers were strongly attracted by classical culture: Rome, Venice, and Florence, in fact, were the main stopping places on the Grand Tour: thus was born the "art of traveling."[55]

The travelers who took to the roads of Europe between the seventeenth and nineteenth centuries can be described as a lay pilgrims who followed the ancient routes of knowledge. Their journeys were motivated by modern concerns that had little in common with the *pietas* of the medieval pilgrims, as Palumbo points out: "In the seventeenth and eighteenth centuries, pilgrimages also became journeys undertaken by those interested in 'curiosities' and works of art; indeed, with regard to the pilgrimage to Rome, it was the slow advent of lay and cultural values that furnished not a few Protestant Europeans with ideological justification for traveling to papal Rome; and little by little the cultural journey supplanted the pilgrimage."[56] The journey as exploration and research, which constituted the link between the pilgrimage and modern tourism, involved a varied assortment of travelers (although the majority were merchants) who opened the way for the aristocrats and intellectuals of the seventeenth and eighteenth centuries.

Pilgrimage languished during these two centuries. With the advent of Enlightenment thought, and its faith in science and progress, individuals concerned themselves more with earthly life, pursuing their desire to find happiness in this world, and no longer regarding themselves as travelers in search of something that lay beyond mundane reality. It was not until the second half of the nineteenth century, in fact, that we find a certain revival in pilgrimage, when the sacred forcefully reemerged, notwithstanding the secularization distinctive of modern society—the most notable examples of this process being Lourdes and the Massabielle grotto.

The circulation of ideas during these three centuries was framed by a heterogeneous microcosm in which the concept of "leisure" moved to the fore. The eighteenth century, and the period of the Enlightenment in particular, saw the predominance of a culture anchored in the dictates of reason—a culture, moreover, now growing increasingly cosmopolitan. With the advent of the nineteenth century and the great social change so distinctive of it—although its origins lay in previous centuries—travel not only became even more frequent but it also underwent further change. This was the period of the sentimental traveler, the romantic attracted by the historical and artistic heritage of the countries visited, and especially by the landscape so well described in the diaries and travel books from which the broad and varied genre of *travel literature* sprang.

Although pilgrimage obviously did not disappear during the period, it nonetheless diminished substantially. The flow toward the great centers of pilgrimage continued, but now to a lesser extent because the ethos of society had changed. Priority was given to the material, and the sacred had necessarily to coexist with this newly discovered value. Material fulfillment, the desire to discover, to travel, and to enjoy, was integral to human behavior in the nineteenth century. Yet only in the 1900s can one talk properly of tourism. A series of innovations, among them the travel agency, gave rise to this new form of behavior. Nevertheless, the sense of the religious persisted: the faithful continued to visit the sanctuaries, and the concept of pilgrimage also remained, although it assumed a value different from the past, now being a form of pilgrimage that was a close reflection of modern culture.

In these three centuries the entire territorial fabric of Europe was transformed: religious destinations were joined by cultural ones, and the culture of the pilgrimage of the past was flanked by the culture of the journey for other purposes. Europe thus witnessed the advent of the "aimless journey"—in the sense that the itinerary could vary at will—in contrast to the pilgrimage, which was instead a journey with an aim. The journey was now optional. It was not imposed, and it was the fruit of free choice. The Renaissance had thus ushered in a new phase in the relationship between man and the sacred, a period that would eventually be marked by conflict, especially in the nineteenth century.

There are various factors that can be cited in explanation of the new human/sacred relationship and of the probably diminished influence of the sacred on the individual. After the fifteenth century, society grew increasingly secularized, a phenomenon that became well-nigh universal for a certain period of time. No longer was the sacred feared, as it had been in the Middle Ages. Now it tended to be marginalized. It was no longer sufficient to curtail the sacred: in certain periods there was an endeavor to eliminate it, albeit with scant results. This endeavor was driven by the new sciences, by a greater spirit of criticism, by a search for individual freedom, and to a greater extent by a different conception of "this worldly" reality. The individual of those centuries was about to become modern, that is, with scant respect for traditions, and especially for the religious tradition. A further factor was a craving for knowledge, a desire that was conceived as fostering growth and as being formative of the person. From the sixteenth century onward, social mobility gave rise to a set of social relations that were the precursors of what is today called the "global" or "cosmopolitan" society.[57]

RELIGIOUS TOURISM

This long period of transition concluded with the advent of the 1900s, a century that saw great discoveries in a variety of fields and whose contribution to the birth and growth of tourism was decisive. The man or woman of that century—the modern individual—was the outcome of diverse social processes but principally of industrialization, one of whose most evident results was the birth of tourism, and of religious tourism in particular.

The improvement of road communications and of transport and greater self-awareness, together with increased social influence were the direct causes of tourism as an *industry*. When tourism becomes a business, the tourist industry follows. Probably the main stimulus to the growth of tourism has been the onset of the concept of "free time": the leisure available to increasing numbers of people without immediate and specific obligations and in search of new experiences.[58]

Once again we are confronted by a new type of society—a society that itself generated tourists because it granted the right to free time. The societies of the nineteenth and twentieth centuries created tourism as they produced mobility and sufficient economic means. Sociology—this, too, a product of the nineteenth century—did not immediately take notice of tourism, preoccupied as it was with the analysis of moral issues. It turned its attention to the phenomenon only belatedly, in the second half of the last century, when a sometimes sterile debate began on defining the concept and propounded a number of conflicting theoretical models.

It is not my intention here to join the debate on tourism.[59] Instead, I shall mention three authors whose pioneering works have made a major contribution to interpretation of the phenomenon, although sociology has yet to develop a theory of tourism in the strict sense. Daniel Boorstin's definition of tourism as a pseudoevent, as an ambiguous truth, contrasts with Dean MacCannell's explanation that the tourist is a pilgrim in a lay world who pays homage to the attractions of modernity.[60] Opposing these theories—too closely tied to a globalizing theory to be realistic—is the work of Erik Cohen based on a phenomenology of tourist experiences which assumes that the modern individual seeks authenticity in different ways.[61]

Although a thorough definition of modern tourism is still not forthcoming, one can nevertheless say that the tourist of the last two centuries has profoundly differed from the individual of previous centuries in that he or she has been dedicated to discovery and in search of comfort, "doing tourism" in a manner utterly different from the typical traveler of the past.

There is, therefore, a profound difference between tourism as it has taken shape in the past two centuries and the mode of travel typified by the Grand Tour. It is a difference that originates from the process of modernity and late modernity. What Cohen calls the "transformation of attractions" and "standardization of facilities" have substantially changed the contemporary lifestyle—as exemplified, for example, by the "weekend break" and the "package tour" with their attendant transformation of values and patterns of consumption.

How does the figure of the pilgrim fit into this context of modernity and late modernity? Although it has certainly not disappeared, amid the values of modernity it has once again been compelled to adjust, and to fashion pilgrimage in the strict sense in a different form.

Obviously, as a burgeoning body of analysis has shown, the desire for the sacred is by no means fading, nor has the modern individual's impulse after the Absolute diminished.[62] Nevertheless, new modes of experiencing the sacred are today apparent, and one of them is *religious tourism*. Although sociology lacks a specific theory on religious tourism, the following is perhaps the most complete definition available:

Theory.

Religious tourism is not tourism *tout court*; rather, it is a form of tourism motivated, partly or wholly, by religious motives and closely or loosely connected with holiday-making or with journeys undertaken for social, cultural or political reasons over short or long distances. . . . In Europe, religious tourism usually takes the form of pilgrimages to sanctuaries or shrines, religious festivals, and the "special events" connected with them. There are thus three types of place concerned: the shrines of holy pilgrimage, religious tourist attractions associated with historical or cultural events, and religious festivals.[63]

This type of religious tourism, however, is not exclusive to Christianity; it is also a distinctive feature of the other great religions like Hinduism and Buddhism. Nor is it confined to Europe, being common in America and in Asia, especially in association with religious events of great importance. As regards Catholicism in particular, Rome, Jerusalem and Compostela still attract millions of visitors each year; and in the course of time they have been joined by other sanctuaries, most notably Lourdes in France, Fatima in Portugal, Santo Nino in the Philippines, Sainte-Anne-de-Beaupré in Canada, Czestochowa in Poland, and Guadalupe in Mexico.

Today, therefore, there is no antithesis between the pilgrim and the tourist; there is no contradiction between piety and relaxation. However, the extent of this intermingling of the traditional with the modern is difficult to quantify in empirical terms: it is hard to distinguish the "curious traveler" from the "religious traveler" and to comprehend his or her identity.[64]

To be sure, pilgrimage is no longer a mass phenomenon; the society of late modernity—although it is not a secularized society but rather one in which humanity proves more than ever before to be religious *by nature* (consider the numerous sanctuaries that open every year in various parts of the world, and the proliferation of new religious movements)—is no longer permeated and shaped by the religious spirit typical of the Middle Ages. Moreover, advances in transport systems, the more efficient organization of travel, and improved accommodation facilities at sanctuaries have modified the meaning itself of pilgrimage. And they have also profoundly altered the *social composition* of pilgrims as a group. Today, pilgrims travel in organized groups, according to age, although the individual pilgrimage has not entirely disappeared. A certain resemblance to the medieval pilgrimage is to be found in the organized groups of the sick and bereft that travel in large numbers to sanctuaries in the hope of being healed or finding help.

Apart from organized events like the special trains to Lourdes, modern pilgrims are generally difficult to distinguish from tourists. Significant in this regard is the following observation by Clara Gallini: "as early as the nineteenth century, guidebooks were printed in Lourdes for 'the pilgrim and the tourist,' with a general information section followed by a further section differentiated for each of the two categories of users."[65]

Nor can modern pilgrims be distinguished by the manner in which they dress, or by any distinctive form of behavior. Perhaps the only feature that marks them out from other travelers is the purpose of their journey, their different *inner disposition*. To reverse the comparison, it seems that modern tourists themselves can be considered pilgrims when they set off to visit places of "holy" significance to them, like museums or art galleries.

One may therefore conclude that, while the form of pilgrimage has changed, its meaning is still the same as it was in the past: the typically human desire to seek out the sacred, though what symbolizes or articulates "the sacred" today may be different from the past, even at the same site, and may be multivalenced among the many visitors. However, in contrast to past ages, the concept of penitence has faded, and so too has the hardship of the journey—the physical pain, that is, of actually walking the road. As Ferrarotti puts it: "The journey has been abolished. Now there is only the point of departure and that of arrival."[66]

The trend apparent in late modernity, with its emphasis on the individual, is toward a relationship with the absolute that mixes the sacred with the profane, a relationship that by virtue of the very nature of society cannot be either solely religious or solely profane. Pilgrimage has therefore been compelled to change its form, although its essential core remains the same: reaching the destination to obtain salvation or grace.

To speak of religious tourism is therefore entirely appropriate, and it is so because the individual of late modernity is more fully complete, in the sense that he or she seeks to experience what society has to offer in a more extensive and multidirectional manner. The contemporary completeness of human existence, the fruit of hard endeavor, places the sacred alongside the other mundane aspects of life. There is nothing deplorable in this, however, because *every age has its own mode of relating to the sacred*. Today, the sacred no longer rests on compulsion or on fear of the imminent end of the world. It is for this reason that the pilgrimage of today is so different from, yet so similar to, the pilgrimage of the past.

Indicative of the growth of religious tourism have been the various Jubilees of the twentieth century:

The convenience of modern transport has brought a much larger number of pilgrims to Rome, although perhaps not all of them have been religiously motivated. While in 1900 there were fewer than 400,000 pilgrims, given the influence of the great Jubilees of the past, in 1925 their numbers rose slightly to around 600,000. For the Jubilee of 1950 the number of pilgrims increased to two and a half million, then to 8,700,000 in 1975, and finally reached more than 10,000,000 in 1983, the Holy Year of redemption.[67]

This growth in numbers has been matched by a diversification of interests:

Modern pilgrims not only participate in religious ceremonies, they act as tourists in the most traditional sense of the term. Package deals include tours of the city and visits mounted specially for the Jubilee; in 1925, for example, the missionary exhibition organized by the Holy See attracted thousands of visitors. Sacred art is no longer part of the penitential and religious, but has become the object of aesthetic communication in museums. In 1950 so many pilgrims flocked to the Vatican museums that the police had to be called to control the crowds.[68]

The distinction between pilgrimage driven by faith and tourism for cultural and recreational purposes no longer holds, because contemporary pilgrimages involve such huge numbers of people that they can only be organized in the same manner as mass tourism. Large numbers of pilgrims pass through travel agencies, accommodation facilities, catering services, and commercial businesses; they are, that is to say, part of the tourist industry.

A striking example is provided by the World Youth Rally held in Rome on 20 August 2000 for the Jubilee, which attracted 2.5 million young people. This was indubitably an occasion of faith and prayer, but it was just as certainly an event of religious tourism. The spiritual component was flanked by the human one. Were these young people tourists, Catholics, the curious, holiday-makers, or pilgrims? It is difficult to say. Perhaps they were all of these and more, and all at once. Guides to Rome mixed with prayer books, and the merging of devotion and tourism was evident; the mingling of religion and religious tourism was obvious. The stone used as a pillow, typical of the pilgrim of the past and symbolic of penitence, had given way to the cellular phone, the paramount symbol of comfort in the modern age, and of the tourist-pilgrim of Jubilee 2000. But yet they came.

NOTES

1. Victor Turner and Edith Turner, *Il pellegrinaggio* (Argo: Lecce, 1997), p. 49.

2. See U. Beck, *Risikogesellschaft: Auf dem Weg in eine andere Moderne* (Frankfurt am Main: Suhrkamp, 1986).

3. Carlo Prandi and E. Turri, "Percorsi della salvezza: Variazioni sul tema della salvezza," in *Lungo le vie della fede* (Piazzola sul Brenta: Papergraf, 1999), p. 3; see also G. Pinto, *I costi del pellegrinaggio in Terrasanta nei secoli XIV e XV: Dai resconti dei viaggiatori italiani* (Florence: Alinea Editrice, 1982).

4. Prandi and Turri, "Percorsi della salvezza," p. 3.

5. See A. Dupront, *Du sacré—Croisades et pèlerinages: images et langages* (Paris: Gallimard, 1987).

6. See Maria I. Macioti, *Pellegrinoggi e giubilei: I lugohi del culto* (Rome: Laterza, 2000), pp. 23–45.

7. Ibid., pp. 3–22.

8. Raymond Oursel, *Pellegrini del Medioevo: Gli uomini, le strade, i santuari* (Milan: Jaca, 1997 [1978]), p. 29.

9. R. Stopani, *La Via Francigena: Una strada europea nell'Italia del Medioevo* (Florence: Lettere: 1998), p. 9.

10. See R. Stopani, *La Via Francigena*; *Le vie di pellegrinaggio del Medioevo: Gli itinerari per Roma, Gersalemme, Compostella* (Florence: Lettere, 1995); Genoveffa Palumbo, "La geografia dei pellegrinaggi," *Iternationale Scuola cultura società* 3, no. 7 (2000), pp. 90–99.

11. Palumbo, "La geografia dei pellegrinaggi," p. 92.

12. A. Musacchio, "La religione come donazione di luoghi: Considerazioni dul tema," in *Lungo le vie della fede* (Piazzola sul Brenta: Papergraf, 1999), p. 182.

13. Oursel, *Pellegrini del Medioevo*, p. 51.

14. Genoveffa Palumbo, *Giubileo Giubilei: Pellegrini e pellegrine, riti, santi, immagini per una storia dei sacri itinerari* (Rome: Rai-Eri, 1999); Thomas Szabò, "Le vie per Roma," in *La storia dei giubilei, 1300–1423* (Florence: BNL-Giunti, 1997), pp. 70–89.

15. Oursel, *Pellegrini del Medioevo*, p. 47.

16. Turner and Turner, *Il pellegrinaggio*, p. 72; cf. E. Rizzi, "Ospizi e pellegrini nelle valli Walser," in *Lungo le vie della fede* (Piazzola sul Brenta: Papergraf), pp. 107–116.

17. J. Vieillard, *La Guide du Pélerin de Saint-Jacques de Compostelle* (Paris: Maçon, 1963).

18. Pierre Barret and Jean-Noel Gurgand, *Alla conquista di Compostela* (Casale Monferrato: Piemme, 2000), p. 11.

19. Prandi and Turri, "Percorsi della salvezza," p. 7.

20. Oursel, *Pellegrini del Medioevo*, p. 63.

21. Turner and Turner, *Il pellegrinaggio*, p. 52.

22. G. Ravegnani, "Venezia e gli altri approdi: sulla via marittima dei pellegrinaggi—Il viaggio in Terra Santa di Felix Faber (1483)," in *Lungo le vie della fede* (Piazzola sul Brenta: Papergraf, 1999), p. 166.

23. Lucetta Scaraffia, *Il Giubileo* (Bologna: Mulino, 1999).

24. Turner and Turner, *Il pellegrinaggio*, p. 77.

25. Prandi and Turri, "Percorsi della salvezza," p. 13.

26. Turner and Turner, *Il pellegrinaggio*, p. 53.

27. Barret and Gurgand, *Alla conquista di Compostela*, pp. 14–15.

28. Turner and Turner, *Il pellegrinaggio*, pp. 14–15.

29. Scaraffia, *Il Giubileo*, p. 20.

30. S. Tenderini, *Ospitalità sui passi alpini: Viaggio attraverso le Alpi, da Annibale alla Controriforma* (Torino: Centro Documentazione Alpina, 2000), pp. 97–98.

31. Franco Ferrarotti, *Paritre, tornare: Viaggiatori e pellegrini all fine del millennio* (Rome: Laterza, 1999), p. 52.

32. Barret and Gurgand, *Alla conquista di Compostela*, p. 35.

33. Ibid., pp. 42–43.

34. Stopani, *La Via Francigena*, p. 11.

35. Turner and Turner, *Il pellegrinaggio*, p. 248.

36. Ibid., pp. 285–286.

37. M. Centini, "La vie alpine fra storia e mito: Appunti per una ricerca," in *Lungo le vie della fede* (Piazzola sul Brenta: Papergraf, 1999), p. 49.

38. Prandi and Turri, "Percorsi della salvezza," pp. 14–15.

39. See Macioti, *Pellegrinaggi e giubilei*; Tenderini, *Ospitalità sui passi alpini*.

40. Centini, "Le vie alpine," p. 49.

41. Tenderini, *Ospitalità sui passi alpini*, p. 143.

42. Ibid., p. 27.

43. Ibid., pp. 37–38.

44. Ibid., p. 78.

45. Ibid., p. 67.

46. Eric J. Leed, *La mente del viaggiatore: Dall'Odissea al turismo globale* (Bologna: Mulino, 1992), p. 13.

47. Ibid., p. 17.

48. Tenderini, *Ospitalità sui passi alpini*, p. 150.

49. Barret and Gurgand, *Alla conquista di Compostela*, p. 203.

50. See N. Paulus, *Die deutschen Dominikaner im kampfe gegen Luther (1518–1563)* (Freiburg im Breisgan: Herder, 1903).

51. Palumbo, "La geografia dei pellegrinaggi," p. 95.

52. Tenderini, *Ospitalità sui passi alpini*, p. 139.

53. See "Grand Tour: The Lure of Italy," in A. Wilton and I. Bignamini (eds.), *The Eighteenth Century* (London: Tate Gallery, 1997).

54. A. Brilli, *Quando viaggiare era un'arte: Il romanzo del Grand Tour* (Milan: Mulino, 1995), p. 13.

55. See A. Brilli, ibid.; A. Brilli, *Il viaggiatore immaginario: L'Italia degli itinerari perduit* (Milan: Mulino, 1997).

56. Palumbo, "La geografia dei pellegrinaggi," p. 95.

57. U. Beck, "The Cosmopolitan Society and Its Enemies," in Luigi Tomasi (ed.), *New Horizons in Sociological Theory and Research: The Frontiers of Sociology at the Beginning of the Twenty-First Century* (Aldershot, UK: Ashgate, 2001), pp. 181–201.

58. See A. Simonicca, *Antropologia del turismo: Strategie di ricerca e contesti etnografici* (Rome: Nuova Italia Scientifica, 1997).

59. See J. Urry, *The Tourist Gaze: Leisure and Travel in Contemporary Society* (London: Sage, 1990); Y. Apostolopoulos, S. Leivadi, and A. Yannakis, *The Sociology of Tourism* (London: Routledge, 1996).

60. Daniel Boorstin, *The Image: A Guide to Pseudoevents in America* (New York: Atheneum, 1961); Dean MacCannell, *The Tourist: A New Theory of the Leisure Class* (New York: Schocken, 1976).

61. Erik Cohen, "Toward a Sociology of International Tourism," *Social Research* 39 (1972), pp. 64–82; Erik Cohen, "Who Is a Tourist? A Conceptual Clarification," *Sociological Review* 22 (1974), pp. 527–555; Erik Cohen, "Rethinking the Sociology of Tourism," *Annals of Tourism Research* 6 (1979), pp. 18–35; Erik Cohen, "The Sociology of Tourism: Approaches, Issues, and Findings," *Annual Review of Sociology* 10 (1984), pp. 373–392; Erik Cohen, "Traditions in the Qualitative Sociology of Tourism," *Annals of Tourism Research* 15 (1988), pp. 377–398.

62. See Yves Lambert, "Religion in Modernity as a New Axial Age: Secularization or New Religious Forms?" *Sociology of Religion* 60 (1999), pp. 303–333.

63. Simonicca, *Antropologia del turismo*, p. 167.

64. See ibid.; Zygmunt Bauman, "From Pilgrim to Tourist—or a Short History of Identity," in, S. Hall and P. DuGay (eds.), *Questions of Cultural Identity* (London: Sage, 1996), pp. 2–36.

65. Clara Gallini, "Penitenti e gaudenti," *Intertionale Scuola cultura città* 3, no. 7 (2000), p. 29.

66. Ferrarotti, *Paritre, tornare*, p. 88.

67. Scaraffia, *Il Giuḫileo*, pp. 105–106.

68. Ibid., p. 108.

Chapter 2

The Holy Man as Traveler and Travel Attraction: Early Christian Asceticism and the Moral Problematic of Modernity

Judith Adler

Why should students of travel at the beginning of the twenty-first century, spurred to understand issues glossed as quintessentially "postmodern"—commodification of culture, fabrication of authenticity, urbanization of the countryside, voluntary nomadism, performed primitivism, or the efface-ment of valued "difference" by the tourism it attracts—concern themselves with Christian ascetics of the late Roman empire? Focusing our gaze upon these holy men of antiquity helps free us from two tenacious illusions: (1) that the history of "mass" tourism and its moral problematic begins with modernism and (2) that this history may be adequately pursued under the rubric of "leisure" or "recreational" travel, neatly distinguished from the history of religious travel, itself identified with overly narrow conceptions of pilgrimage.

TRAVEL AS PERFORMANCE: CONTEXT AND INTERPRETATION

The best scholars of contemporary tourism have consistently avoided mechanistic models of its impact as well as simplistic dichotomies between religious and secular forms of travel. Instead, focusing upon the symbolic mediation of human contacts by travel institutions, they have suggestively couched their analysis of modern tourism in a vocabulary first developed to describe religious practices, while pointing to the mix of secular and sacred motifs to be found in ostensibly secular, or religious, forms of travel. Thus, Graburn provides a pioneering theoretical model of modern tourism as a "sacred journey" and describes the mix of sacred and secular orientations in Japanese domestic travel. MacCannell analyzes tourist rituals as efforts to induce epiphanies of "authentic" social reality. Cohen, Ben-Yehuda, and Aviad write of tourist journeys as modern quests for a sacred "center." Frey describes the multiple goals pursued on the Camino de Santiago. Jokinen and Veijola write of pilgrim sport and adventure.[1]

The recourse of tourism's theorists to a vocabulary drawn from the study of religion may help to ensure that the subject is not trivialized by unreflective classification under narrowly understood rubrics of sport and recreation. Yet, the study of modern tourism will not be advanced by references to pilgrimage if these are allowed to rest upon vague and unexamined preconceptions of pilgrimage itself.

The broad theoretical concern shared by those who hope to understand modern forms of travel glossed as "tourism," as well as modern and earlier styles of travel glossed as "religious," is with human *mobility*, deliberately shaped for expressive and communicative, rather than simply instrumental, purposes. All human mobility involves mutually defining *contact* between social groups, accompanied by a *traffic* in information and goods, and struggles for *control* of these processes; but the specific theoretical concern of students of tourism and religious travel alike is with mobility structured to test and sustain complex cultural constructions of self, group identity, and social reality, geographical space, historical time, or even ultimate reality (God, eternal Truth, etc.).

I have urged elsewhere that we approach travel organized with a view to expressive/communicative purposes as a symbolically charged performance comparable to dance: a play with human bodies in geographical space, calculated to throw both the dancing figure, and the territorial ground against which it can be perceived to move, into enhanced perceptual relief.[2] Such play seems particularly suited to experimentation with social distance and with the relationship between individual or collective identity and territorial domain: a play with experiences of loss and reorientation, estrangement and boundaries of belonging, familiar sameness and frightening or alluring otherness.

Any communicative code (including the enduring codes underlying discrete travel performances) may be used to make statements that have never been made before. The growing wealth of empirical descriptions of varied subcultures of travel sensitizes us to the manner in which stylized mobility speaks about other domains of experience. It is to be hoped that as such descriptive studies mount, they will discourage the still all too frequent theoretical blurring of culturally and historically specific nuances of meaning through recourse to formal, empty categories of purportedly universal (culturally uncontextualized) experience. A model of travel as expressive/communicative performance directs us to social science literature on ritual, on symbolic cultural systems, and—above all—on the multiple institutions and heterogeneous social "worlds" required for the production of any cosmopolitan cultural form. The meanings of any given form of travel are best considered (in relation to differently situated co-producers and audiences) as *plural*, *subject to dispute*, and *changing* over time.

AN ANCIENT "MODERNITY"?

I was first led to an appreciation of the rich symbolic significance of geographical movement when, determined to gain some comparative sense of historically distinctive styles of travel, I decided to learn what I could about early Christian pilgrimage. I discovered a religious culture in which geographical mobility (*peregrinatio*) held core theological significance but was far more complexly conceived than my narrow preconceptions of pilgrimage had prepared me to expect. Furthermore, having set out to gain a contrasting perspective on modern, secular mass tourism by examining a travel culture seemingly distant in time and ethos, I discovered a social world organized to stimulate and support large-scale popular mobility, a world whose moral discourses about such movement bore striking similarities to contemporary debates concerning modern tourism.

In ascetic literature of the fourth to seventh centuries C.E. I began to discern, balanced against expressions of hope that crowds of common people would be edified and strengthened by spiritual sights, a preoccupation with the corruption of such travel attractions as a result of their fabrication for show; anxiety about the moral contamination of host populations by contact with worldly visitors; concern over the degradation of pure sites of retreat by the crowds they attract; struggles for control over markets in travel-linked commodities; an accusing association of travel with unbridled sensual license and material consumption ("gluttony"); and complaint about the relative valorization, confirmed by travel movements, of some places over others.

Above all I discovered a cosmopolitan culture in which freely undertaken geographical mobility, valued as an end in itself, was endowed with rich symbolic significance. An ascetic Christian culture that reached from the Western Mediterranean to Syria, Mesopotamia, and Persia, honing human lives into purified mediums of significance, drew heavily upon the expressive possibilities of geographical movement to make eloquent nonverbal arguments about human nature, time, and the world. The styles of travel it developed may be regarded as forms of folk anthropology and folk theology: ways of testing, symbolically representing, and confirming beliefs. The written texts of early Christian asceticism offer initial formulations of enduring discourses about the psychological, social, ethical, and metaphysical significance of bodily movement in geographical space. And the intrapsychic as well as political struggles of early ascetics over the spirituality of wandering versus the obligation of stability, over the truths to be learned through literal geographical detachment and deliberate estrangement versus the error of errancy (associated with restless idleness, consuming appetite, unbridled sexuality, unstable social loyalties and cognitive commitments, etc.) reveal the deep historical roots of an enduring cultural ambivalence.

For anyone seeking to understand the full significance of geographical mobility for Western culture, perhaps the most important lesson yielded by an examination of the literature of early Christian asceticism is that geographical movement per se was central to its initial constructions of holiness and heresy, purity and sin. Early Christian asceticism was permeated by veritable theologies of mobility and stability: theologies that invite scrutiny as master statements of moral discourses about movement that continue to echo in our own time, transposed into secular keys.

GEOGRAPHICAL MOBILITY, SOCIAL MARGINALITY, AND HOLINESS

Asceticism derives its name from the Greek term *askesis*, denoting a military/athletic contest. And like the military and athletic heroes with whom they were identified, early Christian ascetics or "athletes of virtue" were among the most mobile persons of the late Roman empire. Both as attractions and as hospitalers, they also served as stimulants and sponsors of mobility, the institutions they developed eventually providing the ancient world with a well-developed travel infrastructure. The first Christian hagiographies helped to set many of the conventions of enduring Western genres of travel romance, the lives of star holy men being narratively structured as itineraries, or reported in the frame of a traveler's eyewitness account. Intellectual and administrative elites of the ascetic world shuttled back and forth between the Eastern and Western Mediterranean, endowing marginal desert and wilderness areas with cultural glamor, and linking once peripheral frontiers and backwaters of empire with cosmopolitan centers. The humble, illiterate heroes of asceticism, exalted in their writings, were frequently exemplary wanderers themselves, who mark the stages of their spiritual progress through a series of geographical displacements.

Early formulations of the ascetic calling draw upon Old Testament imagery of the moral superiority of nomadism and take as models both a mobile soldiery and prophets who withdraw to the wilderness for purification. Rhetorically casting the monk as a homeless "soldier of the king," the young Basil of Caesaria writes, "by royal edict, a home lies open to him wherever there are subjects of the king. He is not required to toil at building a house. On the open road is his tent."[3] In continuity with pre-Christian traditions stipulating that a traveling stranger should be treated as a god in disguise, a binding rule of hospitality took central place in emerging monastic theology and practice. A vocation for hostelry, as well as for arduous traveling, became identifying marks of the monk: "Another thing is also the work of those who are called monks . . . who receive and serve with eagerness all travellers, men and women of all conditions, as their monasteries are built on the highways; this is the work of those who are called monks."[4]

Men and women believed capable of mediating relations with the spiritual world are typically called upon to mediate between humans as well. Mobile Christian ascetics, patrolling areas beyond the reach of urban authorities, or shuttling between town and countryside, served as brokers between feuding villages, debtors and creditors, hinterland populations and distant centers of power. It would be overly simple to assume that the services performed by these holy men required their mobility. More precisely, their mobility and geographic marginality to the life of settled communities, while making them serviceable in many ways, was constitutive of their holiness. From the perspective of settled villagers and townspeople, the usefulness (but also fearsomeness) of renowned holy men—the quality that marked them as potential mediators with problematic spiritual and human powers (but also as potential evildoers, agitators, secret agents, and spies)—consisted precisely in their visibly floating, like angels or demons, outside and between other human groups.

As living icons and shifting human "loci" of supernatural and social power, ascetics not only moved themselves but also stimulated considerable popular mobility.[5] Taking up residence in isolated or border areas, holy men attracted visitor traffic to these places—often eclipsing sites, themselves first developed as travel destinations by monks, marked by sacred Scripture.[6] Solitary hermitages in the Egyptian and Syrian wildernesses, as well as settlements of grouped cells that formed veritable cities in the desert, lured disciples, ecclesiastical and civil authorities, and numerous humble clientele on journeys of religious sightseeing, homage, and petition.

Pilgrimages to holy men of the Egyptian desert continued long-standing traditions of Roman pilgrimage to Egyptian shrines.[7] Religious travelers throughout the Eastern Mediterranean used road networks established for military and administrative purposes, and hospices in existence since pre-Christian times. Most of the places visited by early Christian pilgrims to the Holy Land were well-established sites of Jewish pilgrimage associated with Old Testament tales.[8] The frequent reports that ascetics set themselves up in abandoned forts and pagan temples swell the evidence that Christian holy men took advantage of a long-standing travel infrastructure, and that continuities of destination and tribute bearing withstood changes in religious adherence.

A general observation pertinent to modern tourism studies may be drawn here: upon close analysis, even innovative travel institutions and styles rest upon some preexisting conventions. No emergent style of travel will ever prove to be entirely new in all of the conventions that govern its reproduction in recognizable form. With regard to the historical case in point, there is no contradiction between the existence of many long-institutionalized continuities of travel culture and the fact that ascetic lore romanticized the pioneering virtues of holy men, stressing their intrepid penetration of trackless, hostile, and forbidding territory, made passable for others only by their presence. Not only were there long-standing patterns of relationships to outpost spaces, but the very conception of wilderness or desert space was ambiguous, embracing recently abandoned settlements as well as long-settled pagan territories that had not yet been won over to the new religion.

STADIUMS IN THE WILDERNESS

For civil and ecclesiastical officials well-publicized visits to human shrines in the countryside helped to secure popular legitimacy and the political backing of an "army" of monks in the desert. "I was going around the districts to be blessed by the saints," writes one eastern bishop of his travel circuit.[9] But the mere sight of such "athletes of virtue" was touted as salutary for all visitors: "How fine it is to behold the contests of excellent men, the athletes of virtue, and to draw benefit with the eyes; when witnessed, the objects of our praise appear enviable and become desirable, and impel the beholder to attain them."[10] According to well-worn tropes of the period, ascetic stations in the wilderness were the "stadiums of a spiritual wrestling ground" where even illiterate onlookers, moved by nonverbal signs, could draw "benefit with the eyes."

Visitors to popular thaumaturges hoped for more than a glimpse of a glorified sight, seeking contact with reputed saints of multifaceted restorative powers. Holy men (and a few women) exercised informal judicial authority, worked to effect human reconciliations as well as supernatural cures, and—in part, through nonverbal example—offered consolation for social, mental, physical, and reproductive difficulties. Journeys were undertaken to procure the "good and precious merchandise" of a holy man's *eulogia* or blessing (oil, amulet, etc.). And some recorded narratives feature the traveler as a hunter, whose evasive quarry is simultaneously human, wild, and (at a time when the humanity of Christ received less emphasis than in later periods) semi-divine.

> I said to the brother who was with me, "Let us sit down among these trees, and lie in wait for the old man; since perhaps he will come and we shall catch him, and obtain his blessing." ... [A]nd, when we saw him in the distance, we kept ourselves hidden all the more.... When he had approached to about half a furrow's length from us ... as if he scented the smell of us, ... he thereupon like a wild beast turned aside, and set his face to go down the mountain-side at a run.[11]

In one of the most repetitive themes of ascetic lore, travelers in quest of redemptive understanding arrive after great difficulty at a remote ascetic station to ask, "Give us a word, Father." The oracular answer, never followed by further questioning, is simultaneously personal and abstract, taking the form of a general prescription addressed to the needs of a particular petitioner. Ideally, the reward for going the distance was a response to the self, a mirroring, both more disinterestedly individuating and more ethically abstract than responses routinely evoked in familiar home territory.

An ascetic's silence might be deemed to be as salutary as his words, and many texts emphasize the uncompromising, richly communicative silence with which long-distance travelers were sometimes welcomed. "If they are not edified by my silence," one virtuoso insisted, "they would not be edified by my words." Precisely by artfully preserving their distance and avoiding everyday modes of interchange, ascetics held out a promise of contact with otherworldly uncompromised truths.

Some mounted an impressive total theater in the desert, playing to popular audiences with dramatic, nonverbal forms of argument. Visitors who hired camels to reach the abandoned fortress where one internationally famous solitary had taken up residence were greeted by the following scene:

> He [Antony] remained alone in the place, neither going out himself nor seeing any of those who visited. Since he did not allow them to enter, those ... who came to him often spent days and nights outside. They heard what sounded like clamoring mobs inside making noises, emitting pitiful sounds and crying out, "Get away from what is ours! What do you have to do with the desert?" ... At first those who were outside thought certain men were doing battle with him [Antony], and that these had gained entry by ladders, but when they stooped to peek through a hole, they saw no one, and they realized then that the adversaries were demons. They were frightened and they called Antony, and he heard them, but he disregarded the demons.

And coming close to the door, he urged the men to be on their way and not to fear. "In this manner," he said, "the demons create apparitions and set them loose on those who are cowardly. For it is against the cowardly," he said, "that the demons create apparitions in this way. Therefore, seal yourselves with the sign [of the cross] and depart with confidence. And leave them to mock themselves." So they went away, fortified . . . Antony remained and suffered no injury from the demons, and neither did he grow tired of the contest.[12]

After two decades of drawing visitors into the desert by dramatizing his resistance to demonic expulsion from it, Antony emerged from his fortress as though "from some shrine, where he had been initiated into divine mysteries," and allowed himself to be embraced by the large crowd. His biographer does not tell us whether by this time hostelers, victualers, interpreters, stewards, and souvenir peddlers had established themselves at the scene. But we do know from another text that one entrepreneurial deacon of a desert town developed a long-distance transportation and guide service, hiring out "dromedaries . . . on account of the scarcity of water in the desert, to carry travellers who wished to visit Antony."[13]

There is ample evidence from other chronicles that rudimentary hostel services sprouted up near crowd-attracting solitaries; the revenues generated by these human resources supported the disciples who managed the attraction. (John of Lycopolis had a "guest cell" and employed three translators; some of the stylites were flanked by hostels and distributed such *eulogia* as clay medallions and flasks of oil; and well-known anchorites kept gardens for the express purpose of feeding guests, etc.[14])

PEREGRINATIO: A CHOREOGRAPHY OF ESTRANGEMENT

Voluntary exile, or literal spatial withdrawal from home territory and social relations (identified with God's "call" to Abraham to leave his own land), featured as the core "calling" of early asceticism.[15] Independent of any specific destination, the act of leaving home, with its securities, comforts, and confirmations of status, defined asceticism's particular brand of heroism. "[A] monk cannot be perfect in his own country," writes Jerome. "And not to wish to be perfect is a sin."[16]

The Greek term *xeniteia* (from *xenos*, stranger), translated into Latin as *peregrinatio*, is of military origin, referring to a mercenary's stay outside his country. In ascetic usage it denoted voluntary expatriation and a determination to live literally, or figuratively, as a stranger in an alien land. Insofar as homeless vagrancy was the most extreme form of poverty in the ancient world, and expulsion rather than imprisonment was one of the most com-

mon forms of punishment, dramatic acts of voluntary exile served as an eloquent performative discourse about radical renunciation, humiliation, and
reliance upon God alone. Metaphorically conceived as a form of dying,
peregrinatio was a technique and sign of radical disengagement, not only
from "the world" of family, town or village, but from degenerate historical
"times" as well. As a technique for silencing worldly thoughts, or "dying to
the world," *peregrinatio* could be enhanced by movement into a linguisti-
cally foreign territory. Combined with retreat into unsettled, "pure" (virile)
wilderness space where men might try to live in accord with eternal divine
law, it promised escape from sullied human history, soft, effeminate town
life, and corrupting human interchange.

An ascetic theology of disciplined, voluntary estrangement immediately
confronted one obvious moral problem, however: the exile came to feel at
home in the new surroundings and the sharpness of the experience of estrangement dulled. One solution to this threat of spiritual devaluation was to
renew the initial act of estrangement by repeated acts of uprooting and displacement. Virtuoso ascetics became masters of frontier heroics, decamp-
ing and moving on as soon as they perceived the encroachment of "the
world" upon their retreat or the dulling of their passion for the contest. Figures singled out as the spiritual elite of a population of voluntary exiles (by
texts such as the *Lausaic History*, the *Historia Monachorum*, and the
Apophthegmata Patrum) are men distinguished by unremitting nomadism
or pioneering intrusions into remote territory. Such are the sketches of the
Coptic saints John, Bessarion, and Serapion:

> There is a brother of ours called John, a man of another age, who surpasses in
> virtue all the monks of our own time. It is not easy for anyone to find him because he
> is always moving from place to place in the desert.[17]

> The mode of life of the old man [Bessarion] was that of the bird of the heavens.
> . . . He wandered hither and thither like one possessed, in the season of frost [he
> went] naked, and he was consumed with heat under the fierce rays of the sun, and
> at one time he lived among the rocks and at another in the desert.[18]

> [T]here was another, Serapion . . . he wandered about the world and successfully
> perfected this virtue.[19]

Serapion won special praise for his minimalist style. Joining up with a
troupe of comic actors, he journeyed through Egypt, Greece and Italy, carrying no money and wearing nothing but a loincloth, without "shame or
feeling."

The type is familiar. Still today, among modern "nomads from affluence" we find barefoot "Serapions" who wander for years with few clothes, no money, and little shame, attracting attention and gathering prestige among their peers for their perfection of a minimalist travel style.[20]

ASCETIC PRIMITIVISM, IDEAL COSMOPOLITANISM, AND GENDERED SPACE

Centered upon a topos of flight from "the world" (of secular space and time), asceticism posed a challenge to the classical equation of morality and virtue with city life, inverted the moral privilege of citizenship, and gave new ethical significance to socially peripheral, seemingly timeless wilderness spaces. In early formulations of enduring traditions of wilderness romance, Christian ascetic narratives drew upon Old Testament imagery of the desert as a site of divine epiphany and human purification, contrasting the freedom of wild land with the "smoky" air and moral "muddiness" of imprisoning urban space. Jerome writes: "O wilderness that rejoices in intimacy with god! What are you doing in the world, brother . . . ? How long will the shadows of houses oppress you? How long will the smoky prison of these cities close you in?"[21] The association of city space with spiritual constriction and of city "mud" with prostitution is repeated by Gregory of Nazianzus, and by John Chrysostom, bishop of Constantinople, who defends ascetic flight to the countryside by inverting the classical pagan equation of city life with virtue and civility. Because everything is upside down, he argues, and the cities, despite their laws and tribunals, are full of crime and iniquity, those who desire to live virtuously are forced to flee into the wilderness. Only when cities ceased to harbor vice would the exiles be able to return.[22]

The spirituality of the desert played off a moral and gendered opposition between virile, forbidding, yet pure wilderness life and the soft, wet, sinful (female) life of the towns and cultivated lands. Sleeping on the ground or in rude shelters, wearing primitive clothing or no clothes at all, walking barefoot, and eating gathered, wild food, often prepared without the use of fire, male heroes of ascetic narrative dramatized the recreation of a prelapsidarian single-sex paradise, in which a new Adam might repossess the innocence and autonomy of the original, "natural" man, before the creation of Eve, the compromises of sexual interdependency, and the curse of labor. (Rare female heroes of ascetic narrative "became male" in this virile space, or entered it only to die there.) "Eat grass, wear grass, and sleep on grass. Then thy heart will become like iron," advises one Egyptian monk.[23] "Caverns are their palaces, and rocks are their sleeping rooms; heights are their balconies, and ledges their habitations; the herb of the mountains is as their dinner-table," writes an ancient chronicler of the Syrian anchorites.[24]

Like some heroes of nineteenth- and twentieth-century nature travel, these protagonists of ascetic narrative modeled not only a determined escape from sinful human history into an eternal present moment, but the redemption of human relationship with the natural and animal world as well. Transgressing civilized codes of grooming (going naked, allowing hair or nails to grow, forgoing baths), they played with the boundaries of the human, simultaneously associating themselves with animal and angelic existence. Travelers might describe their "hunt" for the blessings of such holy men as the hunt for shy, wild creatures who lived among dangerous beasts without fear: "[T]hey said that he used to go forth from his cell by night and mingle with the wild animals of the desert, and he gave them to drink of the water which he found. The footmarks which appeared by the side of his abode were those of buffaloes, and goats, and gazelle, in the sight of which he took great pleasure."[25]

But the romance of heroic escape from sinful human relations to otherworldly wilderness space was, then as now, inextricably linked to a parallel romance of advancing frontiers. Intrepidly facing down the demons of alien, wild spaces to public acclaim, ascetic heroes made these spaces passable for travelers and habitable for other settlers. Wilderness space invested with religious value, precisely for its presumed purity and emptiness began to be "filled up with monks" and their admirers; the desert was "made a city," with all the moral ambiguity this implied. The famous hermit Antony of Egypt "persuaded many to take up the solitary life. And so, from then on . . . the desert was made a city by monks, who left their own people and registered themselves for the citizenship in the heavens."[26] This passage underlines the ideal urbanity of ascetic wilderness space, where—in line with adapted Stoic ideals—a cosmic citizenship signifying elite spiritual (rather than privileged juridical) status could be enacted. But to a student of tourism in our own day, familiar with the concept of the urbanization of the countryside, it also suggests that a rural hinterland, drawn into the web of a cosmopolitan religious culture, was becoming urbanized, with the moral compromises this would have been seen to entail.

Ideal pure space, capable of sustaining a "perfect" life, proved to be an ever-receding, transcendent goal. As the desert filled up with monks, "true monks" were narratively resituated elsewhere, stimulating ever-renewed acts of distancing by those aspiring to the role, and ever more intrepid acts of search on the part of those (ascetics and lay clientele) seeking contact with them.

Photo 2. Sanctuary of the Peripatetic Celtic Saint Columbano (Columbanus), Rovereto, Italy. *Luigi Tomasi.*

AUTHENTICATION THROUGH DISTANCING

As once peripheral social spaces came to bear a dense human traffic, the problem of maintaining perceptible distance from the world took on public relations, as well as theological, dimensions. Not only did an encroaching "world" threaten territorially maintained defenses against temptation and distraction, but the very accessibility of spiritual attractions also eroded their otherworldly legitimacy. Human "attractions" (or "angels" as they were sometimes referred to and addressed) who failed to protect their impalpable resources of mystery and difference risked finding themselves divested of holiness and the social power it encoded.

Several strategic responses to the dangers of site degradation and spiritual devaluation can be observed. Some human attractions distanced themselves by symbolic acts of ritual flight, delegating visitor management to their associates. One saint constructed an underground tunnel leading from his cell to a nearby cave: "Whenever too many people crowded in on him, he would secretly leave his cell and go to the cave, and no one would find him. One of his earnest disciples told me this, and added that on his way to the cave he recited twenty-four prayers."[27] Others immured themselves behind walls, communicating with the public only through their disciples (a practice calling to mind those pagan Egyptian shrines whose priest-tended statues were never seen by the pilgrims they drew). Stylites of Syria, mounted upon pillars, resorted to vertical rather than horizontal movements of distancing, descending from their pillars only to mount new ones of greater height. And though the biographers of these saints invariably represent their ascents as efforts to escape the crowd, such vertical escape acts were, of course, the principal crowd drawer.[28]

One recommended technique for protecting solitude (best understood as a form, rather than absence, of social relationship) was that of flight into rigorously guarded silence. The richly communicative silence of a human shrine, of a living exemplar of deadness to the world, could be more alluring than any verbal address. But institutionalized license in speech, and deliberately rude forms of visitor repulsion, also took their place in the arsenal of seductive distancing techniques. A certain Arsenius greeted the long-distance travelers who made their way through the desert, hoping to receive a life-giving word from him, as follows: "Will you put into practice what I say to you?" They promised him this. "If you hear Arsenius is anywhere, do not go there."[29]

Some human attractions persuaded visitors to leave the site by threatening to flee themselves; others judiciously lowered the standards of hospitality and imposed long fasts or vigils to hasten the departure of unwelcome guests. At least one saint ordered a woman who insisted on seeing him to return home, promising to appear to her in a dream. The woman meekly obeyed the suggestion, and the dream audience was granted. With respect to human attractions, the drama of sightseeing always hinges in no small part upon uncertainty as to whether the sights, acting as free agents, will allow themselves to be seen. The uncertain favor, if granted, may be understood as an authoritative confirmation of the petitioner's merit.

Some kinds of travelers are considered more damaging to the purity and reputation of sites than others, and hosts take measures to discourage these, while undergoing considerable trouble on behalf of other, more highly valued visitors. Antony, for example, directed his disciple to signal the arrival of learned foreigners ("from Jerusalem"), who were asked to stay for conversation lasting far into the night, in distinction to local day-trippers ("from Babylon"), who were sent away after brief refreshment and blessing.

In early ascetic literature female visitors are disproportionately mentioned as the targets of repelling ploys. Though females have a spotty presence in narratives of the saints, and are likely to have formed a large proportion of many holy men's clientele, female saints do not feature as objects of male quest, and female mobility was widely considered morally undesirable—a threat to the women, but more important, to the men with whom they came into contact. Even in reporting the pilgrimages of rich, high-ranking ascetic women, the narratives put them in their place as visitors who must be made to understand that their very presence at a holy site risks its destruction. That the long-distance female pilgrim turned away in the following anecdote is of high rank only underscores the purported spiritual authenticity of the monk who rebuffs her:

When Abba Arsenius was living at Caopus [Egypt], a very rich and God-fearing virgin of senatorial rank came from Rome to see him. . . . The old man refused to meet her. But when . . . the young girl [was told] this, she ordered the beast of burden to be saddled, saying, "I trust in God that I shall see him, for it is not a man whom I have come to see (there are plenty of those in our town), but a prophet." When she had reached the old man's cell, by a dispensation of God, he was outside it. Seeing him, she threw herself at his feet. Outraged, he lifted her up again, and said, looking steadily at her, . . ."How dare you make such a journey? Do you not realise you are a woman and cannot go just anywhere? Or is it so that on returning to Rome you can say to other women 'I have seen Arsenius'? Then they will turn the sea into a thoroughfare with women coming to see me." She said, "May it please the Lord, I shall not let anyone come here; but pray for me and remember me always." But he answered her, "I pray God to remove remembrance of you from my heart."[30]

Such women might be regarded as the first guilty travelers, made painfully conscious of the damage inflicted upon attractive otherworldly spaces by the mere fact of their having entered them.

For many holy men, repeated literal geographical displacement was the most reliable method for renewing valued estrangement and social distance: "The old man said to him, 'When Scete began to be filled with monks I . . . came to the mountain here, and found that this place was quiet.'"[31] In hagiographic narratives, a sequence of flights, each followed by a period of stability during which the holy man consolidates his clientele and draws an increasing crowd, punctuates progress in spiritual advance as well as popular success. The pattern of these movements suggests a courtship dance of feinting, beckoning retreats, in which mobile holy men lure a mobile clientele into ever more remote distances.

None of the human attractions uproots himself with an explicit avowal that the visitor-generating capacity of a single ascetic station has been fully exploited, or that further expansion of the arena of solicitation is required. All movement is legitimized in personal, spiritual terms as flight from the dangers posed by popularity and increasing density of settlement. Thus, it is written of one Syrian ascetic that "to escape being honored—for he became conspicuous to all and drew to himself, through fame, the lovers of the good—he finally set out for Mount Sinai with a few of those closer to him," and of another, "he had as his wrestling-ground and stadium the tops of the mountains; he did not settle in one place, but now dwelt in this one and then transferred to that. This he did not through dislike of the places, but to escape from the crowds of those who visited him and flocked from all sides."[32]

But if strategic flight from negatively valued social contact was central to conceptions of the spiritual purity and authenticity encouraged by ascetic theology, such flight rested in uneasy balance with equally exalted injunctions to exercise hospitality, and with affirmations of faith that however much a saint might hide himself away, God would ensure his renown for the sake of those he might edify. In short, a purity compromised by human contact simultaneously found its value in the benefit that contact with it could confer upon multitudes. The tension is expressed in numerous anecdotes: model solitaries breach a personal "rule" to observe the rule of hospitality, for example, breaking a fast to eat with a guest, only to resume it with added severity after the guest's departure; but conversely, discerning holy men may dismiss calls to charity, or requests for shelter, as temptations to sin that must be fiercely resisted. The stranger who, according to one long-standing tradition, must be succored as a god in disguise, arrived to test the monk's charity, is presented from another angle as an intrusive demon, who came only to compromise the purity of the monk's retreat and the peace of his mind. Significantly, when Antony tolerates the presence of a crowd of admirers, he explicitly compares them to the demonic host whose assaults he has learned to sustain without damage.

Underlying this normative strain were conflicting interests as well: to be perceived as authentic, a holy man had to appear to disdain the world; yet, the social worlds of asceticism were built upon personal reputation, and exemplary lives could fulfill their redemptive purpose only through social report. Visitors were essential to the transmission of reputation, and (as modern ethnography confirms)[33] long-distance, wealthy visitors, bearing tribute in which others could share, enhanced a saint's local standing.

THE TRAFFICKS OF TRAVEL

Regional elites, boosting holy men whose celebrity became emblematic of regional pride and reflected legitimacy on local persons and institutions, urged travelers to advertise their local saints elsewhere.[34] Saints who did not travel themselves informed visitors of what was expected of them after departure, relying upon a hospitality ethos that obligated guests to spread the good name of their host abroad.[35] Holy men helped to structure the itineraries of their visitors, keeping travelers moving along well-demarcated circuits by reciprocal courtesies of referral, advice, and guide service. John of Ephesus offers a glimpse of such a referral network:

When some men from the territory of the city of Amida were going down for the harvest . . . they heard of that saint, and were eager to go and be blessed by him; and when they had gone and had come to him and been blessed by him, he asked them, "Whence are you, my sons?"; and they said, "From the north of Amida." The blessed man said to them: "But what, my sons, do I for my part really know? . . . If you are from the north of Amida, wherefore did you not go to the pillar of light which stands in the northern country . . . wherefore did you not go to this man . . . ?" But these men on hearing these things from the saint fell on their faces and continued entreating him and saying: "Who, sir, is he . . . ?" But the blessed man . . . says to these men: "This is Simeon the recluse who is living in seclusion on the top of a hill in the village of Kalesh. But go to him, and greet him from me."[36]

Without joint efforts to shape the travel that formed an all-important circulatory system of the back country, recluses risked being overlooked rather than celebrated; and without a flow of gifts and donations, remote ascetic stations faced abandonment. The recluse Simeon, having learned to whom he owed his visitors, could no doubt be counted upon to repay the debt, directing his own south-bound clientele toward the holy man who had asked to be remembered in his prayers.

In addition to its benefits, however, such a circulatory system posed numerous threats. The visitors relied upon to carry reputation were also accused of trying to mar or even "steal" it. Travel itself was suspect as a tactic for invidious personal glorification at the expense of stable, or simply less traveled, ascetic peers. "Be sure," one host greeted newly arrived travelers, "that you have not come 'to spy out our liberty' (Gal. 2:4), that you are not hunting out our virtues for the sake of vainglory, so that like men displaying their talents you may appear to others to be imitators of our works."[37] Men of an oral culture, whose public identities could only be established by faithful report of their holy words and personal practices, were not immune to fears of plagiarism and misquotation. Guests were often suspected of having appropriative designs upon their host's carefully crafted personal practices, memorable words, or even precious disciples: "A brother visiting Abba Theodore of Pherme supplicated him for three days to give him a word; but the abba refused to respond, and the brother left in dejection. Theodore's disciple then asked him, 'Father, why did you say nothing? He left so despondently!' 'Believe me,' the old man answered, 'I said nothing to him because he is a trafficker who only wants to glorify himself with the words of others.' "[38]

In times of sectarian conflict, visits and the provision of hospitality served as performative affirmations of political solidarity. Ascetic lore is rife with advice on evading contact with guests tainted by heresy (and with bishops in a position to define it). Ecclesiastical authorities, like Athanasius of Alexandria, anxious to prevent their enemies from garnering legitimacy through well-publicized visits to popular holy men, sent circulars into the hinterland to warn of "deceivers" who went about the monasteries only in order to be seen visiting them and returning from such visits.[39]

Formally organized ascetic settlements routinized the management of their visitors. Ruling priests and delegated hospitalers maintained a firm control over the flow of guests and the accompanying traffic of information and material goods. The larger Egyptian semi-anchoritic settlements (of solitaries), as well as early communal or coenobitic monasteries, and some of the Eastern stylites, built hostels to house their visitors (xenodochia). The governors of such settlements, sometimes providing interpreters for travelers who were unable to speak the local dialect, also directed these guides to channel their charges toward some human attractions while bypassing others (especially those suspected of heresy). As an ethos of social avoidance and humility made it difficult for any ascetic to solicit visitors openly on his own behalf, the privilege of brokering contacts and distributing tribute was substantial. Ascetic lore provides ample evidence that men who brokered contact between ascetics and their gift- and information-bearing visitors aroused the ire of both. Travelers demanded to know why they had been routed past the cells of men they had hoped to see, while monks scrutinized the distribution of tribute for subtle indications of relative status and favor, or fought with their own disciples over the management of donations.[40]

The development of attractions provided further matter for social conflict. The struggle over land use, revealed by an account of a fifth-century stylite named Daniel from the region of Constantinople, will seem distantly familiar to any observer of modern tourism. Erecting a pillar on another man's property, Daniel mounted it and soon attracted a large crowd. By the time the owner of the property arrived to demand that the business be dismantled, the holy man's wounds had already begun to suppurate. Unable to persuade the authorities to ban the nuisance, the landowner attempted to pull the holy man from the column himself, only to be vanquished by the sight of the wounds (and the mood of the crowd). In the end the landlord not only accepted the *fait accompli*, but agreed to develop the attraction further at his own expense (erecting an even higher pillar on the site), in return for the social honor (and perhaps other tangible rewards) of patronage.[41]

Associates who settled around star attractions were well poised to exercise political influence with high status visitors, as well as to profit from revenues solicited at the site.[42] Any flight of a lucrative or politically advantageous attraction poses a threat to the community poised to exploit it. And a complex social interest in stabilizing such human resources (and the political power they wield or support) is suggested by the immurement of some celebrated hermits, by imperial edicts forbidding stylites to leave their pillars except in time of barbarian invasion, and by reports of villages arming to defend "their" saint against the threat of kidnapping.

Human attractions differ in the kinds of visitor traffic they draw. Star saints, attracting an international, powerful, and rich clientele, may rise in local esteem as regional assets, while their humbler competitors only annoy neighbors by drawing disreputable, unremunerative crowds. In at least one recorded case such neighborly dissatisfaction is narratively linked to the fall of a holy man, calling our attention to the role of perceived collective interest in working either to confirm or challenge the authenticity of an attraction. A Syrian ascetic named James, gaining a reputation as an exorcist, attracted many possessed persons to his monastic community. Its elders, intensely disturbed by the multitudes of both sexes who gathered outside their gates, wailing and frothing at the mouth, demanded that the monk order his admirers to depart. The saint's popularity only grew, however, and "when the numbers of those who used to come there and cause annoyance increased, there were agitations against this blessed man, both on the part of the inmates of his monastery and also on the part of others." Emerging from the monastery as a solo entrepreneur, the healer and an associate moved to another place, followed by their low-status clientele. But divested of its institutional shelter, this thaumaturgic theater soon folded: a local girl, publicly honored by the two holy men as a holy spirit, broke with her role in mid-execution, exposing the monks to mockery and leaving them no choice but to retreat in shame back to the monastery from which they had briefly emerged as solo spiritual entrepreneurs.[43]

SACRAMENTAL STABILITY AND THE HERESY OF ERRANCY

As the ascetic movement was brought ever more firmly under ecclesiastical control, ascetic mobility and the management of host/visitor contact became subject to stringent formal legislation. Monks continued to serve as hostelers, and many monasteries depended upon revenues generated by the travel trade. But bishops and monastic legislators, concerned to secure political and doctrinal stability, the discipline of a monastic labor force, and the inalienability of monastic property, impeded travel movements with numerous restrictions and rigorously separated resident host and itinerant guest populations.

Burgeoning traditions of formal monastic rules, combined with frequently cited passages from Augustine, Jerome, and Cassian, eventually formed a corpus of sacred monastic "scripture" that classified types of monks in a hierarchy of legitimacy with primary reference to their geographical stability: "unstable" or wandering ascetics were castigated as "false monks," vagabonds, parasites, or "gyrovagues." Their traveling was discredited as a mere pretext for relaxation of discipline and unbridled consumption.

The fourth kind of monks, who should not even be called that . . . are called gyrovagues. They spend their whole life as guests for three or four days at a time at various cells and monasteries of others in various provinces. Taking advantage of hospitality, they want to be received every day anew at different places. They oblige their successive hosts, who rejoice at the arrival of a guest, to prepare choice dishes. . . . They force upon their various hosts . . . the precept of the apostle wherein he says, "You should make hospitality your special care." Making use of this precept they demand care for their restless feet after their journey, but using traveling as a pretext, are thinking of their guts.[44]

Caricatured with reference to soft practices that divested their travels of disciplinary significance (for example, the use of pack animals), such monks were said to wander "for the belly's sake," obedient only to their own desires. The bishop of Hippo delineates, only to castigate, the type: "So many hypocrites, under the garb of monks, strolling about the provinces, nowhere sent, nowhere fixed, nowhere standing."[45]

The evolution of the Latin term *stabilitas* reveals the extent to which a calling first centered on the topos of voluntary exile and literal flight became gradually identified with immurement and immobilization. *Stabilitas* had a long history of usage in ascetic culture, tapping Greek philosophical conceptions of the nature of truth and at first signifying a soul in perfect condition, characterized by tranquillity, constancy, and firmness of commitment. With the Benedictine Rule, however, the term underwent a semantic change, coming to indicate literal immobilization and permanent association with a single monastic community for life.[46] *Stabilitas loci* (rather than a vocation for hostelry), and a *professio* made before the concretely local holiness of a monastery's saintly relics, came to define core aspects of the monastic "profession."[47]

As, with formally ruled coenobitic monasticism, all self-willed movement became vulnerable to interpretation as a sign of sinful disobedience, and renunciation of the freedom to move was increasingly idealized as the supreme sign of disciplined sacrifice, obedience to organizational superiors, or even a form of martyrdom.[48] According to the new ethos, every journey, even if commanded by a superior, was to be regarded as a regrettable exception to the rule of cloistering, while immobilization took on nothing less than sacramental significance. The distinctive virtue of the monk, next to obedience to his superior, was to become that of remaining in his place.[49] The most severe applications of rules of enclosure took place with respect to females, with some formal rules forbidding women to leave the cloister alive for any reason whatsoever.[50]

The emergent monastic discipline of stability found support in a parallel epistemology and metaphysics of stability. Truth (God) was conceived, in continuity with pre-Christian neo-Platonic tradition, as eternal and unchanging; those seeking divine knowledge must participate in the nature of that which they sought to know, by "standing still" and remaining "unmovable." The original Fall of man, interpreted as an evil movement away from divinity, was glossed over by some intellectual theorists of the discipline of stability as "the Movement," while Christ was distinguished in relation to such evil precisely by his constancy.[51] He was the only man to remain unmoved though others fell, and his very nailing to the cross figured as an image of cosmic stabilization. Such a characterization of the ideal man could not have posed a greater contrast to the vagabond Christ evoked by the wandering tradition, the Son of Man who had no nest, no hole, nowhere to rest his head (Matt. 8:20).

In place of Basil's soldier tenting on the open road, the image increasingly invoked for inspiration was that of the sentry who remains at his post. Novice ascetics were informed that the proper combat of the monk consisted, above all else, in vanquishing the temptation to leave his cell. A discrete demon even came to be identified—the "noonday demon"—who specialized in tempting monks to a newly defined sin: *acedia*, a spiritual state characterized by a restless urge to move.[52] The "call" to ascetic flight was reinterpreted in strictly allegorical ways. Forbidden to move of their own free will, and tutored to regard the impulse to move as a demonic temptation, monks were urged to "flee" into silence, exploring inner deserts of the self while remaining unswervingly in place.

As godliness came to be associated with literal stability, so heresy, long figuratively understood as a "wandering from the truth" and "instability of opinion," was identified with unauthorized geographical mobility. Ascetic cultures had always concentrated on the enactment rather than verbalization of belief, and practice was more important than creed in defining social boundaries. Hence, as stability became the "orthopraxy" of monasticism, wandering, or "vagabondage," was featured as its principal heresy.

By the late fourth century, an official imperial policy of intolerance called for the prosecution of heretics. One of the first texts of heresiology, developed to guide the policy, offers an intriguing definition of the final heresy of heresies in a list of eighty "concubines of Solomon" to be eliminated.[53] "Messaliens" (subsequently identified as the "wandering people") are described as having "neither roots nor head," being "utterly without character," and "utterly without stability." Virtually nothing else is recorded of them. They may never, in fact, have constituted a self-conscious religious grouping at all, though their condemnation would be periodically reconfirmed in subsequent writings. Rootlessness, ambiguity of identity, masterlessness, and nomadism (modernism?) had become the identifying characteristics of a supreme social evil that recently merged state and religious authority was determined to combat.

MOBILITY AND STABILITY AS PERFORMED ETHOS

Although asceticism, in the course of its incorporation by the state religion, became dominated by an explicit theology of stability, wandering ascetics, bearing alternative conceptions of truth, ideal humanity, and the relationship between spirit and movement, never completely disappeared. Wanderers, claiming moral superiority over settled society, rose to renewed cultural prominence in the Middle Ages with the mendicant friars. And with the transmutation of theological themes into secular culture, voluntary uprooting, wandering and estrangement continued to be endowed with positive cognitive and spiritual value by later romantic and modern traditions.

The morality of mobility will continue to be hotly debated. But, as we have seen, some of the themes raised by present-day writing on tourism have a long cultural tradition: affirmations of the moral superiority of "nomadism" over settled life and of minimalist travel disciplines over softer travel modes; discrediting associations of mobility with moral license, idleness, and consumption; identifications of primitive wilderness spaces, defined in opposition to morally corrupt urban spaces, as privileged sites for self-testing, purification, and contact with timeless law; concern with the degradation of salvatory, "pure" spaces by the visitors they draw; worry about the corruption of human attractions, valued for their difference, by contact with the world; claims that cultural practices lose authenticity and become vain as they are modified for show; and criticism of the destabilizing quest for new experience as an expression of idolatry.

Even some past solutions to some of these dilemmas may be prophetic. There are modern tourist attractions that will not long survive the heavy visitor traffic to which they are subjected. Will policy makers concerned with protecting fragile cultural and natural attractions imitate the holy men who ordered unwelcome visitors to return home, promising to visit them in their dreams?

Now, as in the past, we should expect definitive victories neither for the moral apologists of mobility, nor for their critics. Rather, it is the intense moral ambivalence about mobility, revealed by almost two millennia of debate, that should interest us. Such debate demonstrates the rich, infinitely complex expressive and communicative meanings that the play of the human body in geographical space can encode—meanings that can never be understood without reference to the interests (in wealth, power, prestige, freedom, and even conceptions of truth) carried by such movement.

The fact that men, dedicated to perfecting themselves in the context of a systematic philosophy of Truth, took movement so seriously, as a sign of elite spirituality or of base heresy, should help us to see what they certainly recognized: that human beings think and affirm beliefs about life, not only by verbalizing ideas, but also by contemplating and manipulating things whose endlessly suggestive meanings they only partially comprehend. By the play of their own bodies in culturally conceived space, and by the contemplation of others as they move (or stand immobilized) in such space, people perform, rather than verbalize, core experiences of self, territory, ideal sociality, and Truth. Encoded in even the humblest of travel performances, we begin to discover collectively constructed philosophies—enacted rituals, rather than professed creeds—through which human beings try to comprehend the limits and freedoms of their lives.

NOTES

1. Nelson Graburn, "Tourism: The Sacred Journey," in *Hosts and Guests: The Anthropology of Tourism*, edited by Valene L. Smith (Philadelphia: University of Pennsylvania Press, 1977), pp. 17–31; Nelson Graburn, "To Pray, Pay and Play: The Cultural Structure of Japanese Domestic Tourism," *Les Cahiers du Tourisme*. sér. B, 26 (1983), pp. 1–89; Dean MacCannell, *The Tourist: A New Theory of the Leisure Class* (New York: Schocken, 1976); Dean MacCannell, *Empty Meeting Grounds: The Tourist Papers* (New York: Routledge, 1992); E. Cohen, N. Ben-Yehuda, and J. Aviad, "Recentering the World: The Quest for 'Elective Centers' in a Secularized Universe," *Sociological Review* 35 (1987), pp. 320–346; Nancy Louise Frey, *Pilgrim Stories: On and Off the Road to Santiago* (Berkeley: University of California Press, 1998), p. 42; Eeva Jokinen and Soile Veijola, "The Disoriented Tourist: The Figuration of the Tourist in Contemporary Cultural Critique," in *Touring Cultures: Transformations of Travel and Theory*, edited by Chris Rojek and John Urry (New York: Routledge, 1997), pp. 23–52; Eeva Jokinen and Soile Veijola, "Mountains and Landscapes: Towards Embodied Visualities," in *Visual Culture and Tourism*, edited by Nina Lübbren and David Crouch (Oxford: Berg, 2002), pp. 75–93.

2. Judith Adler, "Travel as Performed Art," *American Journal of Sociology* 94 (1989), pp. 1366–1391.

3. Basil, "Introduction to the Ascetical Life," *Ascetical Works* (Washington, DC: Catholic University of America Press, 1962), p. 9.

4. From Dadisho Katraya's seventh-century work, "On Solitude," quoted in George Nedungatt, "The Covenanters of the Early Syriac-Speaking Church," *Orientalia Christiana Periodica* 39 (1973), p. 208.

5. See Norman H. Baynes, *Byzantine Studies and Other Essays* (London: Athlone, 1960), pp. 27–46; Peter Brown, *Society and the Holy in Late Antiquity* (Berkeley: University of California Press, 1982); Peter Brown, "The Saint as Exemplar in Late Antiquity," *Representations* 1, no. 2 (1983), pp. 1–27; Christiane Saulnier, "La vie monastique en Terre Sainte auprès des Lieux de Pèlerinages (IVe S.)," *Miscellanea Historiae Ecclesiasticae* 6 (1983), pp. 223–248.

6. Hagith S. Sivan, "Pilgrimage, Monasticism, and the Emergence of Christian Palestine in the Fourth Century," in *The Blessings of Pilgrimage*, edited by Robert Ousterhout (Urbana: University of Illinois Press, 1990), pp. 54–65.

7. N. Hohlwein, "Déplacements et Tourisme dans l'Égypte Romaine," *Chronique d'Égypte* 30 (1940), pp. 253–278; J. Yoyotte, "Les Pèlerinages dans l'Égypte Ancienne," *Sources Orientales* 3 (1960), pp. 18–74.

8. E. D. Hunt, *Holy Land Pilgrimage in the Later Roman Empire* (Oxford: Clarendon, 1982), pp. 51–53; John Wilkinson, *Jerusalem Pilgrims before the*

Crusades (Warminster, UK: Aris and Phillips, 1977); John Wilkinson, "Jewish Holy Places and the Origins of Christian Pilgrimage," in *The Blessings of Pilgrimage*, edited by Robert Ousterhout (Urbana: University of Illinois Press, 1990), pp. 41–53.

9. John of Ephesus, *Lives of the Eastern Saints* (Turnhout, Belgium: Brepols, 1974), p. 589.

10. Theodoret, *A History of the Monks of Syria* (Kalamazoo, MI: Cistercian Publications, 1985), p. 3.

11. John of Ephesus, *Lives*, pp. 131–132.

12. Athanasius, *The Life of Antony* (New York: Paulist Press, 1980), pp. 41–42.

13. Jerome, "Life of S. Hilarion," in *Select Works: Nicene and Post-Nicene Fathers*, 2d ser., vol. 6 (Grand Rapids, MI: Eerdmans, 1954), p. 311.

14. Cynthia Horn, "Loca Sancta Souvenirs: Sealing the Pilgrim's Experience," in *The Blessings of Pilgrimage*, edited by Robert Ousterhout (Urbana: University of Illinois Press, 1990), pp. 85–96; *Lives of the Desert Fathers: The Historia Monachorum in Aegypto* (Kalamazoo, MI: Cistercian Publications, 1980), p. 87.

15. Hans Von Campenhausen, *Tradition and Life in the Church* (London: Collins, 1968), pp. 231–251; Antoine Guillaumont, "Le dépaysement comme forme d'ascèse dans le monachisme ancien," *Annuaire: École Pratique des Hautes Études Section des Sciences Religieuses* 76 (1968–1969), pp. 3–58; Emmanuel Lanne, "La Xeniteia d'Abraham dans l'Oeuvre d'Irénée," *Irénikon* 2 (1974), pp. 163–187.

16. Jerome, "To Heliodorus," in *The Letters of Saint Jerome*, vol. 1 (London: Longmans, Green, 1963), p. 65.

17. *Lives of the Desert Fathers*, p. 93.

18. E. W. Budge, *The Paradise of the Fathers*, vol. 1 (New York: Burt Franklin, 1972), pp. 242–243.

19. Palladius, *The Lausaic History* (London: Longmans, Green, 1965), p. 105.

20. See Erik Cohen, "Nomads from Affluence: Notes on the Phenomenon of Drifter Tourism," *International Journal of Comparative Sociology* 14 (1973), pp. 89–103.

21. Jerome, "To Heliodorus," *Letters*, p. 68.

22. Grégoire de Nazianze, *Lettres*, vol. 1 (Paris: Société d'Édition "Les Belles Lettres," 1964), p. 2; André-Jean Festugière, *Antioche Païenne et Chrétienne* (Paris: Boccard, 1959), pp. 192–193.

23. Budge, *Paradise*, vol. 2, p. 17.

24. Arthur Voobus, *History of Asceticism in the Syrian Orient*, vol. 2 (Louvain: Christianorum Orientalium, 1960), p. 26.

25. Budge, *Paradise*, vol. 1, p. 339.

26. Athanasius, *Life*, pp. 42–43.

27. Palladius, *Lausaic History*, p. 57.

28. Paul van den Ven (ed.), *La Vie Ancienne de S. Syméon Stylite le Jeune* (Brussels: Société des Bollandistes, 1962), p. 133.

29. *Sayings of the Desert Fathers: The Alphabetical Collection* (Kalamazoo, MI: Cistercian Publications, 1975), p. 8.

30. Ibid., pp. 11–12.

31. Budge, *Paradise*, vol. 2, p. 6.

32. Theodoret, *History*, pp. 29, 100.

33. Ernst Gellner, *Saints of the Atlas* (Chicago: University of Chicago Press, 1969), p. 152; Bill Porter, *Road to Heaven: Encounters with Chinese Hermits* (San Francisco: Mercury House, 1993).

34. See F. R. Hoare (ed.), *The Western Fathers* (London: Steed and Ward, 1954), pp. 99, 142–143.

35. See Austin B. Ashley, *"Xenia: A Study of Hospitality in Ancient Greece"* (Ph.D. diss., Harvard University, 1940).

36. John of Ephesus, *Lives*, pp. 109–110.

37. *Lives of the Desert Fathers*, p. 55.

38. L. Regnault (ed.), *Les sentences des pères du désert* (Sable sur Sarthe: Abbaye Saint-Pierre de Solesmes, 1966), p. 117.

39. See Athanasius's "Ad Monachos," cited in Brian Brennan, "Athanasius' Vita Antonii: A Sociological Interpretation," *Vigiliae Christianae* 39 (1985), p. 219.

40. Budge, *Paradise*, vol. 1, p. xiv; Antoine Guillaumont, "Histoire des Moines aux Kellia," *Orientalia Louvaniensia Periodica* 8 (1977), p. 198; Hunt, *Holy Land Pilgrimage*, pp. 63–67; André-Jean Festugière (ed.), "Vie de Daniel le Stylite," *Les Moines d'Orient*, vol. 2 (Paris: Cerf, 1961), p. 131.

41. Festugière, "Vie de Daniel le Stylite," pp. 110–111.

42. van den Ven, *La Vie Ancienne de S. Syméon*, p. 166.

43. John of Ephesus, *Lives*, pp. 220–227.

44. *The Rule of the Master* (Kalamazoo, MI: Cistercian Publications, 1977), pp. 106–107.

45. Augustine, "De opere Monachorum," in *Nicene and Post-Nicene Fathers*, 1st ser., vol. 3 (Grand Rapids, MI: Eerdmans, 1971) p. 521.

46. L.Th.A. Lorié, *Spiritual Terminology in the Latin Translations of the Vita Antonii* (Nijmegen, Netherlands: Dekker & van de Vegt, 1955), pp. 118–123.

47. Adalbert de Vogüé (ed.), *La Règle de Saint Benoit*, vol. 6 (Paris: Cerf, 1971), p. 1330.

48. Ernest W. McConnell, "Monastic Stability: Some Socioeconomic Considerations," in *Charanis Studies: Essays in Honor of Peter Charanis*, edited by Aneliki E. Laiou-Thomadiakis (New Brunswick, NJ: Rutgers University Press, 1980), pp. 115–150.

49. Adalbert de Vogüé (ed.), *Les Règles des Saints Pères* (Paris: Cerf, 1982), p. 24; Adalbert de Vogüé (ed.), *Règles Monastiques d'Occident* (Bégrolles-en-Mauges: Abbaye de Bellefontaine, 1980), p. 36.

50. Jo Ann McNamara, "Muffled Voices: The Lives of Consecrated Women in the Fourth Century," in *Distant Echoes: Medieval Religious Women*, vol. 1, ed-

ited by John A. Nichols and Lilian T. Shank (Kalamazoo, MI: Cistercian Publications, 1984), pp. 11–29; Jane T. Schulenburg, "Strict Active Enclosure and Its Effects on the Female Monastic Experience (ca. 500–1100)," in ibid., pp. 51–87.

51. Michael Allen Williams, *The Immoveable Race: A Gnostic Designation and the Theory of Stability in Late Antiquity* (Leiden: Brill, 1985); Antoine Guillaumont, "Un philosophe au desert: Evagre le Pontique," *Revue de L'histoire des Religions* 181 (1972), pp. 29–56.

52. Evacre Le Pontique, *Traité Pratique ou Le Moine*, vol. 2 (Paris: Cerf, 1971), pp. 521–528; Lorié, *Spiritual Terminology*, pp. 126–129.

53. Epiphanius of Salamis, *The Penarion of Epiphanius of Salamis* (New York: Brill, 1987), p. xvii.

Chapter 3

The Sociology of Medieval Pilgrimage: Contested Views and Shifting Boundaries

Lutz Kaelber

Pilgrimage is known to the major world religions as a means of spiritual purification that requires travel. Pilgrimage is not only one of the oldest forms of travel, but continues to be an important form of religious travel in this day and age as well—when, for example, millions of Muslims each year visit Mecca during the month of pilgrimage, and Hindu pilgrims journey to a vast number of holy sites in India.[1]

Pilgrimage is also prominent in Christianity and, in a broad sense of the term, has been an integral aspect of Christian religion from its inception. One of Christianity's basic tenets is that earthly life is but a small part of existence, after which the uncertainty of the afterlife awaits a person—ultimately, heaven or hell. A person journeys toward that end from the beginning of his or her existence. Hence, as ecclesiastical doctrine maintains, "earthly life was a phase of the journey, the *peregrinatio*, the pilgrimage, in which individual Christians sought to merit, even earn, the reward of Heaven; to make a bargain, perhaps a contract, with God to secure eternal felicity."[2] To merit salvation and to help earn the reward of heaven, a pilgrimage, in the more narrow sense of the term, could be undertaken. In Europe, pilgrimage as a normative model of travel had its heyday in the Middle Ages, when a great many people traveled to shrines and other places that had a special, sacred meaning.[3]

This chapter provides a sociological account of medieval pilgrimage.[4] It has two major theoretical foci. First, it conceptualizes pilgrimage as a contested activity. Following John Eade and Michael Sallnow's path-breaking elaboration of Victor Turner's notions on liminality in pilgrimage, it describes cultural agents' competing discourses about the form and the content of medieval pilgrimage.[5] Medieval heretics and women, I show, were particularly adept at generating alternative meanings of pilgrimage that were at odds with ecclesiastical discourse. Second, the chapter thematizes such discourses, to borrow a term used in the sociology of knowledge, as "boundary-work." I describe and analyze shifting cultural boundaries between pilgrimage proper and other religious or related forms of travel. These boundaries not only were contested and shifted over the course of the Middle Ages, but also became particularly blurry in early modern and modern times.

PILGRIMS' LIMINALITY AND PILGRIMAGE AS A CONTESTED ACTIVITY

Based on his prolific studies of the major world religions, the anthropologist Victor Turner has provided comprehensive analyses of pilgrimage over time and in different periods.[6] Turner relates pilgrimages to "liminal" activities. These are activities by which people escape from the confinements of their ordinary lives. They enter new fields of experience that differ from those in their past. Liminality may denote radical changes in personal conduct, but it can also be a transient and fragmentary experience, allowing people to revert back to their previous ways of life. Liminal activities, thus, are transitional activities of a world-transcending nature.

Besides release from mundane structure, Turner attributes other characteristics to the liminality of pilgrimage.[7] Pilgrimage provides for the homogenization of status. Liminality severs the ties to past activities and positions, which tends to level status differences and role structures. Hence, during the transitional period of pilgrimage, horizontal rather than vertical ties predominate. Lack of social stratification in pilgrimage provides a leveling experience. Pilgrimage's transcendent nature also creates a new sense of community among the participants. As old social ties are loosened, new ones develop. Attachments form among the pilgrims themselves and the communities around them. Communal experiences of liminality contribute to an egalitarian social structure.

Finally, liminality in pilgrimage leads to the shaping of new identities. The self is reconstituted around liminal symbols and practices that once were peripheral to the pilgrim. In religious pilgrimage, the constitution of a pilgrim's identity, Turner points out, is most often linked to a physical object or location that represents the sacred. Objects or locations, such as

holy shrines, provide "evidence for the faithful that their religion is still in-
stinct with supernatural power and grace; that it has objective efficacy derived from the founder's god or gods and transmitted by means of miracles,
wonders, and signs through saints, martyrs, and holy men."[8] In short, the
constitution of identity in pilgrimage is tied to place as locus of supernatural forces.

While Turner's work became the dominant account of pilgrimage in the
social sciences over the last three decades,[9] sharp criticism has come from
the anthropologists John Eade and Michael Sallnow. Reviewing a broad
range of anthropological literature, they dispute the importance of shrines
and sacred centers as loci of sacredness for pilgrims and argue that Turner
overemphasized the anti-structural elements of community in pilgrimages.
Moreover, they deconstruct Turner's account by pointing to the contested
nature of pilgrimage. Pilgrimages should be viewed as what they call a
"realm of competing discourses" by which opposing groups attach different
meanings to pilgrimage. Thus, rather than providing descriptions of pilgrimage, social scientists should investigate a multiplicity of discourses
about pilgrimage.[10] Far from providing shared experiences and attitudes toward this religious activity, pilgrimage has multiple meanings. It also represents a variety of religious actions and experiences.

The deconstruction of Turner's account leads Eade and Sallnow to pro-
pose a new paradigm that depicts pilgrimage as contested activity and any
account of it as contested knowledge.[11] Contested knowledge reflects contesting and competing notions about what such religious travel is or should
be. These notions can come from different groups, including the pilgrims
themselves, clerics, and heretics, and they can also derive from tradition or
innovative practices.

In the following sections, I intend to broaden the focus of Eade and
Sallnow's deconstructionist paradigm of pilgrimage to medieval religious
travel, and address diverse discourses and perceptions that existed about
such travel. Since discursive structures reflect, at least in part, social structure and are shaped by it, a complete analysis needs to go beyond discourse.
I focus on inequalities in power to sustain and socially implement such discourses and perceptions, which allows me to include gender inequalities in
the analysis.[12] Moreover, the analysis will show that some of the
contestation centered precisely on the issue of liminality in pilgrimage.[13]

BOUNDARY-WORK AND PILGRIMAGE

Discourse is often used to delineate positions and may reflect the boundary-work of cultural agents. The term "boundary-work" originated in the

sociology of knowledge.[14] It refers to activities that uphold social boundaries between institutions and social spheres, activities by which groups and
institutions seek to establish their social status and affirm their societal position vis-à-vis competing claims. Boundary-work serves to legitimize a status or activity by setting a boundary around, or a limit to, the types of
activities that are considered legitimate. Thus, boundary-work involves a
process of demarcation. In science, following the pioneering work of
Thomas Kuhn on paradigm shifts, this process has been thematized as "the
demarcation of science from non-science."[15] I have previously applied the
concept of boundary-work to the religious sphere in an analysis of the shifting boundaries between magic and religion, as well as orthodoxy and heterodoxy, and the demarcation of the former from the latter.[16]

The concept of boundary-work can also be employed in the analysis of
medieval pilgrimage. Boundary-work in this chapter refers to activities of
pilgrims and other agents or institutions to delineate the liminal or world-
transcending qualities of pilgrimage, and to defend—or to challenge—the
appropriateness of pilgrimage as a religious activity. Such contesting views
can be found in orthodoxy, but they are particularly relevant to religious heresy, and to the pilgrimage of women. Boundary-work furthermore refers to
the delineation of religious pilgrimage from other related or similar activities. Foremost among such activities are postmedieval pilgrimages that
blend religious and secular purposes.

SHIFTING BOUNDARIES OF MEDIEVAL PILGRIMAGE

Pilgrimage in medieval religion was a multifaceted phenomenon. The
analysis of its forms and varieties begins with three ideal-typical depic-
tions: pilgrimage as itinerancy displayed by saintly ascetics; as orthodox religious practice taken up by large numbers of worshipers; and as expression
of popular adherence to a type of folk religion that, on occasion, came into
sharp conflict with ecclesiastical authorities.

Pilgrimage in Medieval Religion

Around 1205, in the chapel of San Damiano near Assisi, Francesco di
Bernadone, the son of a wealthy cloth merchant, heard a voice. It came
from the crucifix above the altar. "Francis, go and repair my house." Francis followed the orders he received in his vision. He gave away everything
he had, devoted himself to preaching, and wandered around in poverty.
Gradually, other men joined him, rejecting the ownership of goods, sleeping in barns and shacks, begging or working in menial jobs to support
themselves. Guided by their leader, Francis of Assisi, they embraced per-

manent travel—itinerancy—as their lifestyle. To them, renunciation meant not to dwell in the pleasures of this world; instead, they attempted to emulate the early apostolic communities, living without a fixed abode. This led Jacques de Vitry in 1216 to write down the following observations: "they live after the manner of the primitive Church, of which it is written: 'The multitude of them that believed were of one heart and soul.' By day they go into the towns and village in order to win others by setting them an example. At night they retire to some hermitage or lonely place and give themselves up to meditation."[17]

About two hundred years later, in Jerusalem, one of the travelers to the Holy Land was a woman named Margery. Margery was about forty years old and had borne fourteen children. After struggling with her husband to allow her to live a different life, she emerged victorious and made a vow of chastity. From then on, she began to travel frequently, both to places in her native England, and to countries like Italy, Spain, Norway, Germany, and the Holy Land. Later, she reflected on her travel experiences in her autobiography, *The Book of Margery Kempe*, a book that made her one of the most famous mystics of the Middle Ages.[18]

Roughly in the middle of the time period between Francis of Assisi and Margery Kempe fall the somewhat peculiar events pertaining to a third person to be mentioned here, Armanno Pungilupo. Pungilupo was a citizen of Ferrara, Italy. On the surface, he displayed the marks of a pious Catholic: in the last twenty-five years of his life—before his death in 1268—he went to confession regularly, and he undertook a local pilgrimage. People in the town of Ferrara mourned his death; after he was buried in the bishop's cathedral, people in the town undertook little pilgrimages to his grave where they witnessed miracles. It became a much-frequented shrine visited by people believing in the miraculous powers of the dead Armanno. It is important to note that such local people included both orthodox Catholics and supporters of Catharism, a dualist heresy with strongholds in southern France and northern Italy that was stamped out by the early fourteenth century. Apparently neither the local pilgrims nor the cathedral clergy questioned Armanno's sanctity, at least not until a Dominican inquisition revealed him to be a heretic. He was a lay believer of Catharism who, in spite of his outward appearance of pious orthodoxy, was sharply critical of the institutions of the Catholic church. To squelch any further travel to Armanno's grave as a pilgrimage site, in 1301 his bones were exhumed, burnt, and disposed of in a river. His shrine was dismantled.[19]

Francis of Assisi, Margery Kempe, and Armanno Pungilupo relate to medieval pilgrimage in different ways. St. Francis exemplifies the life of a religious virtuoso, one who tries to surpass worldly morality through other-worldly asceticism. For such a religious virtuoso, pilgrimage is one of the means of renouncing the world and transcending its boundaries. In the Middle Ages, such pilgrimage was part of, to use a phrase coined by Max Weber, "the medieval economy of salvation."[20] In this salvation economy, there were two tiers of ethical demands: the *consilia evangelica*, or evangelical counsels, and the *præcepta*, or commands. Nuns and monks were held to the higher ethical standards of the evangelical counsels, according to which monastic life was disciplined and systematized. The counsels, which came to be understood as being identical to the obligations expressed in the monastic vows—poverty, chastity, and obedience—rendered salvation more assured and expeditious, and were thus seen as the primary ways and means to the perfection of Christian life. Those who had been successful in this quest, the saints, having attained perfection and entered into the presence of God, not only had surpassed worldly morality through other-worldly asceticism, but also were believed to have procured a surplus of good works (*opera supererogationis*) that was accumulated by the monastics as well. In the later Middle Ages, orthodox doctrine referred to this surplus as the "thesaurus of merits."[21]

While the saintly achievement of merit reflected, in Weber's terms, an "ethic of heroes," there was also a medieval "ethic of the average."[22] The ethic of the average was reflected in the commands that, according to Church doctrine, were to reign over mundane life. The commands, as expressed in the Ten Commandments, concern the basic ethical precepts that all Christians ought to follow. If they failed to do so, medieval Catholics could compensate for their own ethical shortcomings by tapping the thesaurus of merits of the saints and by partaking in the supererogatory works of the monks and nuns administered by the Church.

Pilgrimage, in medieval Catholicism's moral economy, thus had two primary functions. First, among religious virtuosos, particularly at the beginning and toward the end of the Middle Ages, pilgrimage was one of the means of renouncing the world and transcending its confinements. It allowed religious virtuosos to enter into a liminal state that was linked to increased status in the community. Not only canonization and legend, but also pilgrimage, as Alexander Murray so aptly puts it, "could accord to an ascetic hermit a reputation which many an ancient hero might have envied."[23] Ascetic hermits were not the only ones, however, whose reputation might be enhanced by pilgrimage, as the enthusiastic response of the populace to the mendicant orders showed. The mendicant orders were successful at least in part because they broke with received monastic traditions and left the seclusion of the cloister for the busy streets of the city. Instead of collective stability they chose individual mobility, as was the case for the group around St. Francis and many other religious communities who emulated the apostolic life.[24]

If pilgrimage for virtuosos was a means to display signs of sainthood, it could for the masses also be a means to express devotion to these saints and their earthly remains, as evidenced in the travels of Margery Kempe and the cult of Armanno Pungilupo. Devotional pilgrimage was tied to shrines and relics. The principal pilgrimage site was Rome, where St. Peter and St. Paul are buried, but in the high and late Middle Ages other major sites gained in importance, including Jerusalem, and the shrines of St. James at Compostela, St. Thomas at Canterbury, and the Three Kings of Cologne. Yet ordinary people in the Middle Ages could usually not afford to go on long-distance travel to such grand sites, many of which were located in the periphery of Western Christianity. They were most likely to go on pilgrimages to one or several of the myriad local sites devoted to national and local saints.

As Patrick Geary has shown in a seminal essay on the mobility of sainthood, up to the High Middle Ages the physical proximity of saints in relics and other holy objects was of great significance to the pilgrimage process.[25] Unlike in the eastern Mediterranean, where the object of devotion was the artistic representation of a saint in an icon, in the West the link between people and the sphere of the divine was the corporeal remains of the saints. In early Christianity, such remains were typically those of Christian martyrs. They were not to be moved from their locations. However, contrary to the Roman tradition to have sites of religious worship and ritual in the cities, Christianity in late Antiquity and the early Middle Ages placed its centers of sanctity outside the confines of the cities. Moreover, in the process of Christianizing the rural hinterlands of Europe, Carolingian ecclesiastical authorities allowed relics, as visible representations of sanctity, to be relocated to such remote sites, where popular religious practice could be better controlled by the Church. There it reflected the earthly relations between lords and serfs on a divine plane, bringing together supplicants expecting worldly favors and their favorite mediators to the holy. At the shrines miracles tended to occur fairly regularly, as they, Geary notes, "advertised the virtues and importance of saints and thus increased the number of pilgrims to their shrines. . . . [S]aints by their physical presence were a primary means of social integration, identity, protection, and economic support for the communities in which they were found."[26]

The nature of such local pilgrimage underwent significant changes in the eleventh and twelfth centuries. First, pilgrims and crusaders to Palestine brought back an increasing number of relics, lessening the reliance on local saints. Second, as the social landscape of Western Christianity became more urbanized and commercialized, the association between a local protector and pilgrims tended to get replaced by a larger bond between translocal saints and their clientele. Third, the cult of Mary and the Eucharist, the former a universal saint, the latter a practice with a focus on consecrated objects, took away from the importance of corporeal remains of local saints.[27]

Depending on the distance and the time of year, pilgrimages could be arduous undertakings. One can distinguish four phases of pilgrimage: the departure, the journey, the encounter with the holy at the shrine, and the return.[28] Preparation for departure could begin many months before a pilgrimage. Most important were sincere contrition and confession of sins to the pilgrim's parish priest, without which a pilgrimage was considered worthless. The priest gave a blessing as well. Wealthy pilgrims could make a will, and they were expected to give to charity before departure. Pilgrims were also to wear a distinctive garb, and badges, which could take on the function of an amulet with a protective charm. During the pilgrims' absence, their assets were immune from civil lawsuits, and their families were placed under ecclesiastical protection.

Similar civic and ecclesiastical protections also extended to pilgrims on their journey, at least in theory. Among the longest journeys were those to Jerusalem. In the eleventh century, due to the conversion of Hungary and Byzantine's revival, it could be reached via an overland route, but increasing political instability in the areas along that route made sea voyage the preferred way of travel thereafter. Either type of travel could be very hazardous, and even when travelers were physically safe, they often had to endure difficult conditions. Osterrieth provides this instructive example of a French pilgrim at sea:

> It would do to be fussy
> About food for it happens
> Many times and quite often
> That stinking food must be eaten
> Badly covered and sunbaked,
> Eating dishes nearly rotten,
> And wines with sorts of foul tastes,
> Them many, they drink often.[29]

After arrival at the shrine, pilgrims were often described as being in a state of elation. Such elation could last for days, and it could be bolstered by the pilgrim procuring some of the merchandise offered around a shrine, including medals, badges, and rosaries, as well as jewels and drapery for the wealthier pilgrims. Fairs on the feast days of saints were common, even though clergy viewed them negatively because of their carnivalesque character, with little effect on the mood of the participants.[30] The return of the pilgrim from the holy site was the last phase of the pilgrimage, which in some cases took years to conclude.

Yet not all pilgrimages were taxing, nor were all undertaken voluntarily. Pilgrimages could be imposed by ecclesiastical or secular authorities, in which case they took on a mandatory penitential character. Secular authorities, which included civil courts, guilds, and other corporations, began to prescribe pilgrimage as one outcome of the juridical persecution of heterodoxy. When the Inquisition against Waldensians and Cathars commenced in full in southern France in the 1240s, heretics were condemned to go on pilgrimages to sites as far away as the Holy Land, England, and Germany. In one case, the inquisition by Bernard de Caux and Jean de Saint-Pierre in 1245–1246, of 207 condemned heretics, twenty-three were condemned to perpetual imprisonment, whereas the remaining 184 were compelled to wear a yellow cross and to go on minor or major pilgrimages. Pilgrimage as punishment continued in later inquisitions.[31] Many civil authorities thereafter used pilgrimages as the equivalent of banishment, to rid themselves of members who seriously disturbed the peace or committed other acts that threatened their communities.[32]

Moreover, ecclesiastical authorities employed pilgrimage as a punishment for sin. After contrition, confession, and absolution, the sinner had to do penance, and pilgrimage became one of the most common forms of penance. On some occasions, such pilgrimages could span long periods, as in this punishment, found in an Irish canon (ca. 1000), for a tyrant (king): "If a tyrant binds anyone attached to a bishop, he shall release him safe and sound and make restitution, and . . . he himself shall remain in the penance of a hard pilgrimage alone for a period of ten years; and if he touches him so as to wound him, . . . he himself shall remain alone on pilgrimage for the space of twenty years."[33]

The penitential character of such pilgrimages was not always upheld, however. In the later Middle Ages pilgrimages increasingly attained a ritualistic character in popular religion, in that the notion became popular that sins were remitted by the very act of formally visiting a particular shrine, regardless of the internal state of the penitent. At least in the eyes of some clerical observers, this sometimes left the state of penitence wanting and turned pilgrimage into a sightseeing tour. When the German friar Felix Fabri journeyed to Jerusalem in 1480, he observed: "We did not spend more than nine days in the Holy Land, and in that time we were rushed around the usual Holy Places both by day and night, and were hardly given any time to rest. . . . When we had hurriedly visited the Holy Places . . . we were led out of the

Holy City by the same road by which we had come, down to the sea where our galley waited."[34] Such travelers were prone to display what Christian literature excoriated as "curiosities," the morally useless exercise of wandering around, signaling instability and waywardness.[35]

Fabri's complaints about the touristic nature of religious voyages and the quick and superficial tour he got are reflective of related practices that detracted from the original purpose of pilgrimage. The wide availability of indulgences that could be obtained by paying a sum of money allowed penitents to substitute them for other, more traditional kinds of penance, including pilgrimage. Even pilgrimage by proxy became possible, to the extent that professional pilgrims were employed to perform pilgrimages vicariously for recompense. Such practices, in the extreme, all but eliminated the liminal character of pilgrimage.[36]

Contesting Medieval Pilgrimage

While the boundaries between pilgrimage as a liminal stage and other penitential or mundane activities became increasingly blurred in the late Middle Ages, contesting discourses existed throughout the Middle Ages, both in orthodoxy and in heterodoxy, about the appropriateness of pilgrimage as a penitential practice. In late Antiquity and the early Middle Ages, there was no shortage of exhortations from ecclesiastical authorities not to abuse pilgrimages. One such exhortation was presented by the Council of Châlons in 813. Its decreed that

grave error is committed by some who go thoughtlessly to Rome or Tours and to certain other places on the pretext of prayer. There are priests and deacons and other clergy who, living carelessly, think that they are purged of their sins thereby and may perform their ministry, if they go to these places. There are laity no less, who think they can sin, or have sinned, with impunity because they are going to pray at these places. There are some powerful men, who acquire a great deal by levying taxes on the pretext of a journey to Rome or Tours and who do it solely out of cupidity, pretending that they are doing so by reason of a visit to a church or holy places. There are poor people who do the same in order to have a better pretext for begging. Of this number are those who, wandering around falsely, claim that they are on a pilgrimage, or who are so stupid that they think that they are purged of their sins simply by the sight of holy places.[37]

Pulling no punches, the council members included all social strata in their criticism. This may be seen as an indication of how concerned ecclesiastical authorities had become about the widespread abuse of, and misconceptions about, penitential pilgrimage.[38] Critics continued to rebut popular views of an automatic efficacy of pilgrimage as time went on, with a sharper focus on the intentions of pilgrims than their actions after the eleventh century.[39] As the objects of criticism, two types of pilgrimage deserve particular attention: first, the pilgrimage of orthodox religious women; second, penitential pilgrimage as viewed by heterodox groups.

Within orthodoxy some of the harshest discourse and contestation focused on the pilgrimage of women. Female pilgrims had been part of the ascetic movements of late Antiquity, immediately facing objections by Church authorities.[40] In the Middle Ages, these objections continued. They were motivated in part by the view that women were less adept at withstanding the temptations of the world to which pilgrimage would inevitably expose them, and in part by the fact that virtuoso religion had, according to tradition, its outlet in the monastic life. Monastic life entailed that those who participated in it, as a contemporary commentator put it, "were forever enclosed within the prison of [their] own heart[s]." It also meant a cloistered life. Strict enclosure was the norm for Benedictine, Cluniac, and Cistercian establishments for women.[41]

Even though the advent of the mendicant orders signified one of the most distinctive discontinuities in medieval monasticism, it did not bring about a different view of women's pilgrimage.[42] St. Dominic established a cloister for women at Prouille in 1206, some nine years before the first male religious community of Dominicans was founded. Unlike St. Francis, the founder of the Franciscans who remained reserved toward the idea of women affiliating with his order, Dominic accepted women wishing to join the religious life. In spite of a quota system to regulate demand, 141 Dominican convents for nuns existed by 1303. At the same time, Franciscan convents, inspired by the saintly example of Clare of Assisi, proliferated as well. Yet mendicant nuns lived a religious life quite different from that of the friars. Most important, they continued the monastic tradition of strict enclosure for women. In principle never allowed to leave the convent, nuns were prevented from preaching and begging and had limited personal contact with the outside world. Their religious voyage, so to speak, was internal, one that happened in the form of a secluded life of simplicity and contemplative devotion. While Franciscan and Dominican friars were free to roam the world, their female counterparts often turned inward, contributing greatly to the mystical and devotional literature in the later Middle Ages.[43]

Much of orthodox discourse, then, was intent on confining women's liminality to the cloister. Yet, as Caroline Bynum argues, to leave it at that would mean to present history from the point of view of those who write about medieval women, rather than with them.[44] Women joined religious groups not closely affiliated with religious orders in large numbers in the late Middle Ages to be able to prevail in their spiritual journey in the world rather than outside of it, but they appear to have had a different view of their spirituality from the men who wrote about them: they often saw their religious practices not as liminal but as a continuation of their everyday lives. Unlike their male counterparts, most religious women—as liminal personae—did not experience a sharp break with the past. Still, to continue their worldly activities they typically had to obtain male approval and protection, as was the case for Margery Kempe and the fifteenth-century mystic Dorothy of Montau. When those two went on their extensive pilgrimages, they were seen as fit to travel only when they took their husbands or other protectors along.[45] Women's travel in general was morally suspect and was not to be conducted without male supervision—views and practices criticized, if only implicitly, by women.[46] Travel, in the more general sense, was therefore certainly a reflection of the gendered social structure of the time.[47]

Orthodox and heterodox religious movements also addressed pilgrimage as a controversial topic that served to establish boundaries on both sides. Lambert le Bègue, the archetype of a charismatic, devoted, and puritanical village priest, who lived in the diocese of Liège in the late twelfth century, found himself the center of controversy and charged with heresy when he took on what he perceived as abuses of popular piety, including pilgrimage. Money for pilgrimages abroad, Lambert maintained, could sometimes be better used at home. This was particularly true for parish priests who journeyed to Jerusalem instead of attending to the needs of their flock at home. The charges against Lambert did not prevail, and he died a vindicated man.[48]

Criticism of pilgrimage took on a much stronger form in heretical movements. For the largest two heresies of the High Middle Ages, the Cathars and the Waldensians, pilgrimage had no redeeming value. For the Cathars, one of the differences between their belief system and that of Catholicism was that they negated the notion of penance as soteriological practice. Cathars believed that in the Fall souls had fallen from the spiritual realm, leaving behind a good part of them, the spirit. Souls, according to Cathar mythology, were now trapped in earthly bodies and awaited the reunion with the spirit. The reunion required that Cathars receive the central sacrament of spiritual baptism (*consolamentum*) and conduct themselves afterward in a pure manner until death, upon which their souls would be able to return to the spirit in the spiritual realm. The notion of pilgrimage as a way to lessen God's punishment, as well as to seek the intercession of a saint on behalf of the pilgrim—a practice so prominent in Catholicism—was in principle alien to Cathar faith, even though it did not prevent some, as shown by the case of Armanno Pungilupo, from mingling heterodox faith with orthodox practices. This appears to have been rather uncommon, however, for Catharism's leadership stratum, the "perfect."[49]

For the Waldensians, the denial of the spiritual value of pilgrimage had different religious roots. Waldensianism had its origin as a reform movement within the Catholic church, from where it was quickly driven to its fringes and found itself anathemized. The push into heresy did not prevent the Waldensians, however, from adopting the view that they represented the true Christian church, and that the basis of salvation was faith. They believed faith expressed itself in being poor, in preaching, and in practicing scriptural commandments to the letter, not in rituals. Especially after they had become the target of inquisitions from the 1230s onward, Waldensians increasingly renounced major facets of orthodox religious beliefs and practices, such as confession, veneration of saints, suffrages for the dead, and the belief in purgatory. Pilgrimage can be added to this list. For example, the Dominican inquisitor Anselm of Alessandria wrote of the Waldensians: "they see no worth at all in pilgrimages."[50] Similarly, the *Passau Anonymous*, compiled in the mid-thirteenth century by an anonymous Dominican friar about an inquisition in the diocese of Passau and perhaps one of the most illuminating writings on heresy in all of the Middle Ages, explicitly mentions pilgrimage as a practice abhorred by the Waldensians.[51] In its rejection of pilgrimage as well as other orthodox practices, Waldensianism was thus, in the words of one historian, "reactionary in its piety when compared to the high and late medieval tendency toward increasing the means and ways of attaining grace."[52]

In the pre-Reformation period, heretical groups continued to voice views critical of pilgrimage and to demarcate themselves from orthodoxy. Pilgrimage became so contested that the medieval Church responded by making adherence to the practice of pilgrimage an indicator of fidelity. When made to abjure heresy in 1395, the English Lollard William Dynet swore that he "shal nevermore despise pylgremage."[53] Yet this did not stop Lollards from attacking pilgrimage. A year earlier, in 1394, Lollards had publicly proclaimed that

pilgrimages, prayers, and offerings made to blind crosses or roods, and to deaf images of wood or stone, are pretty well akin to idolatry and far from alms. . . . [W]e ask you, pilgrim, to tell us when you offer to the bones of saints placed in a shrine in any spot, whether you relieve the saint who is in joy, or that almshouse which is so well endowed and for which men have been canonized, God knows how.[54]

In a similar vein, when examined by his archbishop in 1407, the Lollard William Thorpe asserted he had examined the motives and conduct of men and women who went on pilgrimages, only to find that such fond people waste blamefully God's goods in their vain pilgrimages, spending their goods upon vicious hostelers, which are oft unclean women of their bodies; and at the least those with which they should do works of mercy, after God's bidding, to poor needy men and women. These poor men's goods and their liveli-hoods these runners-about offer to rich priests, who have mickle more livelihood than they need; and thus those goods they waste wilfully and spend them unjustly, against God's bidding, upon strangers, with which they should help and relieve, af-ter God's will, their poor needy neighbors at home.[55]

While heretical criticism did not stem the proliferation of smaller cults and pilgrimage sites, critical voices continued to follow the tenor of Lollard sen-timents, including those of Jan Hus, Erasmus, Thomas More, and Martin Luther. Contested views on pilgrimage marked the boundaries not only be-tween orthodoxy and heterodoxy, but also between critics of popular prac-tice and those defending it in the Catholic religion itself.[56]

POSTMEDIEVAL PILGRIMAGE: DISENCHANTED PILGRIMS?

With Protestant Reformation theology hostile to pilgrimage and a re-formed Catholic church that tempered what it considered excesses of penitential rituals, it is tempting to write the history of the early modern age as if the practice of pilgrimage was fading and rituals were giving way to inward expressions of religious faith and even indifference. Had Luther himself not proclaimed that "the true Christian pilgrimage is not to Rome, or Compostela, but to the prophets, the Psalms, and the Gospels," a notion the post-Tridentine Catholic church did not entirely ignore when attempt-ing to impose order on traditional pilgrimages and to curtail what it consid-ered excess?[57]

Accounts of postmedieval pilgrimages suggest, by contrast, that pilgrim-age continued to be popular. In regard to not only this activity, but also other religious practices, a Weberian "disenchantment" came about rather slowly, if at all, or so it seems.[58] Historical scholarship on religion in the early mod-ern era shows that old and new pilgrimage sites continued to be major at-tractions. In Nîmes, Huguenots no less than Catholics went on pilgrimages, and shrines in England still attracted their share of pilgrims.[59] Pilgrimages in both Protestant and Catholic regions in Germany continued to be popular well into the twentieth century.[60] Eugen Weber's seminal study of the mod-ernization of rural France provides ample examples for the resilience of pil-grimage in the French countryside. He also shows that there was more to pilgrimage than religious activity. In its modern forms, it included social and economic aspects: "Pilgrimages were festive occasions involving food and drink, shopping and dancing. . . . 'It's more a pleasure trip than a pious action,' caviled an eastern teacher in 1888. What was wrong with its being both? At this unexalted level, the pilgrimage and traveling were one and the same thing. Indeed, in the Dombes *vyazhou* (voyage) was a synonym for pilgrimage."[61] At least in this case voyage, festive travel, and pilgrimage had become difficult to distinguish.

De-Centered Religious Tourism and Pilgrimage

The increasing fuzziness of the boundaries between pilgrimage and related types of travel, and even between religious travel and tourism, has been noted by a great many observers who find it difficult analytically and empirically to distinguish between the two.[62] These observers agree, however, that the erosion of boundaries is linked to the expansion of various forms of travel. As recently as the early 1970s, the majority of Americans, one of the most mobile peoples on earth, had never spent a night away from home in a hotel or motel. A quarter-century later, in 1995, Americans logged about 800 billion long-distance travel miles and completed about 650 million household trips for business or pleasure.[63] For religious travel, Catholic pilgrimage sites as far away as those in Goa and Velankani, India, draw about 1.5 million pilgrims annually, not to mention better-known places such as Lourdes, which attracts up to four million visitors per year. Many more sites could be added to this list.[64] In many such cases, the simultaneous expansion of tourism and religious travel has led to the amalgamation of the two. This has been pointed out in a comprehensive survey of traditional European religious sites:

Although the impact of mass tourism may effect dramatic changes on small festive pilgrimages, there is no evidence to suggest that tourism and pilgrimage are intrinsically incompatible. For example, there is a growing interest in a form of religiously oriented tourism that is emotionally satisfying, whether it involves visiting architecturally significant shrines, participating in retreats, or hiking along Europe's Medieval pilgrimage routes. In some cases, shrine administrators view tourists as potential pilgrims; thus the integration of the traditional religious focus with secular interests becomes a missionary challenge. In addition, the acceptability of secular visitors varies regionally, with a tendency toward greater tolerance of nondevotional spectators at Mediterranean Europe's festive pilgrimages, which historically mix the sacred with the profane. Even in these regions, however, too many outsiders with no interest in a festival's religious significance can erode the event's traditional characteristics, and missionary efforts can fall on barren ground. As a result, the event may become largely secularized, or it may go underground to reemerge in a new form, often at a different date.[65]

In this time and age, the blurring of boundaries does not end at sites that were once exclusively religious in nature but now function to address both sacred and profane needs of travelers whose motivations may or may not be religious. The sphere of cultural and religious travel has become fragmented in many ways. For example, modern travel includes provisions for those who wish to go on a political pilgrimage, to pay homage to their political heroes of the past and present.[66] Moreover, in his illuminating analysis of American pilgrimage landscapes, Juan Campo has recently demonstrated just how de-centered this landscape has become. While traditional religious pilgrimage remains vibrant in the United States, it has been complemented by cultural journeys and popular quests to a plethora of national shrines such as Mount Rushmore and Graceland. These shrines are sacralized by the commemoration of national heritage, the seamless interconnection of God and country, and the attribution of patriotic significance to natural landscape or other physical space. In the example of Graceland, the postmortem Elvis reemerges as a sanitized saintly figure whose portrait is modeled after those of a white, Euro-American Jesus.[67]

POSTMODERN PILGRIMAGE—*QUO VADIS?*

The purpose of this chapter has been to give a sociological account of medieval pilgrimage. The chapter focused on pilgrimage as a religious activity that was at times highly contested in the Middle Ages. The center of contention was the liminality of pilgrimage. In that period, it was also an activity that was demarcated from other, related forms of religious travel in changing ways. The findings presented in this chapter therefore caution against painting a conventional but perhaps all-too-rosy picture of medieval pilgrimage, as if medieval pilgrimage had always been a sacred, hazardous, and strenuous religious enterprise that was based on a shared theological framework—a framework that has since been gradually but steadily lost. The analysis here rejects the appropriateness of this conventional but inaccurate paradigm by demonstrating the existence of multiple religious frameworks of pilgrimage and a plurality of particularistic meanings that were attached to it, based on the finding that there existed an abundance of heretical perspectives on pilgrimage in the later Middle Ages and ample internal dissension about it in the Catholic church throughout the Middle Ages.

This is not to deny, of course, that societal transformations in the advent of modernity have led to a further mixing of the sacred and the profane in travel, and that most recently there has been, as postmodernists would argue, an *implosion* of boundaries between pilgrimage and other forms of travel. The notion of liminality in pilgrimage vis-à-vis life in general is certainly much more problematic in the postmodern era than medieval times, and it seems impossible to conceive of a "center" in postmodern travel or pilgrimage, and of some meta-narrative to reflect on its forms.

Nor can one deny that the postmodern religious sphere, which includes organized religion as well as civil religion and implicit religion, is much more fragmented than in earlier times.[68] Correspondingly, what can be observed in religious/cultural/heritage travel is a plurality of sacralized places that give rise to often diverse and sometimes very contentious interpretations of their cultural meaning.[69]

Such contention is also characteristic of other forms of travel, and of the boundaries between them. If, as Zygmunt Bauman has argued, postmodern identity is not only fragmented but also transitional and disembedded from spatial and temporal contexts, then identity itself assumes a permanently transitional, perhaps even liminal, character.[70] Daniel Boorstin once remarked, in a stinging criticism of modern and specifically American tourism, that "the more we move around, the more difficult it becomes not to remain in the same place."[71]

More than thirty years after those words were first written, we move around a lot more; and as global pilgrims, travelers, and communicators we encounter different cultures that seem increasingly less different from ours.[72] Georg Simmel's figure of a "stranger" who acquired the attribute of strangeness by virtue of mobility has now mutated into the "temporary stranger" who is perhaps more and more temporary and less and less strange.[73] Conversely, as indicated in a recent essay about the cult of the most popular science fiction series ever on American television, which the author subtitled, interestingly enough, *Star Trek Convention Attendance as Pilgrimage*, we seem to like to sanctify those who explore the next frontier.[74] That frontier or destination of pilgrimage could be outer space, or the seemingly endless possibilities of virtual travel and tourism in cyberspace, where the boundaries between pilgrimage, cultural voyage, and tourism truly implode.[75]

Yet postmodern pilgrims' destinations, in a figurative sense, could also be their own selves, their bodies, and their public personae. That possibility did not escape a journalist of the *New York Times* when describing travelers to the Miss America Pageant in 1999: "To them, the trip is a pilgrimage."[76]

NOTES

1. See Gisbert Rinschede, "Forms of Religious Tourism," *Annals of Tourism Research* 19 (1992): 51–67.

2. Ronald N. Swanson, *Religion and Devotion in Europe* (Cambridge: Cambridge University Press, 1995), p. 191; cf. Gerhard Ladner, "*Homo Viator*: Mediaeval Ideas on Alienation and Order," *Speculum* 42 (1967): 233–259.

3. A comprehensive treatment of medieval pilgrimage is provided in Diana Webb, *Pilgrims and Pilgrimage in the Medieval West* (New York: Taurus, 1999), which supersedes Jonathan Sumption, *Pilgrimage: An Image of Mediaeval Religion* (Totowa, NJ: Rowman & Littlefield, 1975). Norman Housley, "Pilgrimage, Western European," *Dictionary of the Middle Ages*, vol. 9 (New York: Scribner, 1987), pp. 654–661, gives a short but valuable overview.

4. The only existing sociological accounts of medieval pilgrimage I know of are two essays by Anne Osterrieth: "Medieval Pilgrimage: Society and Individual Quest," *Social Compass* 36 (1989): 249–260; "Pilgrimage, Travel, and Existential Quest," in *Sacred Places, Sacred Spaces: The Geography of Pilgrimages*, edited by Robert H. Stoddard and E. Alan Morinis (Baton Rouge, LA: Geoscience Publications, 1999), pp. 25–39. They address ways in which pilgrimage as an individual quest was framed by social conditions, a topic that is not explored in this chapter.

5. John Eade and Michael J. Sallnow (eds.), *Contesting the Sacred: The Anthropology of Christian Pilgrimage* (London: Routledge, 1991), pp. 1–29.

6. Victor Turner and Edith Turner, *Image and Pilgrimage in Christian Culture: Anthropological Perspectives* (New York: Columbia University Press, 1978); cf. Victor Turner, *The Ritual Process: Structure and Anti-Structure* (Chicago: Aldine, 1969); Turner, "Pilgrimage and Communitas," *Studia Missionalia* 23 (1974): 305–327.

7. Turner, *Ritual Process*, pp. 94–130; Turner and Turner, *Image*, pp. 1–39.

8. Turner and Turner, *Image*, p. 34.

9. For a review and general critique of Turner's work from a sociological perspective, see Mathieu Deflem, "Ritual, Anti-structure, and Religion: A Discussion of Victor Turner's Processual Symbolic Analysis," *Journal for the Scientific Study of Religion* 30 (1991): 1–25.

10. Eade and Sallnow, *Contesting*, p. 5.

11. On deconstruction and contested knowledge as themes in social theory, see Stephan Fuchs and Steven Ward, "What Is Deconstruction, and Where and When Does It Take Place?" *American Sociological Review* 59 (1994): 481–500; and Steven Seidman, *Contested Knowledge: Social Theory in the Postmodern Era* (Oxford: Blackwell, 1994).

12. See also Eade and Sallnow, *Contesting*, pp. 26–27.

13. As Eade and Sallnow's perspective has found considerable support, the scholarly debate continues as to which of the two paradigms is better suited to analyze religious activities. In fact, it has been pointed out that they may be seen as complementary rather than conflicting, with the liminal approach perhaps better suited to modern industrialized nations and Eade and Sallnow's to pre-industrial societies; see Gerard Hersbach, "De Bedevaart: Turner na Twintig Jaar Opnieuw Bezien," *Antropologische Verkenningen* 13 (1994): 8–21. This issue cannot be re-

solved in this chapter, but my point here is that the two theoretical approaches need not necessarily conflict.

14. Thomas F. Gieryn, "Boundary-work and the Demarcation of Science from Non-science," *American Sociological Review* 48 (1983): 781–795.

15. Thomas F. Gieryn, *Cultural Boundaries of Science: Credibility on the Line* (Chicago: University of Chicago Press, 1999); Charles A. Taylor, *Defining Science: A Rhetoric of Demarcation* (Madison: University of Wisconsin Press, 1996); cf. Thomas S. Kuhn, *The Structure of Scientific Revolutions*, 2d ed. (Chicago: University of Chicago Press, 1970).

16. Lutz Kaelber, *Schools of Asceticism: Ideology and Organization in Medieval Religious Communities* (University Park: Pennsylvania State University Press, 1998).

17. Much of what is known about Francis's early life derives from the biographies written by Thomas of Celano, an early Franciscan who wrote the First and Second Lives of Saint Francis, from which the first quote is taken (David Burr, *Thomas of Celano's First and Second Lives of Saint Francis* (<http://dburr.hist.vt.edu/Celano.html> 2000). The de Vitry quote appears in John Moorman, *A History of the Franciscan Order* (Oxford: Clarendon Press, 1968), p. 30.

18. The life and travels of Margery Kempe, as well as the social context of her spirituality, are explored in Clarissa W. Atkinson, *Mystic and Pilgrim: The "Book" and the World of Margery Kempe* (Ithaca, NY: Cornell University Press, 1983), and Richard Kieckhefer, *Unquiet Souls: Fourteenth-Century Saints and Their Religious Milieu* (Chicago: University of Chicago Press, 1984), pp. 182–201; cf. Margery Kempe, *The Book of Margery Kempe* (London: Penguin, 1985).

19. See Gabriele Zanella, *Hereticalia: Temi e Discussiioni* (Spoleto: Centro italiano di studi sull'Alto Medioevo, 1995), pp. 3–14; Carol Lansing, *Power and Purity: Cathar Heresy in Medieval Italy* (Oxford: Oxford University Press, 1998), pp. 92–95; Malcolm D. Lambert, *The Cathars* (Oxford: Blackwell, 1998), pp. 281–282.

20. Max Weber, *From Max Weber* (New York: Oxford University Press, 1958), p. 273.

21. For this and the following, see Kaelber, *Schools*. Also see E. Dublanchy, "Conseils Évangéliques," cols. 1176–1182, *Dictionaire de théologie catholique*, edited by A. Vacant and E. Mangenot (Paris: Letonzey et Ané, 1938); Franz Lau, "Evangelische Räte," in K. Calling, *Die Religion in Geschhichte und Gegenwart: Handwörterbuch für Theologie und Religionswissenschaft*, 3d ed. (Tübingen: Mohr, 1958), cols. 785–788.

22. Weber first used these terms in a letter to Else Jaffé in 1907; see Max Weber, *Briefe 1906–1908* (Tübingen: Mohr, 1990), p. 399. The relevant part of the letter is translated in Kaelber, *Schools*, p. 21.

23. Alexander Murray, *Reason and Society in the Middle Ages*, rev. ed. (Oxford: Clarendon Press, 1985), p. 358. On the status-enhancing qualities of pilgrimage for religious virtuosos, see also Giles Constable, "Opposition to Pilgrimage in the Middle Ages," *Studia Gratiana* 19 (1976): 126–127.

24. Lester K. Little, *Religious Poverty and the Profit Economy in Medieval Europe* (Ithaca, NY: Cornell University Press, 1978), pp. 146–169; M.-D. Chenu, *Nature, Man, and Society in the Twelfth Century* (Chicago: University of Chicago Press, 1983), pp. 202–269; C. H. Lawrence, *Medieval Monasticism*, 2d ed. (London: Longman, 1990), pp. 238–273.

25. Patrick J. Geary, *Living with the Dead in the Middle Ages* (Ithaca, NY: Cornell University Press, 1994), pp. 163–176.

26. Ibid., p. 171.

27. Ibid., pp. 174–176; Sumption, *Pilgrimage*, pp. 114–136, 217–256; Rosalind Brooke and Christopher Brooke, *Popular Religion in the Middle Ages* (London: Thames and Hudson, 1984), pp. 21–29. For studies on local pilgrimages in the Middle Ages, see the extensive bibliography by Linda Kay Davidson and Maryjane Dunn-Wood, *Pilgrimage in the Middle Ages: A Research Guide* (New York: Garland, 1993).

28. Osterrieth, "Medieval Pilgrimage"; idem, "Pilgrimage, Travel." For the following, see also Sumption, *Pilgrimage*, pp. 168–210, from whom I draw extensively.

29. Osterrieth, "Pilgrimage, Travel," p. 34.

30. Sumption, *Pilgrimage*, pp. 211–216.

31. Yves Dossat, *Les crises d l'Inquisition toulousaine au XIII siècle* (Bordeaux: Bière, 1959), pp. 257–258; see also James B. Given, *Inquisition and Medieval Society: Power, Discipline, and Resistance in Languedoc* (Ithaca, NY: Cornell University Press, 1997), pp. 67–90.

32. See Sumption, *Pilgrimage*, pp. 98–113; Webb, *Pilgrims*, pp. 51–56.

33. John T. McNeill and Helena M. Gamer, *Medieval Handbooks of Penance* (New York: Columbia University Press, 1990), p. 425.

34. Quoted in Simon Coleman and John Elsner, *Pilgrimage: Past and Present in the World Religions* (Cambridge, MA: Harvard University Press, 1995), p. 206.

35. See Christian K. Zacher, *Curiosity and Pilgrimage: The Literature of Discovery in Fourteenth-Century England* (Baltimore: Johns Hopkins University Press, 1976).

36. J. J. Jusserand, *English Wayfaring Life in the Middle Ages*, 4th ed. (London: Benn, 1950), p. 225; Sumption, *Pilgrimage*, pp. 288–302; Webb, *Pilgrims*, pp. 68–72.

37. Webb, *Pilgrims*, p. 32.

38. However, the Church actively promoted pilgrimages to those sites and shrines it approved, which on occasion replaced those of pagan origins. "When non-Christian shrines were destroyed, they were wherever possible replaced by Christian ones . . . erected upon the selfsame spot and made up sometimes of the very same materials" (Valerie I. J. Flint, *The Rise of Magic in Early Medieval Europe* [Princeton: Princeton University Press, 1991], p. 254).

39. Webb, *Pilgrims*, pp. 235–254; Constable, "Opposition."

40. Susanna Elm, *Virgins of God: The Making of Asceticism in Late Antiquity* (Oxford: Oxford University Press, 1994), pp. 272–281.

41. The statement was made by Venantius Fortunatus, as quoted in Constable, "Opposition," p. 130; see also Sumption, *Pilgrimage*, pp. 261–263; Webb, *Pilgrims*, pp. 13–14. For the enclosure of women in medieval monasticism up to the early thirteenth century, see Sally Thompson, "The Problem of the Cistercian Nuns in the Twelfth and Early Thirteenth Centuries," in *Medieval Women*, edited by Derek Baker (Oxford: Blackwell, 1978), pp. 227–252; Jane Tibbetts Schulenburg, "Strict Active Enclosure and Its Effects on the Female Monastic Experience (ca. 500–1100)," in *Medieval Religious Women*, vol. 1, edited by John A. Nichols and Lillian Thomas Shank (Kalamazoo, MI: Cistercian Publications, 1984), pp. 51–86; Jane Tibbetts Schulenburg, "Women's Monastic Communities, 500–1100: Patterns of Expansion and Decline," in *Sisters and Workers in the Middle Ages*, edited by Judith M. Bennett, Elizabeth A. Clark, Jean F. O'Barr, B. Anne Viley, and Sarah Westphal-Wihl (Chicago: University of Chicago Press, 1989), pp. 208–239.

42. For a more extensive account of the issues discussed below, see Kaelber, *Schools*, pp. 74–93.

43. See Brenda M. Bolton, "Mulieres Sanctæ," in *Sanctity and Secularity: The Church and the World*, edited by Derek Baker (Oxford: Blackwell, 1973), pp. 77–85; Herbert Grundmann, *Religious Movements in the Middle Ages* (Notre Dame, IN: University of Notre Dame Press, 1994), pp. 92–137; Webb, *Pilgrims*, pp. 236–239. Catholic nuns' withdrawal from the world was encouraged long into the modern era; see Patricia Wittberg, *The Rise and Fall of Catholic Religious Orders: A Social Movement Perspective* (Albany: State University of New York Press, 1994), p. 90.

44. Caroline Walker Bynum, *Fragmentation and Redemption: Essays on Gender and the Human Body in Medieval Religion* (New York: Zone Books, 1991), pp. 27–51.

45. Ibid., pp. 41–42.

46. Diana Webb, "Women Pilgrims of the Middle Ages," *History Today* 48 (1998): 20–26.

47. See also Dorothea French, "Ritual, Gender, and Power Strategies: Male Pilgrimage to Saint Patrick's Purgatory," *Religion* 24 (1994): 103–115, which, *pace* Turner, depicts a medieval pilgrimage that strengthened social distinctions and the established hierarchies of males over females and of nobles over common people. For a general overview of travel in medieval times, see Marjorie Rowling, *Everyday Life of Medieval Travellers* (New York: Dorset Press, 1971).

48. R. I. Moore, *The Birth of Popular Heresy* (London: Arnold, 1975); *The Origins of European Dissent*, rev. ed. (New York: Blackwell, 1985). Interestingly, Constable, "Opposition," p. 144, notes that in regard to criticism of pilgrimage, "the views of the future were voiced by heretics," but does not give any further examples. Aryeh Graboïs's otherwise comprehensive review of medieval pilgrimage, *Le pèlerin occidental en Terre sainte au Moyen Age* (Brussels: De

boeck Université, 1998), does not mention the topic at all. Webb, *Pilgrims*, pp. 241–245, gives a concise overview.

49. See Lambert, *Cathars*; Lansing, *Power*.

50. In Walter L. Wakefield and Austin P. Evans, *Heresies of the High Middle Ages: Selected Sources* (New York: Columbia University Press, 1969), p. 371.

51. Wilhelm Preger, "Beiträge zur Geschichte der Waldesier im Mittelalter," *Abhandlungen der königlich bayerischen Akademie der Wissenschaften* 3 (klasse 13/1, 1875): 245; Margaret Nickson, "The 'Pseudo-Reinerius' Treatise: The Final Stage of a Thirteenth Century Work on Heresy from the Diocese of Passau," *Archives d'histoire doctrinale et littéraire du Moyen Âge* 34 (1967): 301; Alexander Patschovsky and Kurt-Victor Selge (eds.), *Quellen zur Geschichte der Waldenser* (Gütersloh: Mohn, 1973), p. 101.

52. Kurt-Victor Selge, *Die ersten Waldensen*, vol. 1 (Berlin: de Gruyter, 1967), p. 317.

53. Jusserand, *English Wayfaring*, p. 205.

54. Edward Peters (ed.), *Heresy and Authority in Medieval Europe: Documents in Translation* (Philadelphia: University of Pennsylvania Press, 1980), pp. 279–280.

55. Webb, *Pilgrims*, p. 253.

56. See Étienne Delaruelle, *La piété populaire au Moyen Âge* (Turin: d'Erasmo, 1975), pp. 555–561; Sumption, *Pilgrimage*, pp. 55, 301; and Webb, *Pilgrims*, p. 245.

57. See Roland H. Bainton, *Here I Stand: A Life of Martin Luther* (New York: Mentor, 1950), p. 288; Anthony D. Wright, *The Counter-Reformation: Catholic Europe and the Non-Christian World* (New York: St. Martin's, 1982), pp. 68, 251.

58. See Kaelber, *Schools*, pp. 102–105; Philip S. Gorski, "Historicizing the Secularization Debate: Church, State, and Society in Late Medieval and Early Modern Europe, ca. 1300–1700," *American Sociological Review* 65 (2000): 138–167.

59. Keith Thomas, *Religion and the Decline of Magic* (New York: Scribner, 1971), pp. 70–71; William Monter, *Ritual, Myth, and Magic in Early Modern Europe* (Athens: Ohio University Press, 1984), p. 51.

60. See Lenz Kriss-Rettenbeck and Gerda Mohler (eds.), *Wallfahrt kennt keine Grenzen* (Munich: Schnell und Steiner, 1984).

61. Eugen Weber, *Peasants into Frenchmen: The Modernization of Rural France, 1870–1914* (Stanford, CA: Stanford University Press, 1974), p. 351.

62. See Jean Rémy, "Pilgrimage and Modernity," *Social Compass* 36 (1989): 139–143; Zygmunt Bauman, "From Pilgrim to Tourist—or a Short History of Identity," in *Questions of Cultural Identity*, edited by Stuart Hall and Paul Du Gay (Thousand Oaks, CA: Sage, 1996), pp. 18–36; Luigi Tomasi, "Pilgrimage/Tourism," in *Encyclopedia of Religion and Society* (Walnut Creek, CA: AltaMira, 1998), pp. 362–364.

63. Cathy Greenblat and John H. Gagnon, "Temporary Strangers: Travel and Tourism from a Sociological Perspective," *Sociological Perspectives* 26 (1983): 92; U.S. Department of Transportation Bureau of Transportation Statistics, *American Travel Survey: Long-Distance Leisure Travel in the United States* (<http://www.bts.gov/ats.pdf>, 1999).

64. See Rinschede, "Forms."

65. Mary Lee Nolan and Sidney Nolan, "Religious Sites as Tourism Attractions in Europe," *Annals of Tourism Research* 19 (1992): 77; cf. Mary Lee Nolan and Sidney Nolan, *Christian Pilgrimage in Modern Western Europe* (Chapel Hill: University of North Carolina Press, 1989); Klaus Guth, "Pilgrimages in Contemporary Europe: Signs of National and Universal Culture," *History of European Ideas* 20 (1995): 831–835.

66. Paul Hollander, "Durable Significance of Political Pilgrimage," *Society* 34, no. 229 (1997): 45–55.

67. Juan Eduardo Campo, "American Pilgrimage Landscapes," *Annals of the American Academy of Political and Social Sciences* 558 (1998): 40–46. For heritage tourism and travel, see also Wiendu Nuryanti, "Heritage and Postmodern Tourism," *Annals of Tourism Research* 23 (1996): 249–260; Peter S. Hawkins, "American Heritage," in *One Nation under God? Religion and American Culture*, edited by Marjorie Garber and Rebecca L. Walkowitz (New York: Routledge, 1999), pp. 258–279.

68. See Robert N. Bellah, "Civil Religion in America," *Dædalus* 96 (1967): 1–21; Edward Bailey, *Implicit Religion in Contemporary Society* (Kampen: Kok Pharos, 1997).

69. See Campo, "American Pilgrimage Landscapes," p. 53, for a discussion of the Indian writer Gita Metha's cynical label of "the trance-inducing industry" for American travels to spiritual gurus in India. John Eade, "Pilgrimage and Tourism at Lourdes, France," *Annals of Tourism Research* 19 (1992): 18–32, and Adolf Ehrentraut, "Maya Ruins, Cultural Tourism, and the Contested Symbolism of Collective Identities," *Culture* 16 (1996): 15–32, provide further examples of locally contested tourism.

70. Bauman, "From Pilgrim to Tourist."

71. Daniel J. Boorstin, *The Image: A Guide to Pseudo-Events in America* (New York: Harper & Row, 1964), p. 110; Such notables as Umberto Eco, *Travels in Hyperreality* (San Diego: Harcourt Brace Jovanovich, 1986), and Jean Baudrillard, *America* (New York: Verso, 1989) have since emulated this criticism.

72. Rinschede's estimate ("Forms," p. 57) that 200 million people annually engage in international, national, and supraregional pilgrimage journeys seems far too low by now, especially for the Jubilee, when more than twenty million visitors were projected to visit the Eternal City alone. One might sympathize with, but fear the futility of, the recent exhortation of the pastor of Rome's Church of Santa Susanna, which has a special ministry for Americans, that the pilgrims remind themselves of the holy in pilgrimage and expect to find it. However, "while the expectation is authentic," he notes, "sadly the tools and opportunities for such

an experience are few. Surrounded by professional travel consultants, bus schedules, group dinners, and frozen itineraries, many Americans [and others] during the Holy Year will be quickly hurried past the spiritual richness of Rome. While their trip might be called a pilgrimage, they will be little more than religious tourists with great expectation and little spiritual direction." Quoted in Paul Robichaud, "Tourist or Pilgrim? Rescuing the Jubilee," *America* 181, no. 20 (1999): 11.

73. Georg Simmel, *The Sociology of Georg Simmel* (New York: Free Press, 1950), pp. 402–408; cf., Greenblat and Gagnon, "Temporary Strangers."

74. Jennifer E. Porter, "To Boldly Go: Star Trek Convention Attendance as Pilgrimage," in *Star Trek and Sacred Ground: Explorations of Star Trek, Religion, and American Culture*, edited by Jennifer E. Porter and Darcee L. McLaren (Albany: State University of New York Press, 1999), pp. 249–274.

75. See also the thematization of Disney World as a pilgrimage center in Alexander Moore, "Walt Disney World: Bounded Ritual Space and the Playful Pilgrimage Center," *Anthropological Quarterly* 53 (1980): 207–218.

76. Maria Newman, "Updating the Permissible for the Feminine Ideal," *New York Times* (27 Sept 1999): A27.

Chapter 4

Pilgrimages of Yesterday, Jubilees of Today

Maria I. Macioti

Christian pilgrims were plentiful in the Middle Ages; plentiful, too, were the indulgences promised to them. They would go to the tomb of a saint: to look for grace, to beg forgiveness of their sins, to release themselves from a vow. They would go on foot, with difficulty. The journey, the long, hard and risky route, was the most meaningful thing; Marcel Mauss defined that as a total experience: the journey meant leaving one's house, one's family, one's well-known environment.[1] One's own existence and body were exposed to risk. The return was a far and unsure destination, hard to achieve for many of them. The journey, with all its risks and discomforts, meant both the parting and the approaching of the destination: the journey had a "liminal" function.[2]

The Jubilee is justified by the acquisition of indulgences. Actually, from a historical point of view, the Jubilee indicates some sort of "rationalization" of the indulgences, including the "plenary indulgence." Indulgences existed since the first centuries of the Christian age. More precise documentation goes back to the eleventh century, when bishops of France and northern Spain used to grant them to those who made pilgrimages to some sanctuaries or who gave money for charity. Apparently the first pope who granted indulgences was Nicholas II (1058–1061) on the occasion of the consecration of an altar in the Abbey of Farfa (Latium). Later, indulgences were connected with the Crusades: they were granted to those who died in the effort to conquer the Holy Land.[3] At a still later stage, indulgences were related to the Jubilee in such a way as to become its strongest attraction. At the same time the commerce of indulgences acquired relevance. Even today the issue of the indulgences tied to the Jubilee causes problems and disagreements between the Roman Catholic and the other Christian churches, since in part the reformed churches were born in the fifteenth century above all as a protest against the commerce of indulgences that was going on in Rome at that time.

MEDIEVAL PILGRIMAGES: TOWARD
THE HOLY LAND

First among the destinations of medieval pilgrimages was the Holy Land, where people have gone since the early Middle Ages. The attraction for the places where Christ had lived and died was strong. It appears that the Holy Land was reached by departing from Gaul, Britain, or other places of the empire: testimony to this is the graphic designs that date back to the third century and recollections, such as those of the author of the *Itinerarium Burdigalense*. So ancient were these pilgrimages, that the term *romeo*, which would indicate the pilgrim bound for Rome, seemed to be used initially to refer to those who, coming from different parts of the empire, had gone to the Holy Land as pilgrims. Only later did the appellative *palmieri* become a common term; it also was used by Dante Alighieri.

Once the difficulties borne by these pilgrims on their visits to the Holy Land were recognized, the West conceived of the idea of the crusade, that is, an armed expedition or pilgrimage carried out in order to return to the believers those lands of Christ. Indulgences followed: first awarded to the warriors who had answered the appeal made by the Church, the indulgences were extended also to the warriors' wives, maybe to reward them for the long absences of their husbands. Then indulgences were awarded to all those who had lavished their money on the Crusades, and to the preachers who had encouraged participation, as well as other cases.

In the Middle Ages, Rome would also be considered a destination for pilgrimage. Starting from the seventh century at least, people would go to the tombs of the Apostles, as various guides and *itineraries* testify. According to different historical interpretations, the Constantinian basilicas represented, above all, the main destinations for pilgrimages: the catacombs had been buried, and every trace lost.

Arsenio Frugoni, who has dedicated various studies to the period of the Middle Ages, talks about the veneration of pilgrims for the wood of the Cross on which Christ died. He also highlights the importance attributed to the nails and to other relics such as "Veronica's veil."[4] It should be mentioned that there are various explanations as to the origin of this veil. According to tradition it is the veil used by a young woman (Veronica) for cleaning and drying Christ's face. A second explanation is based on etymology: Veronica derives from *vera icona* (real icon). And indeed it was considered to be an icon (a very important one) more than a historical object. A similar question concerns another object, the *Sindone*, a sheet on which the features of the Savior are apparently preserved. This relic, according to Archbishop Severino Poletto, was visited in Turin by a million pilgrims between 2 August and 22 October 2000. It is also worth recalling the Holy Steps and the Flagellation Column. As the journey to the Holy Land became increasingly difficult, the attraction for Rome as the New Jerusalem started growing.

TOWARD ST. JAMES OF COMPOSTELA

The "House of Galicia" and the Basilica of Santiago de Compostela directly refer to Christ, to the Apostle James, and to his journey of proselytism, which led him to far-off lands. The cult of St. James would be well known starting from the ninth century, with the "discovery" of its relics. It seems that an old monk, Pelayo, living in the woods of Libredon, saw some mysterious lights, similar to a rain of stars. At his request, Bishop Teodomiro apparently sent a small expedition to investigate; it was later called the "journey to Santiago." Following the starlight, this expedition reached a sepulcher made of stone containing the bodies of Santiago or James the Great, and of Theodore and Athanasius, his disciples. King Alphonse II, called "the Chaste," was informed, arrived there, and, realizing how reassuring and identifying an element the relics could be for the Christians, developed the cult and encouraged the pilgrimages.

Ever since, St. James has been linked to the Milky Way, and his tomb has become increasingly loved. The Islamic threat strengthened the cult, emphasizing the holy warrior image, the *matamoros*, and Santiago, "the Thunder." The pilgrimage started in the tenth century and was reinforced in the twelfth and thirteenth centuries. It declined during the Renaissance and the Reformation, but it gained momentum with Leo XIII's bull *Deus Omnipotens* in 1884.

People went to pay homage to St. James, going on foot or horseback, depending on their social status. They arrived there by different routes, of which the best known was the *Camino francés*, using one of four initial paths—the Turoniensis from Paris through Tours and Poitiers; the Limousin, from Vezelay passing through Limoges; the Podiensis, from Le Puy through Moissac and Conques; and the Tolosana from Arles—meeting in Puente de La Reina, in Navarra, passing through Roncisvalle, and then winding toward Galicia, along an eight hundred-kilometer route. It is a journey that still attracts pilgrims, either on foot or horseback. Others cycle or drive, but in this case it is a different pilgrimage, where some important aspects are lost. It is the walking that is considered meaningful. The walking itself leads to friendships and solidarity among fellow travelers and those who give *refugios* (shelter).[5] The body and the concepts of time and distance traveled are considered the main elements of all pilgrimages.

As a rule, people passed through Roncisvalle, a place reminiscent of the battle led by Roland, the nephew of Charlemagne—a battle celebrated throughout the centuries, in which the French people fought for Christ against the pagans. Archbishop Turpino waited for them, representing heaven, where they would sit at the right of God the Father. Fighting for the spread of Christianity would open the way to heaven. It stands to reason that the *matamoros,* the armed warrior risen from the waters—waters that are beyond the extreme borderline of the well-known environment, the place to which so many Celtic legends referred as the world of the dead—was a strong attraction. Muslims invaded Spain, Christians were escaping, and the emir of Cordoba was imposing his power everywhere, when the body of the saint was miraculously found.

Later it would not be the *matamoros* who would be the most beloved, admired, and worshiped; it would be the saint, capable of healing, linked to the revealing moonlight of the "Milky Way" (the *Via lattea*). Even nowadays people keep looking for a performer of miracles, and it is the route, the carrying out of the vow, that is important, rather than the return home. The pilgrimage to Compostela is so well known that many people have gone there from all over Europe. From Paris people start from Rue Saint Jacques, now one of the most charming of Parisian roads. In those times, it was "a wide dirty road . . . from which the pilgrims headed for the Shrine of Santiago de Compostela, the farthest end of the Iberian Peninsula," a muddy and dirty route, where pilgrims traveled together with swine, horses, and donkeys.[6]

The pilgrim came back with a shell (today the very well known scallop shell of St. Jacques [hence the menu entrée, *coquilles St. Jacques*]), as testimony of having reached the sanctuary, the extreme limits of the world— Vieira. The shell was closely linked to this pilgrimage and to pilgrimages in general: today it is associated with the Catholic Jubilee of the year 2000. However, starting from the thirteenth century, the shell was placed beside the probatory letters. These were followed by the *compostela*, a sort of credential that had to be shown in order to be admitted to the Fundacion del Hospital Real, the most important hostelry in Galicia, built on request of the Catholic kings during the sixteenth century. Along the way the pilgrims carried a notebook with them in which the seals of the churches they passed by were affixed. Today an official document is given to those who reach the sanctuary on foot or horseback, having traveled at least a hundred kilometers, and to those who have cycled for at least two hundred kilometers, either for spiritual or for religious reasons.

The pilgrimage to Compostela, in a specific context, sets forth the modalities of the pilgrimage in general: the typical clothing of the pilgrim at Compostela—a short cloak, a broad-brimmed felt hat, a stick or a pilgrim's staff, and a gourd used for carrying water—became the pilgrim's general style of attire. These pilgrimages were characterized by crosses put up along the way, stones brought to the cathedral, and fragrances. Herbs were strewn on the cathedral floor in order to adorn it and offset the unpleasant stench coming from the tired and dirty pilgrims. All this was reported in the chronicles. On the way to Compostela the pilgrims could also have risky encounters: thieves, vagabonds, and prostitutes who tried to interrupt the journey: sometimes there were even worse encounters, as the film director Buñuel reminded us in his *The Milky Way* (1969).

Today, as in the past, there is a continuous flow toward those saints with healing virtues, figures linked to the spirituality of the New Age. Today pilgrims in the *refugios* have some herbs placed against their tired legs, which are no longer used to covering long distances; the herbs are able to soothe the pain of their tired feet and their sore muscles. In the twelfth century, thanks to the *Regis Aeterni* papal bull of Alexander III (Orlando Bandinelli, 1159–1181) Santiago City enjoyed a Jubilee year. It was established that if 25 July, St. James's feast day, fell on a Sunday, that would be considered a year of Jubilee. The Jubilee indulgence of Compostela is still in force.

For this kind of Jubilee it is essential to visit the cathedral and the mortal remains in Santiago, to say prayers (the Lord's Prayer and the Creed, at least), and to receive the sacraments of penance and communion. Here too, through the Jubilee, a plenary indulgence for all prior sins is obtained.

TOWARD THE YEAR 1300

Before the year 1300 there had been many partial indulgences, in addition to the plenary indulgences conceived in Compostela. Why was the end of the thirteenth century different, with the Jubilee proclaimed by Boniface VIII Caetani? Why was the idea of the end of the world taken into consideration only in that period, and not earlier?

Arsenio Frugoni, the historian and the author of a study of the Jubilee of Boniface VIII, reminds us that during the years prior to 1300, there was the preaching of St. Francis, typical of a spirituality whose main topic was Christ as described in the gospel accounts. Frugoni also recalls the eschatological vision of Gioacchino da Fiore, whose strength of vision inspired religious changes.[7]

The papacy of Celestine V (Pietro Angelari da Murone, 1294) followed, and it was characterized by a period of anxiety and the need for spiritual salvation. Because of the changing times, Celestine conceded the "forgiveness of L'Aquila" (*perdonanza aquilana*) to those who would go, penitent and in God's grace, to the Church of Santa Maria di Collemaggio on the day on which the decollation of St. John the Baptist was commemorated. This indulgence is probably linked to the Franciscan indulgence of Porziuncola and to others conceded by the same pope: on the very first day of his papacy and again seven days later. According to Frugoni, both the indulgence linked to the Church of Santa Maria di Collemaggio and the others should be connected to the apocalyptic fear of the end of the world, together with the spirituality of many anchorites who surrounded this atypical pope. They were, above all, Benedictines and Franciscans who had joined the movement of Spirituals, which was closely tied to the teachings of Joachim of Fiore, and which had been condemned by both the Lateran Council of 1215 and Alexander IV in 1256. Frugoni says that Celestine "had allowed God into the Church on earth with no more barriers than he had felt with mystical abandon during his hermit life. And for his contemporaries this had been a brief emotion, a shiver of sanctity."[8] This period was very short, and in fact Celestine died soon after his abdication. On the other hand, the idea of the indulgence, of the *remissio gratiosa*, survived him, because of the idea of the "Treasury of the Church" (a spiritual treasury). The Celestinian indulgences were quickly suppressed by Pope Caetani, and his action was subsequently confirmed by Church councils.

BONIFACE VIII CAETANI (1294–1303)

As soon as Boniface VIII was elected pope, he quickly repealed every act of his predecessor, including the forgiveness of L'Aquila. He did, however, establish a plenary indulgence in connection with special Jubilee pilgrimages every hundredth year: an important step and one that recalls memories of the Jewish Jubilee and the hundredth year. In fact, according to Jacob Caetani Stefaneschi (Iacobi) this was a powerful year to concede an extraordinary forgiveness to all the pilgrims of Peter. The idea of spiritual salvation—of Hebrew origin—is very strong. Many people attribute a spiritual meaning to the Jubilee, although Boniface VIII was never considered a spiritual pope. He was a pope who wanted to show both his own *plenitudo potestatis* and that of the Roman church.

The indulgence he promised differed from the previous ones, because it did not refer to a particular period; it was a plenary indulgence concerning the remission of all sins. Frugoni says that it was a sign of power: the year 1300 was a brilliant period for this pope. The Jubilee was considered the culminating point of his papacy: the defeat in Anagni, the humiliation of the "slap," the victory of France, and the destruction of the Colonna family followed quickly. It was time to proclaim a Jubilee, the first Christian Jubilee. It was a great and unique event that was able to widen and highlight the power of the pope and to discourage his enemies. But there was no peace on earth during this year, as this pope did not forgive his enemies; he knew his power and his role. All of the following Jubilees would be carried out more or less in the same way.

THE CALL OF THE ROMAN JUBILEE

The publication of the bull *Antiquorum habet fida relatio* marked the beginning of the Jubilee on Christmas Eve 1299 (although this date must be considered retroactive because the publication is actually dated 22 February 1300). The Jubilee finished in December 1300. In order to obtain grace the pilgrim had to repent and go to confession; moreover, he had to visit two churches according to the prescribed rules. These were two visits a day for thirty days. One visit a day was allowed, but in that case it prolonged the time period. The rule for foreigners was different; they could shorten the period to fifteen days. Later, for this kind of Jubilee, the indulgence would also be extended to the dead: it referred perhaps to those people who died en route to Rome.

A Political and Religious Mission

Historians have studied the calling of this Jubilee with reference to Boniface's political and religious point of view. He had a particular opinion about his papacy and the papacy in general. Frugoni discusses political games that required, at different times or occasions, an "unrestrainable and excessive rigor," "realistic arrangements," and "fiery impulses"—games to be carried out by a pope well known for the awful grudges he bore and his ambition to be considered the judge of all kings.[9] Boniface is the pope who recognized forgiveness for sins, but he is also the pope who excommunicated the Colonna family on 23 May 1297, for having hampered his election. He imposed the *Lapis abscissus*. A real crusade was called against the Colonna family, who had obstructed and fought him, and against those nobles considered "heretical, schismatic, and blasphemous." It was established that those who decided to fight these people would be conceded the same indulgence awarded to the crusaders bound for the Holy Land. Boniface destroyed Palestrina, the Colonnas' land and its churches, and ordered the spreading of salt all over the land. The victory obtained over the Colonnas was complemented by the subsequent canonization of Louis IX, which was considered a sign of improvement for the critical relationship with France. The king of France at the time of the Crusades and leader of a Crusade himself, Louis was canonized in 1297, the eve of the first Jubilee, after which he is referred to as St. Louis of France.[10] The call of the Jubilee with pilgrims coming on foot, horseback, or mule; the abundant flow of money; the success of the Jubilee; and the new relations with France all apparently strengthened Boniface's power. Nevertheless, catastrophe was very near.

The Pilgrims of the Year 1300

Sovereigns did not go on pilgrimages, but single pilgrims belonging to different social classes joined others on their way, and they, in turn, joined many other merchants: the most important thing was to be in company in order to avoid risky encounters, not to become a victim of a thief or be killed en route. The routes, narrow and winding, gave rise to traps: there were no longer those wide Roman routes where the legions could quickly pass. According to the chronicles, there was a flood of pilgrims, about 10,000 a day, with a greater flow in particular periods. According to Frugoni, however, it is difficult to quantify the phenomenon, as the numbers are, in his opinion, all imagined, although they nevertheless reflect the widespread amazement at the flow of pilgrims prevailing in Rome during that period.

Although the sovereigns were absent, their subjects were present. There were ambassadorships from both Persia and Mongolia, whose presence was commemorated by a stone that still exists in Florence in Via Giovanni da Verrazzano. Such an uncommon flood of people probably caused great logistics problems—concerning supplies and accommodation. Pilgrim hospices were built together with the various *Scholæ*, which were often named after the places of origin of the pilgrims: there were the Schola Francorum, the Schola Saxonum, the Frisonum, and others. Disciplinary actions were perhaps taken to regulate the flood: Dante Alighieri wrote about a division on the bridge of Sant'Angelo between those who were going toward St. Peter's and those who were returning.

There was no lack of problems. Three months later there was a threat of famine. The Tiber overflowed; the whole area was flooded. This would happen again and would force pilgrims to go to the Basilica of Santa Maria in Trastevere rather than to Saint Paul Outside the Walls, which was often flooded. Problems of an economic nature were also involved. Controversy about the use of offerings arose as these amounted to a great deal of money. They were used to buy estates, which in turn enriched the basilicas.

Afterwards

A Jubilee every one hundred years: that was the timing fixed by Boniface VIII. It was reduced to fifty years by Clement VI (Pierre Rogers, 1342–1352) and then to thirty-three years, representing the life of Christ, by Urban VI (Bartolomeo Prignano, 1378–1389). Nowadays it is fixed at every twenty-five years, without considering the "extraordinary" Jubilees. John Paul II (Carol Wojtyla, 1978–), for example, proclaimed an extraordinary Jubilee in 1983–1984 with his bull *Aperite portas Redemptori*. It was a period of papal travels and attempts at dialogue with the other Christian churches. On 13 April 1986, there was the encounter with the Jewish community and afterward, on 27 October 1986, one in Assisi, where the pope prayed together with the Dalai Lama and representatives of other religious faiths.

THE JUBILEE OF THE YEAR 2000

The Jubilee proclaimed for the year 2000 follows the scheme that Alexander VI (Rodrigo Borgia, 1492–1503) had determined for the celebrations of the year 1500, but with some variants: for example, the gold or silver hammer with which, in the past, the pope opened the Holy Door no longer exists. As well as this small formal change other more drastic ones have occurred. Both organizational and communications details have become so important as almost to obscure the spiritual messages from the pope and other clerical representatives.

Individual Pilgrimage and Collective Pilgrimage

At one time there was the lone pilgrim. He would decide on the journey by himself; he would leave his own place of origin, his family. The journey had been long considered; he had probably supplied himself with food, and arranged everything for the family he was leaving behind. Yet the pilgrimage experience itself was an encounter that was generally spontaneous and unexpected. It was highly regarded and meaningful. But risk was also always present. One could become a victim of a thief or be assaulted on the road. One could die under the sword or of an illness, possibly consumed by the plague in some improvised quarantine hospital. Nature concealed some traps: mountains covered with snow and clefts, rough seas, deceiving waves. The body itself was at risk. The luckier ones could go on horseback or ride in a carriage or go by boat, but generally a pilgrimage meant hard work for the body, walking for days or even months. Then there was the spiritual search: one pilgrim would look for reassurance, while another might ask for grace. The pilgrimage is a reproduction of what real human life should be: the Christian is a pilgrim on this earth. Life itself is a pilgrimage, a route to God, whose aim is reconciliation.

In the Jubilee of the year 2000, however, a global business dimension also seems to prevail. Pilgrims usually come in groups organized by travel agencies. The medieval pilgrim fought against the fatigue, risk, and other troubles that would probably occur. The modern pilgrim pays for a package tour, which means that, of course, he or she has a different attitude: possible problems and mistakes, long waits at the airports, and traffic jams on the highways give rise to irritation and intolerance. Most likely these will not be considered as a possible occasion for penance and expiation! For this Jubilee, pilgrims' stays are organized and planned in religious institutes, in parish rooms, as well as in the small towns surrounding the city of Rome. To be hosted by a family is difficult. The Italian hotel trade in general, and in particular the Roman one, seems not to have been positively influenced by this Jubilee. Apparently, during the first few months of the year 2000, the city of Rome registered a decrease in the number of tourists, compared to the previous year. Restaurants also reported a negative trend: pilgrims are supposed to buy an all-inclusive journey, which covers all expenses such as board, accommodation, and transport.

This Jubilee appears to be managed by religious institutions, parishes, travel agencies, and banks: the individual who gets to Rome alone, with no reservation, maybe on foot, risks exclusion from some religious events and celebrations. To attend some Jubilee events the pilgrim may need an invitation; only tickets with special colors allow admission. A reservation through the Internet becomes essential; it gives access to Scoop, the system set up for this purpose by the Roman agency for the Jubilee that also allows access to museums.

Among the operators involved, banks and financial institutions are particularly relevant. For this special event, Banca di Roma has granted economic bodies a subsidized credit, aiming to implement welcome facilities as well as envisaging opportunities of payment by installment for pilgrimage purposes. In addition, more bank counters have been reserved for pilgrims along with shop windows dedicated to the sale of Jubilee items. The bank has also provided the Holy See with its central premises, located in Via del Corso, to be used as a Jubilee reception center. Subsidiary credits have been granted by Rolo Banca to all trade associations, tour and trade operators; and different initiatives, such as memorial medals, are being offered by

Comit Bank and Banco di Sardegna. Banca Intesa acts as an intermediary for the collection of the "Pilgrim Journal." This enormous change, beyond the multitude of small differences, represents not only the loss of "liminality" (related to the loss of the real essence of the journey), but also the change of attitude of the pilgrim. Franco Ferrarotti has already mentioned the shift from the individual pilgrimage to mass tourism.[11] Moreover, it seems that "the group" has become the main element. The Jubilee is now institutionalized. If individuals previously took the initiative, nowadays a collective management prevails. The pilgrims have lost their autonomy, their capacity of thinking or acting by themselves; today they depend on top management and their decisions.

Pilgrimage as Total Experience

The individual pilgrimage, the one requiring total participation, the one able to involve the whole self, is still alive and present. We can find it in other lands and religions, for instance in those countries where it is connected to the magnificent Kailasa Mountain of Tibet. This is a mountain that has been a traditional haven for pilgrims of the ancient religion Bon. It is still a sacred place for Hindu and Buddhist pilgrims in spite of the fact that it is not easy to reach. The trip might require weeks, if not months, on the road—encountering very cold weather and all sorts of natural difficulties from floods to climbing. Once at the foot of the Kailasa one begins the pilgrimage: for about fifty kilometers one goes on foot through abysses and rocky paths around the mountain. A series of prostrations to earth must be performed. It is forbidden to climb to the very top of the mountain because it was once regarded as the dwelling of the gods. The meaning of going in a circle around the mountain—the same happens at Mecca—has to do with its sacrality and total otherness. This kind of pilgrimage is also related to waters considered redemptive, such as the Varanasi (Benares), a continual destination of Hindu and Buddhist pilgrimages. The belief in the purifying power of Ganges waters is such that people go to Varanasi in order to pray, to make ablutions, and also to die or to lay the body of a loved one on a pyre. In the past, according to widespread popular beliefs, to die at Varanasi, after being purified in body and spirit, implies the breaking up of the chain of births and deaths. The concept of an all-involving pilgrimage in which the spiritual dimension reigns also remains dominant in Islamic belief.[12]

The pilgrimage to Mecca (*Hajj*)—one of the pillars of Islamic religion—is deeply felt at the individual level, but at the same time it has a collective dimension. All Muslims—regardless of nationality, geographical location, ethnicity, language, or culture—aspire to make this pilgrimage. Leonardo

Capezzone, a professor of Arabic language and literature, writes that the annual voyage to Mecca—in order to visit the places where the teaching of the Koran started—is composed of people of all countries and social classes, called together by an ecumenical and universalistic message.[13]

The same also happens in Catholic lands. In Italy, for instance, the pilgrimage in which people go on foot to the "Author Mountain" (*Monte Autore*) in central Italy, still carried out on the weekend of Trinity Sunday, usually in early June, represents a clear example. People walking in groups, singing songs, praying, and carrying flags reach the mountain during the night. It is cold and the pilgrims sit by the fires: sometimes residual snow remains on the ground. The mountain is alight from fires the pilgrims have lit. It echoes with songs addressed to the Holy Trinity. The following morning, at dawn, the pilgrims have to stand and wait a long time in order to enter the cave containing the sacred image, to touch, even for a single moment, the door architrave, the window protecting the image. Then, they return, walking backward, never showing their back to the Holy Trinity, singing all the way songs praising the sacred image. It is also possible to be present at "the spinsters' cry," at about six o'clock in the morning, where the scene is dominated by the Madonna gone into mourning and the Magdalene, both desperately crying for the dead Christ. Plenary indulgences are not envisioned.

For the time being, this kind of pilgrimage, deeply felt by the neighboring people and beloved by well-known figures of the arts and literature, does not need to be booked on the Internet. It is not broadcast world wide: to see this pilgrimage it is necessary to participate, which proves uncomfortable and demanding.

Jubilee Pilgrimage and Communication

Since the beginning of the twentieth century, communication related to the Jubilees has increased. A color poster shows the image of Bernini's angel saying "*Pax Christi in regno Christi.*" It was first published in the year 1900. Many editions followed, and later it became a postcard. In 1933 the radio first appeared. At the end of 1949, Pius XII (Eugenio Pacelli, 1939–1958) used it to announce world wide the opening of the Holy Door in the presence of radio commentators and journalists. proclaiming the Jubilee of 1950. On this occasion, polychrome postcards were created, together with stamps, special cancellations, and memorial medals (the issuance of medals, however, can be dated back to Martin V Colonna, 1417–1431).

Present-day mass-media communication is especially extensive: in 1998 and 1999 Italian Radio-Television (RAI) broadcast videos and films regarding pilgrimages, the Exodus of Jews from Egypt, and the lives of Moses and

Christ. RAI also opened a Web site, started a publication called *RAI Jubilee News*, and made arrangements with the Vatican Press Agency and the Roman Agency for the Jubilee to enable joint use of the available facilities. Publications have markedly increased, in particular those dealing with artistic topics, the Jubilee in general, and the Jubilee routes. This Jubilee has been strongly present in Roman newspapers for two main reasons: one is linked to the spread of information about transportation—the rail yards and highway projects in progress (a problem that upset Roman life throughout the year 1999); the other relates to gifts and fancy goods (wedding rings, pens, medals, and so on, bearing the Jubilee logo).

But most of all, the Jubilee is found on the Internet, with more than 650 Web sites. They are different in terms of type and number but can be divided into three main categories: institutional (few), informative in general (particularly connected to travel agencies or to the voluntary service), and commercial (the most numerous). An intranet Jubilee also exists, that is to say, there is an Internet among organizations—essential, nowadays, for reservations, connections, and so on.[14]

TO BEAR WITNESS THROUGH CONVERSATION AND WORKS

The pope has determined that it is not necessary to come to Rome to get the indulgence. One can go to Jerusalem or one can visit other appointed basilicas, located in places closer to home. But if the Jubilee journey has lost its meaning, would it not be more appropriate to follow those who simply want to grant a privilege to the converted? Those who want the testimony of faith to be borne through works, such as remission of debts to poor countries, aid to the needy, a common commitment to peace? This is a proposal that has been made by many Catholics, including Gerardo Lutte, a psychologist of human growth and development, who promoted the initiative already launched by the newsletter *Times of Brotherhood*. At his initiative an e-mail was sent to many correspondents. This e-mail talks about a worldwide proposal called "Jubilee Pilgrimage with Street Boys and Girls." The aim is to donate to Guatemalan children the monetary equivalent of the cost of the journey to Rome. He argues that this serves a far more important purpose than a "pleasure trip justified by 'religious' reasons." He hopes that the money that would be spent by three or four pilgrims in a month, as mentioned in the e-mail, would go to the children. It would be used for housing and food expenses, to spread literacy skills among the population, for professional training, for teaching children, and so on. The e-mail also recalls that once people organized "fasting dinners" to support different initiatives, from the campaigns against the war in Vietnam to the support of small missions in Latin America. Similarly, people could renounce an increasingly tourist Jubilee.

Christian Resistance to the Jubilee

The current Jubilee gives rise to many reservations, to a certain resistance because it is too linked to outward appearance. The commercial aspect is evident, particularly at a communicative level, both in newspapers and magazines, and on the Internet. Just as Glassman points out that the media have both a charismatizing and decharismatizing effect on politicians, so the media here serve both to promote Jubilee 2000 and to provide a forum for criticism.[15]

Not all the other religions and the other Christian churches have welcomed these celebrations; not all of them have taken part in common prayers or rituals. Rome's central role and the Jubilee indulgences are particularly subject to critical discussion. In some ways this Jubilee, so much a media captive, especially the new media, seems to go back to the wishes and intentions of Boniface VIII Caetani. The difference is that in those times the aim was to assert the Pope's strength, while nowadays John Paul II insists on penance, on forgiveness, on a continuous recall to spirituality. But his voice does not always prevail, and the Jubilee transmits different messages more and more often. Resistance on the side of Catholic dissent and of other Christian churches has been noticed, and is still in progress. Other religions now present on Italian territory, such as the Muslims and Buddhists, keep themselves on the fringe of all these events.

Dissent Outside the Church

Outside the Church, dissent has been relatively weak, but it showed a sign of life and became somewhat vocal for the commemoration of the killing of Giordano Bruno, the Dominican friar and philosopher who was burnt alive in Campo dei Fiori approximately four hundred years ago (17 February 1600), in a Jubilee year. (The pope was Clement VIII [Ippolito Aldobrandini, 1592–1605].) In commemoration of this, there have been publications and reprints of or about Bruno, together with scholarly conferences and lectures sponsored by prestigious institutions. Even more spontaneous events took place in Campo dei Fiori, where on the base of a statue dedicated to Bruno people have placed flowers and writings. Marching demonstrators arrived, coming from the nearby Tor di Nona's Tiber embankment. This march reproduced the procession of that time, when Bruno, led in shackles, had his face muzzled so he could not speak. The same once happened to witches sentenced to death.

In general, dissent has come from believers of some Christian creeds, while the larger world would rather enjoy the numerous restorations established for this occasion, the numerous Jubilee exhibitions of photographs, and, above all, the paintings. As a matter of fact, the much feared flood of pilgrims has not been registered so far; the city of Rome seems to be the same as ever, with the advantage of so many restored façades, enlarged pavements, and flowered squares. If anything is to be noted, we can highlight the decrease of tourists compared to the preceding years at least through springtime. With the arrival of summer, and especially with the World Youth Day, both pilgrims and tourists appeared to be increasing in number.

Issues and Questions to be Investigated Further

The Jubilee is coming to its end. This is the time for a critical evaluation. Does pilgrimage need to be a difficult journey, a traveling still connected with its etymological meaning of fatigue, danger, and uncertainty? At present, modern and efficient mass transportation has profoundly changed the nature of pilgrimage. But, what about the psychological, inner nature and expectations of the individual pilgrims? Are they real pilgrims or simply tourists?

Franco Ferrarotti has already considered that a pilgrimage to Rome could easily be transformed into a tourist trip. He also views pilgrimage or the penitent's trip as a common feature of the three monotheist religions (Judaism, Christianity and Islam) that by no historical accident see in Abraham their original father.[16] Lucetta Scaraffia's thinking moves in the same direction.[17] Present-day pilgrims visit basilicas and churches as various kinds of art exhibitions—more like eager tourists than persons who are moved by some spiritual need. This means that pilgrimage is about to lose its original nature of a penitentiary and redeeming experience, aimed at a profound inner reorientation or "conversion" in Paul's meaning of μετάνοια. Needless to say, it seems obvious that the liminal and conversion dimensions so strongly supported by Van Gennep and Turner are about to disappear in the Jubilee of 2000.

No doubt local parishes have been working for the past three years preparing for the event. But, perhaps, organizational efforts have prevailed over, or against, spiritual readiness and acquisition. Inner persuasion has probably a price to pay, in terms of concentration, to the all-pervading noise of the media. This has especially become apparent in the World Youth Day. Moreover, this Jubilee was conceived as an excellent occasion for an inter-religious dialogue. In this respect, some doubts are in order for the real spiritual efficacy of the Jubilee.

NOTES

1. Marcel Mauss, "Essai sur le don" (1923–24), in *Teoria generale della magia*, edited by Marcel Mauss (Torino: Einaudi: 1991), pp. 155–292.

2. See Victor Turner and Edith Turner, *Image and Pilgrimage in Christian Culture: Anthropological Perspectives* (New York: Columbia University Press, 1978).

3. Marcello Morgante, *Le indulgenze: Cenni storici, Dottrina, Norme e il Giubileo dell'anno 2000* (Cinisello Balsamo: San Paolo, 1999).

4. Arsenio Frugoni, "Riprendendo il 'De Centesimo seu Jubileo anni liber' del Cardinale Stefaneschi." *Bullettino dell'Istituto Storico Italiano per il Medioevo e Archivio Muratoriano* 61 (1949): 163–172; "Il giubileo di Bonifacio VIII," *Bullettino dell'Istituto Storico Italiano per il Medioevo e Archivio Muratoriano* 62 (1950): 1–121.

5. See Elena Zapponi, "Pregare con i piedi: Santiago e Finis Terrae," *La Critica Sociologica* 133 (2000): 131–132; Nancy Louise Frey, *Pilgrim Stories: On and Off the Road to Santiago* (Berkeley: University of California Press, 1998).

6. Abraham B. Yehoshua, *Viaggio alla fine del Millennio* (Torino: Einaudi, 1998), p. 93.

7. Arsenio Frugoni, *Il Giubileo di Bonifacio VIII* (Rome: Laterza, 1999).

8. Ibid., p. 45.

9. Ibid., p. 35.

10. See Jacques Le Goff, *Saint Louis* (Paris: Gallimard, 1996).

11. Franco Ferrarotti, *Partire, tornare: Viaggiatori e pellegrini alla fine del millennio* (Rome: Laterza, 1999).

12. Maria I. Macioti, *Pellegrinaggi e Giubilei: I luoghi del culto* (Rome: Laterza, 2000), esp. ch. 3.

13. Leonardo Capezzone, "Pellegrini alla Mecca," *Iter* d, no. 4 (2000): 21–25.

14. Some of the most important Internet sites include: <www.vatican.va> with many items from the Holy See; <www.jubil2000.org/osservatore/indice.it.html>, the Vatican newspaper *L'Osservatore Romano* online; <www.jubil2000.org>, in eleven different languages, prepared by the "Comitato del Grande Giubileo dell' Anno 2000"; <www.viafrancigene.com>, the famous Francigena road, a cultural itinerary suggested by the Council of Europe; <www.jiubileo.com>, history, roads, events, and dates of the Jubilee, also the Apostolic Letter of Pope John Paul II; <www.jubilee.it>, history and meaning of the Jubilee; <www.miriam.org/profets>, a Catholic link, with more than 3,740 links; <www.newadvent.org/cathen>, many items about Catholicism, and some about Protestant churches.

15. See Ronald M. Glassman, "Manufactured Charisma and Legitimacy," in *Charisma, History, and Social Structure*, edited by Ronald M. Glassman and William H. Swatos, Jr. (New York: Greenwood Press, 1986), pp. 115–128.

16. Ferrarotti, *Partire, tornare*.

17. Lucetta Scaraffia, *Il giubileo* (Bologna: Mulino, 1999).

Chapter 5

New Canterbury Trails: Pilgrimage and Tourism in Anglican London

William H. Swatos, Jr.

In his seminal entry on pilgrimage and tourism in the *Encyclopedia of Religion and Society*, Luigi Tomasi addresses the interplay of tourism and pilgrimage that characterizes our times. He points out that "the old pilgrimage sites have begun again to attract masses of pilgrims," but today "the pilgrims also come across tourists on holiday. . . . Without a doubt," he adds,

the tourist industry and the media are offering pilgrimages as consumerism. Given that tourists share the same attitudes as pilgrims—in other words, the search for authenticity at different levels of depth and involvement—it could be said that pilgrims are partly tourists and that tourists are partly pilgrims. . . . [T]he promotion of "religious" tourism today, seen as both devotional and cultural, is proof of the existence of this common search. . . . This means that the modern individual is seeking transcendental values to overcome the fragments, the discontinuity, of modern society and that he or she is the "pilgrim tourist" of modern times.

Tomasi sees modern pilgrim tourism, however, as contrasting with the medieval period when "pilgrimages were a collective phenomenon that was an integral part of the Christian world."[1]

Tomasi is not alone in pointing to the significant "rediscovery" of pilgrimages. Grace Davie has also noted "the growing popularity of sacred places in contemporary Europe" as a part of creating the "memory" that, following Hervieu-Léger, she sees as crucial to defining the nature of religion—at least in Europe. "The argument," Davie writes, leads naturally to the relationship between tourism and pilgrimage and the importance of the aesthetic (architecture, art and music) as a carrier of the sacred. It is not an exaggeration to consider Europe's cathedrals as a form of European museum. But for the faithful, they are more than this—they are *embodiments* as well as carriers of memory. . . . [S]o, too, is the contemporary significance of Europe's religious festivals, many of which are able to draw significant numbers of young people together at least in the short term, even if regular churchgoing has all but disappeared in this generation.[2]

Yet Davie is quite aware that by no means did the young people who went to hear the pope in Paris in 1997—or went to Lourdes (*n.b.*) in 2000—necessarily come with motives that could undeniably be called devout or even Christian. Indeed, no test of faith was imposed upon those who heard the pope saying Mass, as no test of faith is imposed upon the tourist who comes to Europe's great cathedrals, medieval or otherwise.

In the contemporary pilgrim tourist—whether traveling to a historic site like Chartres or an event like a papal youth rally—singularity of motive shared across the field cannot be presumed. At the same time, however, there is no basis for discounting religious motivation, nor need it necessarily be the case that *religious* motivation conform to historic *theological* categories. The search for "transcendental values" overarches any particular set of theological presuppositions. To call this "secular," however, is to miss the "quest" dynamic that underlies spirituality—which is a human dynamic that can be as much "at home" in the consciousness of a medieval pilgrim as a postmodern one. Nancy Frey's treatment of pilgrimage to Compostela particularly highlights the confrontation of these dynamics. In a curious inversion of the broad contemporary cultural preference for the language of spirituality over that of religion, "true" Compostela pilgrims (those who make the journey more or less on foot, stopping at designated sites and performing specific rituals) assert the primacy of religion over spirituality; yet Frey also has recounted a case where a Japanese tourist fulfilled the obligations of the religiously orthodox only to be denied the *indulgencia* because she was not a Christian.[3]

This chapter will focus on the interplay of various levels of pilgrimage and tourism at sites large and small within the Church of England, principally in London. It will be based on observations accumulated over a decade and a half of travel, but with special intentionality within the last two years, as well as interviews with key personnel responsible for coordinating aspects of tourist visits as well as the worship life. I will describe in particular a single festival observance in one parish church, St. Mary's Bourne Street, as indicative of an intensity of devotion within a religious tradition, but also as part of a larger trend that manifests itself at the Church of England's great cathedrals, not least St. Paul's London. But let us first look backward for a moment.

PILGRIMS ON THE CANTERBURY TRAIL

What is it that makes Geoffrey Chaucer's *Canterbury Tales* one of the world's great literary classics and the jewel of England's pre-Shakespearian era? It is not its devotionalism. It is, rather, its sociology—specifically, what today might be called its ability to articulate latent functions. In the *Canterbury Tales*, the manifest "sacred" functions of pilgrimage pale before the "secular" concerns of the pilgrims. It is precisely the secularity of Chaucer's account that gives it literary immortality. All of the pilgrims display "mixed motivations." Indeed, the Kantian postulate of motivational singularity has never sustained an empirical test in the world of everyday life. Even the high social regard of which Tomasi speaks must be understood in this mixed motivational context. The "valuing" of spirituality may well, in fact, have had higher this-worldly benefits in the medieval period than our own. Anthony Blasi has written of the tentative, "casuist nature of much religious conduct," and Rodney Stark has noted the dangers of using "Age of Faith" assumptions in conjuring secularization-type explanations.[4] There is no reason to believe that the underlying human dynamic of mixed motivation arose only after the Enlightenment. Over and over again in religious history it has been the case that religion has been used and abused for ends that are far from devotional or theological.

This is not to single out the medieval period—or even Chaucer's late-medieval period—for particular attention. It is well known in English church history, for example, that the Caroline seventeenth-century archbishop of Canterbury, William Laud, during his years as bishop of London complained of the noise in Old St. Paul's: "like that of Bees . . . mixed of walking, tongues and feet." Indeed, Jay Jacobs notes, "For much of its life St. Paul's was market place, employment agency, factory, playground, and flophouse for the city." A lay vicar in 1589 noted that services were disturbed by the rounds of "Porters, Butchers, Waterbeareres, and who not," and the precincts of it were used for various pursuits: "The south alley [aisle] for usurye and poperye; the north for simony and the horse-fair; in the midst for all kinds of bargains, meetings, brawlings, murthers, conspiracies." Jacobs continues:

Varlets seeking employment and prospective masters met at St. Paul's. Lawyers staked out pillars as offices. Books, tobacco, and tailoring were hawked there. Trunks were hammered together; glass, lumber, wine, and other goods were stored on the premises. Plays were given. Beggars and drunks slept in the church. Rubbish and dung collected there in heaps. . . . The antics of children were a constant distraction. As early as 1385 a bishop of London spoke of boys shooting birds, playing ball, and breaking windows in the cathedral.[5]

Indeed, even the "fully secular" tourist of today, simply whisked through St. Paul's during a bus-tour stop on a predetermined itinerary, is likely to find far less secularity than may have been the norm through much of the cathedral's history.[6] In fact, one might argue that, although Charles I and Archbishop Laud were staunchly anti-Puritan theologically, it was their great religious purism that ultimately cost them their lives. Perhaps there was no dyad in history that more closely approximated the model of singularity of motive than these men. Its failure was not nearly so much about Puritan theology—because that was not popular—but because real people do not live real lives with the singlemindedness of the Laudian policy of "Thorough."

While London was more cosmopolitan than Canterbury even at the time Chaucer wrote (in Chaucer's Miller's Tale, for example, the dandy Absolon has "Paul's window carved on his shoes"—that is, the "rose" east window of the old cathedral), there is no reason to believe that when his pilgrims arrived at their goal they found any greater purity of religion than might have been the case at St. Paul's two centuries later. Indeed, Henry VIII managed to get away with the destruction of Becket's tomb based on the superstitions and abuse that occurred there. The symbolic aspects of the tomb's desecration as a tool of royal hegemony notwithstanding, theologically pure devotionalism was not the only order of the day at Canterbury and other shrine sites in either Chaucer's time or Henry's—for example, St. Swithun's shrine at Winchester was destroyed in the same purge as Becket's, without any corresponding association between Swithun and hierocracy. The association between cathedrals and shrine activities is long standing, hence "[c]athedrals were centres of tourism from a very early date," inasmuch as it was to the tombs of saints, rather than to architectural sites, that pilgrims came to connect to the miraculous charismata believed to be associated with the remains of the deceased. It was the shrine that brought both holiness and temporal wealth to the cathedral, much more than the reverse.[7]

This is not by any means to say that the characters Chaucer puts on the Canterbury trail were "not religious" or "purely secular." The richness of Chaucer's work is precisely the way it highlights the mixing of motivations within the human personality, hence in the process of social interaction. To presume singularity or simplicity of motive, rather than multiplicity and complexity, is to posit a theologico-philosophical model of human behavior that cannot be consistently sustained in empirical research. Rather, with Max Weber, we should recognize that a clear consciousness of motives by

Photo 3. Contemporary Shrine of St. Thomas Becket, Canterbury Cathedral. *William H. Swatos, Jr.*

participants is a great rarity, and that the normal mode of human action is worked out in a cacophony of motives—some conscious, some not—that must be interpreted with the utmost care by social scientists: "In the great majority of cases actual action goes on in a state of inarticulate half-consciousnesss or actual unconsciousness of its subjective meaning. The actor is more likely to 'be aware' of it in a vague sense than he is to 'know' what he is doing or be explicitly self-conscious about it."[8]

Furthermore, in a specific action setting, motives and meanings may change during the action sequence, such that one cannot assume that the motivations and meanings that caused an actor to set out on a particular trail are necessarily sustained through to its conclusion, nor even during the journey. The constantly shifting action field offers a virtually infinite series of motivational permutations and combinations. Consider, for example, Jacobs's description of the effect of establishing the shrine of St. James at Compostela (which remained sufficiently important to attract, *inter alios*, the pilgrim Walter Raleigh, in spite of the separation of the Church of England from that of Rome): "The effects of the pilgrimage route cannot be overestimated. Markets bustled, building and shipping industries boomed, churches throve, and customs, songs, and tales were exchanged. Souvenirs and art objects carried by the pilgrims helped to spread artistic styles from country to country, and the necessity of accommodating huge crowds of pilgrims gave rise to a series of new churches along the route."[9]

For then as now, we may follow Eade and Sallnow and say that the pilgrimage process is characterized by an "essential heterogeneity" such that the pilgrimage experience becomes "an arena for competing religious and secular discourses." There are "varied discourses with their multiple meanings and understandings, brought to the shrine by different categories of pilgrims, by residents and by religious specialists," and there are also "mutual *mis*understandings, as each group attempts to interpret the actions and motives of others in terms of its own specific discourse." Hence, "if one can no longer take for granted the meaning of a pilgrimage for its participants, one can no longer take for granted a uniform definition of the phenomenon of 'pilgrimage' either." Thus,

[A] pilgrimage shrine, while apparently emanating an intrinsic religious significance of its own, at the same time provides a ritual space for the expression of a diversity of perceptions and meanings which the pilgrims themselves bring to the shrine and impose upon it. . . . As well as perhaps being a symbolic power-house productive of its own religious meanings, a pilgrimage shrine is also . . . an arena for the interplay of a variety of imported perceptions and understandings, in some cases finely differentiated from one another, in others radically polarized.[10]

But this is also not to say that there are no differences between those who set out on Chaucer's trail and pilgrim tourists of today's London. These might be categorized broadly as those who are relatively external to the religious system of action, versus those who are more specifically theological—notwithstanding that these two dimensions constantly interact.

Not the least important among the external dimensions is precisely the absence of the shared frame of theological reference of which Tomasi speaks with respect to the medieval world. The central dicta of Western Christianity, though not necessarily understood in depth, nevertheless provided a common cultural arena in which shared meanings could reasonably be inferred among participants. Even after the Reformation, the presence of state churches tended to maintain a common theological core among the population. Today this is no longer the case. Within contemporary England itself, religious pluralism ensures that a diversity of meanings characterizes the cultural frames of reference that will occur as persons visit the same site. Extensive globalization of tourism simply magnifies this phenomenon, as persons from all over the world visit sacred sites. Contestation over Jerusalem is the most obvious example.

The duration of the pilgrimage experience is also altered. While a few sites, like Santiago de Compostela, attempt to preserve the tradition of walking as a qualification for true pilgrimage, tourists nevertheless stream in; hence the "authentic" pilgrims become part of the attraction. It is now easily possible to visit a dozen holy sites in as many days, so at least the temporal journey is dramatically shortened. It is the combination of these two elements—pluralism and temporal shortening—that creates the external conditions for the peculiarities of modern tourism to religious sites under the conditions of high technology, multinational capitalist society and culture. One can conceive a continuum between those who come to a site having no real idea why it is on a tour, at one extreme, as contrasted with those who have hoped and dreamed and planned to fulfill a religious commitment.

However, there is also a significant internal change, at least as far as Western Christianity is concerned: namely, the relative decline of asceticism and rise of mysticism that characterizes contemporary spirituality. As Eade and Sallnow note, "[i]n the Catholic tradition, pilgrimage has always been seen as a form of penance. . . . The hardships and dangers of the journey and the bodily privations which pilgrims were obliged to undergo were thought to win the penitential pilgrim God's forgiveness and grace."[11] Although some shrines of Roman Catholic provenance attempt to preserve this in a local cult, the clear drift of post-Vatican II theology is to deemphasize the penitential aspect of Catholic tradition—particularly in regard to the earning of merit, now further repudiated by the Catholic-Lutheran concordat on justification. People now come to pilgrimage centers to receive benefits, in the nature of physical healing or a spiritual "charge." The shift from asceticism to mysticism radically alters the pilgrim experience and is fully consistent with the concomitant individualization of religious experience that is associated with postmodernity.[12] People come for what they "get out of it," and what they get is what *they* determine they get. This is quite different from a quasi-authoritarian organization predetermining the qualifications that are associated with obtaining a writ of absolution. In phrases that float around contemporary Anglicanism in various contexts, today's pilgrim tourist may potentially experience "all of the joy, and none of the guilt," encountering "preferences rather than rules." However, this is not to say that penitence is not a possible motive, nor the joy of forgiveness an opportunity the site offers. Members of the verger's staff at St. Paul's, for example, report "a lot" of people come to them seeking to have a confession heard (which ministry is provided throughout the day).

Sites like St. Paul's London, Westminster Abbey, All Saints Margaret Street, and St. Mary's Bourne Street—to name but a few—are all also working, living religious institutions. While Grace Davie may well be right that the great cathedrals are in some ways museums of Europe, there can be no question to anyone who has done comparative observations that what happens among the pilgrim tourists in these living religious institutions is quite different from New York City's Metropolitan Museum of Art's medieval site, The Cloisters. Both can evoke memory, but something qualitatively different separates the two. The ongoing worship life of the cathedrals and parish churches distinguishes them from the intentionally aesthetic-educational functions of The Cloisters, regardless of how "medievalized" it is in its appearance. In the London churches, pilgrim tourists of all hues are confronted by a worship experience and the exercise of the religious life. Religion continues as an activity, not merely a memory, though it certainly is an activity with memory.

On the other hand, comparative tourist statistics suggest that Davie is correct in saying that there is a quality about the European cathedrals that is distinctive, at least in comparison to those in the United States. "Heritage" is a leading category for defining the tourist quest in the United Kingdom, and the cathedrals and other leading churches fall within that rubric. A 1984 survey, for example, found that 72 percent of overseas tourists "had visited cathedrals, churches and other religious sites, which was a higher proportion than for any other attraction." In 1992 St. Paul's was the fifth most visited site in England that charged admission, and Westminster Abbey was among the top ten free attractions. The abbey, which instituted general charges for tourists in 1998, nevertheless continues to receive more visitors than any church in Great Britain, being the fifth most popular site nationally and the third in London. "As many as half of the Anglican cathedrals (21) attracted over 200,000 visitors in 1992, a feat equalled by only 7 percent of the 5,500 tourist attractions in the UK." Among English cathedrals, St. Paul's, which is the seventh most popular site in London, reports the highest proportion of overseas visitors, at 70 percent.[13] Roberto Cipriani similarly reports the Vatican among the most visited sites in Rome.[14] The most visited site in Washington D.C., by contrast, is the National Air and Space Museum, followed by other museums, even ahead of such potentially civil religious sites as the Lincoln Memorial, Mount Vernon, Arlington National Cemetery, and the Vietnam Veterans Memorial. Washington's National Cathedral ranks eighteenth.[15]

LONDON: THE GREAT CHURCHES

St. Paul's Cathedral and Westminster Abbey symbolize both the quintessence of classical Anglican praxis and simultaneously the "soul" of England. Both continue, also, to have a regular round of daily worship, including the daily offices and Eucharistic celebration. Choral evensong almost daily at both churches particularly epitomizes Anglican tradition in contemporary imagination (even though, in fact, current choral practice does not extend over much more than a century, prior to which singing the offices had gradually fallen into desuetude after the Reformation). Both are immensely popular tourist sites and have throngs of tourists going through them through much of the day, though neither allows tourist access on Sundays. Both charge admission, except during service times. The principal clergy of both churches are Crown appointees, though the significance of that has changed over time. Much more consultation was done with St. Paul's chapter and staff, for example, in regard to the selection of the current dean than was the case previously. The abbey—strictly speaking, the Collegiate Church of St. Peter—is neither a cathedral nor a diocesan church, but is rather a "royal peculiar," and that has historically given its dean a unique status.[16]

St. Paul's is the cathedral of the diocese of London, next in seniority to York, following Canterbury. In recent history, it has also been in that same position regarding number of annual visitors, though in 1998 it showed a 14 percent increase, drawing ahead of York.[17] Diocesan functions take place here throughout the year, as do other activities of various religious and charitable organizations. During these times the church is closed to tourists. A gift shop and café are in the basement, as is the crypt. The café is managed by an outside, for-profit firm. A separate charge must be paid for access to the galleries and dome. A weekly organ recital late on Sunday afternoons is the only regular public activity that has no explicitly religious component. In addition to the specific services of corporate worship, prayer is said hourly during the "tourist" times, along with a welcome to the visitors. Photography is not permitted during services at either site.

The forming of the congregation for evensong at St. Paul's helps distinguish levels of pilgrim tourists. Those who actually indicate a desire to attend the service are permitted to enter seating in the crossing or in the choir itself, and they are provided with an order of service and a psalter. Except on Saturday evenings, Sundays, and some holy days, when a hymn may be sung, the congregants do not themselves sing anything. Kneeling pads are provided with the chairs in the crossing, and there are kneeling benches in the choir. Three clergy, whose ability to sing is one of their selection criteria, are specifically employed to conduct the daily round of services. Recently one of these has been a female; however the cathedral has reaffirmed its intention to continue to restrict its choir to men and boys. No formal monetary collection is taken except on Saturday evenings and Sunday, but a person normally stands with a receiving dish as the psalters and service orders are returned. The size of the congregations who specifically choose to attend the service has remained stable over the past two decades. Virtually all of the participants follow the printed directions regarding standing and sitting, but the majority will not kneel, notwithstanding the kneeling pads (which some attendees use instead as back supports)—though perhaps the most curious posture, seen on rare occasions, is those in the crossing who kneel facing into their chairs, rather than toward the altar.[18]

But those who specifically choose to attend the service are not the only persons who in fact attend the service. Farther back in the nave a congregation that may well by the end of the service equal or exceed in number those who choose formally to attend the service also is present, at least for part of the service. This congregation does not receive the service materials, and is not expected to follow directions regarding standing and kneeling. There is greater coming and going among this group, but at least some stay through the service once they are seated. At greater remove are those who continue to walk about the side aisles and rear of the church during the service. As long as these people do not take pictures, make noise, or attempt to move forward into the crossing or beyond, their presence is accepted. This group of people constitutes a significant tourist-pilgrim blend. Technically the cathedral "closes to tourists" at 4:00 P.M., but at 4:15 P.M. people may again enter the cathedral. These people do not pay for tickets since the cathedral is then "open for evensong," but in fact may visit on a limited basis from 4:15

to approximately 6:00. St. Paul's also offers matins and a celebration of the Eucharist daily before 8:30 A.M., which is when the tourist flow starts, but these services are in a more remote chapel. A noon Eucharist is said daily in the choir, while tourists are free to roam elsewhere throughout the building. The services thus create a liminal situation in which pilgrims, locals, and tourists mix—though it is doubtful that Victor Turner's *communitas* is thereby achieved.[19]

St. Paul's has far fewer monuments to British leaders and historical events than the abbey, but it is not without them. Memorial tablets, some quite elaborate, adorn the walls. A chapel in the northwest corner is set aside for private prayer (though this is not universally honored by visitors). There is also a memorial chapel. As a post-Reformation structure, however, St. Paul's lacks the extensive side chapels that one finds in the medieval cathedrals. On the other hand, Wren's architectural genius combines with a spectacular mosaic display of angelic hosts that defies deist rationalism. In earlier times, St. Paul's was frequently attended by royalty, and Queen Anne, in whose reign the building was completed, is immortalized in a statue outside the west doors. Today, however, the royal family does not worship with any regularity at St. Paul's, and Westminster Abbey is the site for most royal functions—though Prince Charles and Princess Diana broke with this pattern to be married at St. Paul's. This Paul's did not to become the site of "traffick" as did its predecessor, though one of the shifts from the "tourist" period to the "service" period is a shutting down of stalls in the nave that sell tourist items (the downstairs gift shop remains open). The stairs up to the west doors, however, have become a significant mingling place as tourists, persons who work in the area, and pilgrims use them in good weather as a place to meet, eat, sun, and chat. Perhaps a hint of *communitas* occurs here and in the garden sections adjacent to the north and east ends.

Much more than St. Paul's, Westminster Abbey, standing adjacent to the Houses of Parliament, represents England's "civic" religion. Many of England's most prominent politicians, military leaders, and intellectuals, as well as royalty, are interred (now inurned) or memorialized here. A permanent war memorial is a central feature at the west doors, and the grounds are strewn with poppies for Remembrance Sunday. The abbey differs from St. Paul's architecturally in that it was originally a medieval structure. The architectural differences between the abbey and the cathedral tend also to minimize the size of a potential "second congregation" at the abbey, and abbey staff work to restrict the presence of tourists during services. Thus, there is significantly less activity outside the choir and crossing than there is at St. Paul's at these times. Abbey staff also try to stress the length of the service to potential congregants to avoid coming and going, which would

Photo 4. A Tour Bus Pulls Away from St. Paul's Cathedral, London.
William H. Swatos, Jr.

Photo 5. Tourists, Locals, and Worshipers Mingle on the Steps of St. Paul's. *William H. Swatos, Jr.*

again be more obvious due to the seating arrangements that are imposed by the medieval architecture.

Perhaps because of its "civic" quality and, hence, the potential of some tourists to discount it as a worship site, the abbey takes some pains to emphasize that "it is first and foremost a church." Indeed, according to one abbey official, the decision to institute a general admission charge (whereas previously the main structure had been open for free, with only side areas carrying charges) was because the nave was being used too much "as a waiting room, where people were shouting, eating ice cream, meeting their friends, not giving a damn that it was a church." In other words, the abbey position on its institution of charges was that it took this step to protect the building's *religious* character, rather than to capitalize on its value as a tourist venue. Hourly public prayer is offered during the tourist hours, and a separate entry is maintained for those who wish to pray; yet it is also the case that the staff "watch for people who try to use that as an excuse for a free visit."

Lay attendants at the abbey are more formally dressed than those at the cathedral, but the abbey clergy make it a practice to be available in the nave following services, which is not the case at St. Paul's. Again, psalters and printed orders of service are available, but in different ways and places, depending on how, where, and when one enters.[20] The orders of service are virtually identical between the two churches, with the exception that abbey services much more frequently include a general confession and absolution at the beginning (i.e., except for principal feasts, when a hymn is added at the conclusion), which may be preceded by a word of welcome. At the abbey a welcome is often, but not always, broadcast over the loudspeaker system, prior to admitting worshipers to seating. This "welcome" also has the function of reminding worshipers to turn off their cell phones. No receiving basin for offerings is evident at the conclusion of the weekday service; collections are taken Saturday and Sunday. At St. Paul's a word of welcome may occur prior to the reading of the first lesson, at the discretion of the member of the clergy doing the reading; one or both lessons may be provided with a brief contextualizing commentary, are also at the discretion of the reader. On principal feasts there are also a homily and a hymn. At the abbey distinguished laypersons, such as Commonwealth consular officials, may occasionally be appointed to read a lesson. On the other hand, when the congregation at the abbey is small, lessons may be read with the clerical lector remaining in his choir stall rather than using the lectern; at St. Paul's the lectern is used consistently. Contextualizing comments are not a part of the abbey's routine. The abbey also offers special prayers nightly on weekday evenings for the royal family and the Order of the Bath.

A certain amount of coming and going before the service at the abbey makes it clear that some non-English-speaking tourists have not understood what they were getting into when the marshals outside the entrance asked them "Service?" or even "Do you wish to attend the service?" This occurs because even as the marshals are explaining that the abbey is closed, people are in fact going in at that very same spot to attend evensong. This leads some of the more persistent tourists to try to enter, and if a series of miscommunication cues takes place, they do. At least some leave, then, when they are escorted to and placed in seats, once they realize that they are, in effect, going to have to sit there for a time, on the one hand, and they will not be allowed to walk around the abbey, on the other. It is possible to remain outside the choir and hear evensong there—perhaps actually acoustically better than in the crossing—but milling about is not permitted. Unlike the cathedral, where the "second congregation" may be as large or even larger than the first, only a handful of people sit in the nave during the service. It is made clear that those who are unable to stay for the entire service but who wish to hear some of it should sit in the nave. Yet the abbey reports that more and more people are staying for services, with its major services "completely oversubscribed."

Evensong, of course, represents only one small portion of the day. Except for principal holy days, Sundays, and a limited number of ecclesiastical or state functions, however, it is the one daily service for which the abbey consistently formally ceases to be a tourist site. At the cathedral, by contrast, tourists are allowed a limited presence virtually all the time except during the major Sunday liturgies, as long as they remain respectful of the religious significance the liturgical performance may have for others present. Thus two different models have developed: at the cathedral worship and tourism tend to be more blended, while at the abbey they tend to be more separated. One might call the cathedral model more of an "open performance" type, while the abbey is more "pastoral-congregational." Neither of these is a pure type: tourists at the cathedral may not, for example, walk into the crossing or choir during service, and tourists may attend service at the abbey without actually having to meet any religious test—though like Paul's, the abbey tourists are expected to, and almost universally will, sit and stand at appropriate points; the practical line is drawn at kneeling. At the abbey, I have also seen marshals walk into the nave and make hand gestures suggesting that persons stand at appropriate points in the service (and then sit again). I have never seen this with regard to the "second congregation" at St. Paul's.

During much of the rest of the day, tourism is the visible order of the day, though one must not assume that tourists come with no religious motivations. Indeed, at least some tours will be church groups, although one must also not assume that all of those persons included in these church groups come with religious motivations. I often mark what the many photographer tourists choose as their subjects: do they photograph each other, principally ("Now here's Lin Ying at Westminster Abbey. Now she's standing at the war memorial. Here she is at the Houses of Parliament."), or do they photograph the site itself? If the latter, do they seem to be focusing on specific religious objects or on architectural features? Of course, it cannot be denied that these all blend together. There is a *gestalt* to the experience—at least for some. Nevertheless, given that there is much to see in London or any other major European capital, the decision to choose a religious site has some significance. As a counterpoint to this, however, Salisbury Cathedral has recently been dropped from one major London operator's day tour that once included it with Stonehenge and other area attractions, simply on the basis of time. This not only created a loss of revenue for the cathedral and community, but it also suggests that some of the decisions as to who tours what are not in the hands of the tourists themselves. One might assume, then, that sites like Canterbury, Salisbury, Winchester, and Ely, for example, are more likely to draw pilgrim tourists (rather than "secular" tourists) than those in London, since the tourist must make a greater effort to seek them out.

THE SHRINE CHURCHES

Along with the great cathedrals, the Church of England also has a variety of smaller pilgrimage sites. These include both ecclesiastical ruins and sites of current religious activity. Holy Isle (Lindisfarne) may be mentioned among the former, Walsingham among the latter. Somewhat like Glastonbury, Walsingham is a contested sacred space, inasmuch as there is both a Roman Catholic Walsingham and a Church of England Walsingham. In this context may also be mentioned All Saints Margaret Street (London), which has a long-standing reputation as a center of Anglo-Catholic devotion. A sign at its entrance inviting passers-by says, "This Famous Church is Open 7 A.M.–7 P.M. Welcome." In one sermon challenging the congregation to greater activity, I heard the vicar ask whether All Saints would have a place in the future other than that of "a field-trip site for the Open University"— clearly implying that it already is a field-trip site for the Open University and probably several others.

Less well known than All Saints, but equally a center of Anglo-Catholic practice with an extended set of "friends," is the parish church of St. Mary's Bourne Street. Although in some ways similar to All Saints, St. Mary's remains simultaneously a pilgrimage center for Anglo-Catholic devotion and

Photo 6. Concluding Procession of the 125th Anniversary Celebration at St. Mary's Bourne Street, London. *William H. Swatos, Jr.*

a geographical parish, while All Saints sees itself as a "nonresidential parish." St. Mary's, for example, will take its Mary procession into the streets and has a close relationship with a school immediately across the street. In 1999 St. Mary's celebrated its 125th anniversary with a four-day liturgical extravaganza that drew not only locals but pilgrims from both the British Isles and the United States. St. Mary's history has been distinguished by a limited number of clergy, including two who served for over thirty years each, one of whom was a man of personal means who generously benefacted the church, not only its trust, but also donating vestments and paintings, and making contributions to architectural projects.[21]

In both its own 125th anniversary publication and in the sermon the bishop of London preached as a part of that observance, St. Mary's is referred to as a "shrine church" and a "wonderful shrine." That designation suggests the pilgrimage style that is a part of its current image. But that image is in part created by a unique confluence of architecture and interior design that engulfs the visitor upon entry. Housed in an undistinguished brick shell—but one that now has some remarkable features in its interior brickwork—the building has a quality that gives it a kinship with Italian sites:

I wandered in one day to look at the church. It was like straying into another world—or, at least into another country; I was immediately struck by the soft, remote daylight, by the coolness, the mysterious dark corners, by the stillness (broken every so often by the rumble of an underground train, [as it still is]) and by the rich glow of gilded furnishings against red-brick walls. It was an experience akin to entering such churches as San Zanipolo or the Frari, in Venice. . . .

There is very little in St Mary's of the specially designed "ecclesiastical" furnishings that make other churches seem so dull and conventional; the polished wood-work, the gilded gesso—even the wood block flooring of the sanctuary—combine to suggest a private house of unusual sumptuousness; and one, of course, that has been continuously lived in by the same family over many generations. . . . [It is] infinite riches in a little room.[22]

In this little room worship is conducted in vestments of museum quality, with high masses featuring classical musical settings of excellent caliber. At the anniversary masses the settings include an orchestra. No longer offered, but a feature very consistent with the church's "living room" atmosphere was the "Hangover Mass" celebrated at 12:15 P.M. on Sundays during the interwar period, "when gentle music . . . was played on the violin to a suitably subdued organ accompaniment."[23]

In St. Mary's one finds the interplay of local parish church and pilgrimage center. St. Mary's both serves as a gathering place for Anglo-Catholic devotees and sends pilgrims forth to Walsingham and Santiago de Compostela. The global and the local interpenetrate in the daily, weekly, and seasonal activities of the corporate life of the parish and its friends. This is complemented by an active publishing program that has had several instantiations. For a number of years the Anglican theologian Eric Mascall lived in the presbytery, and the parish published a significant collection of edited collections of theological essays. This same spirit of communication appears also in the fact that St. Mary's was among the first London parishes to establish a Web site (<www.stmarythevirgin.org.uk>).

The pilgrimage quality of St. Mary's and All Saints may be profitably contrasted to that of St. Martin in the Fields, also an internationally known Anglican congregation. Whereas St. Mary's attempts something of a resacralization of at least its neighborhood, if not the world, by its Mary procession, for example, one may say that St. Martin has largely formulated its program to meet a different demand. St. Martin is certainly known internationally for its high quality classical music program, which includes pay "candlelight" concerts several nights a week and free concerts on some weekdays. Nevertheless, these programs are totally secularized. A nonliturgical musical service is held on Sundays, principally for "visitors," but the rest of the worship is not well attended and musically uninspired. The congregation operates a café in its undercroft, along with a brass-rubbing center and an art gallery, at which artists display works for sale. There is also a chapel in the undercroft, but I have never seen it in use. Thus, the integration of quality musical presentations and worship which is seen at All Saints and St. Mary's (and other congregations) is not a part of the life at St. Martin, and the passer-by tourist who stops at St. Martin to see the building will much more likely find the homeless sleeping than people praying. The building gives an aura of by-gone glory rather than living faith.

At the same time, the church of St. Mary-le-Strand, near St. Martin, perhaps the masterpiece edifice of English Baroque ecclesiastical architecture in London, has a trickle of visitors throughout the day, even though it does not maintain anything as elaborate as the programs of All Saints and St. Mary's Bourne Street. One suspects that the differences between St. Martin and St. Mary-le-Strand represent divergences in theology and ecclesiology between these two parishes over recent decades, rather than a "secularization of the world" per se. The semi-free-form intercessions at St. Mary-le-Strand, under the control of the celebrant, have explicitly included, for example, a petition for those "on holiday or on pilgrimage," and I have never attended worship there when there has not been some coming and going of visitors (i.e., "tourists"). St. Mary's offers a weekly free concert through much of the year but also a weekday sung mass (on a different day as well as on Sunday). While the homeless may sleep in St. Martin during the day, it is the priest-in-charge of St. Mary-le-Strand who has been the bishop of London's chaplain to the homeless. Specific figures in leadership positions among both the clergy and laity serve as *agents* of the secularization process—hence St. Martin is a case of internal secularization, rather than the result of external "system variables."

NOW AND THEN

The purpose of this chapter has been to highlight the complexities of the interplay between tourism and pilgrimage in several Church of England worship sites in London. Not only motivationally, but also practically, at many points it becomes difficult to distinguish in the great cathedrals between the religious pilgrim and the secular tourist. In smaller congregations, conscious decisions have determined whether the site is primarily a tourist venue (St. Martin in the Fields) or a pilgrimage site (All Saints Margaret Street, St. Mary's Bourne Street). In the large churches, particularly, the phenomenon of pluralism plays a significant role. It is this, rather than an inherent secularity, that distinguishes the present pilgrimage/tourism complex from earlier times. In short, when we compare the pilgrimage experience of Chaucer's England with that encountered in London (or Canterbury) today, it is not the case that Chaucer's pilgrims were necessarily any more spiritual than those of today, but that they brought a common spiritual meaning system to their activities—and this meaning system was in turn shared between them and those around them on the Canterbury trail.

Today, unlike the Middle Ages, individuation and privatization virtually ensure that one person's pilgrimage is another's tourism, and vice versa. The multiplicity of meaning complexes—both of tourist meanings and pilgrim meanings—among a larger context of multiple meanings creates a web that is practically impossible to untangle. Rather than a collective phenomenon, the pilgrimage is more likely mystical in character, having "spiritual" meaning for the individual seeker—even if that seeker comes in a religious tour group. There is no socio-religious equivalent to "the Christian world" of the Middle Ages. The tomb of the king St. Edward the Confessor, though still lodged at Westminster Abbey—Henry VIII would not have destroyed the tomb of a king—is not what people come for today, even less so that of the now virtually unknown Eorconweald, the seventh-century fourth bishop of London, whose tomb at St. Paul's was a place of pilgrimage throughout the Middle Ages. It may well be this set of overarching meaning systems, rather than any putative "Age of Faith," that serves to distinguish that unique geohistorical period in human civilization.

This is not to say that there is not a world culture of advanced high technology and multinational capitalism. Indeed, as John Meyer notes:

Modern world culture is more than a simple set of ideals or values diffusing and operating separately in individual sentiments in each society. . . . The power of modern culture—like that of medieval Christendom—lies in the fact that it is a shared and binding set of rules exogenous to any given society, and located not only in individual sentiments, but also in many world institutions.[24]

One hallmark of this culture is *religious pluralism*, and this religious pluralism is thrown into sharpest relief when it is compared to the religious monopolism of medieval Europe. It is not that medieval people were more religious than people of any other time and place, but that there was "a shared and binding set of rules exogenous to any given society" that were articulated in the language of the Western Church. Those rules assumed religious monopolism, whereas today the rule system to which Meyer refers assumes religious pluralism, hence individual liberty of religious profession—including no profession at all. There may be no less *spiritual* quest today than there was in Chaucer's day, but the context for articulating that quest is inchoate: "there will be many who arrive unskilled in holy things."[25] Thus it becomes easier to speak in the secular language of tourism than the religious language of pilgrimage, even if, in fact, there is a spiritual dynamic at some level manifest in the experience, perhaps only implicitly.[26] "[T]hose who enter a cathedral [or other historical religious site] as tourists are sometimes beguiled by place, mood and size into a mode of wonder. They can acknowledge a desire to understand, to question, even to confront the God whose inspiration has made possible both the building and the moment. In this way, the tourist may indeed be transformed into a pilgrim."[27]

NOTES

1. Luigi Tomasi, "Pilgrimage/Tourism," in *Encyclopedia of Religion and Society* (Walnut Creek, CA.: AltaMira Press, 1998), p. 363.

2. Grace Davie, *Religion in Modern Europe: A Memory Mutates* (Oxford: Oxford University Press, 2000), p. 36; cf. Danièle Hervieu-Léger, *Religion as a Chain of Memory* (Cambridge: Polity Press, 2000).

3. Nancy Louise Frey, *Pilgrim Stories: On and Off the Road to Santiago* (Berkeley: University of California Press, 1998); cf. T. Davis Bunn, "A Baptist Goes to Lourdes," *Clarity* (Aug./Sept. 1999), pp. 28–32; Annie Paisley, "Joyful Journeys with Kindred Companions," *Spirituality & Health* (Fall 1999), pp. 56–60.

4. Anthony J. Blasi, "Problematic of the Sociologists and People under Study in the Sociology of Religion," *Ultimate Reality and Meaning* 13 (1990), p. 151; Rodney Stark, "Secularization, R.I.P.," in *The Secularization Debate*, edited by William H. Swatos, Jr., and Daniel V. A. Olson (Lanham, MD: Rowman & Littlefield, 2000), pp. 47–52.

5. Jay Jacobs, "The Land's Epitome: A St. Paul's Profile," in *The Horizon Book of Great Cathedrals*, edited by Jay Jacobs (New York: American Heritage, 1968), p. 179.

6. As the Report of the Archbishops' Commission on Cathedrals observes, one of the problems in discerning the comparable "secularity" or "sacrality" of cathedral life in earlier times is that the evidence of secular "use is largely derived from the records of complaints about it." On the one hand, these certainly suggest that some people thought the cathedrals should be reserved for sacred purposes, while others used them more widely; but the nature and occurrence of both sentiments cannot be clearly stated. See *Heritage and Renewal: The Report of The Archbishops' Commission on Cathedrals* (London: Church House, 1994), p. 191.

7. Ibid., p. 189.

8. Max Weber, *Economy and Society* (Berkeley: University of California Press, 1978), p. 21.

9. Jacobs, "Land's Epitome," p. 257.

10. John Eade and Michael J. Sallnow (eds.), *Contesting the Sacred: The Anthropology of Christian Pilgrimage* (London: Routledge, 1991), pp. 2–4, 10. Like Jacobs, Eade and Sallnow (pp. 25–26) also point out that "mirroring the intensive sacred commerce mediated by a pilgrimage shrine, one frequently encounters equally intensive secular commerce taking place in or around the sanctuary precincts," and note that "[i]n the Old World, supershrines . . . have developed more permanent economic infrastructures for dealing with the continual influx of pilgrims." The Report of the Archbishops' Commission on Cathedrals in the Church of England similarly gives significant attention in both its tourism chapter and appendix to the monetary role of tourism in cathedral operations, and by extension to the surrounding community (*Heritage and Renewal*, ch. 12 and Appendix 4).

11. Eade and Sallnow, *Contesting*, p. 21.

12. It should be remembered that when Weber writes about the Protestant ethic, he is describing a shift *within* the ascetic mode from other-worldly to inner-worldly—hence a change in the external locus of soteriological accomplishment, but not in its essential dynamic. From a religious point of view, the shift from asceticism to mysticism is much more profound. I refer to this elsewhere as "romantic Protestantism," following Colin Campbell's analysis of the shift from capitalist to consumerist society, but it can equally well be applied to other religious traditions. This shift in economic production styles has important implications for contemporary tourism. See Max Weber, *The Protestant Ethic and the Spirit of Capitalism* (New York: Scribner, 1930); William H. Swatos, Jr., "Western Hemisphere Protestantism in Global Perspective," in *"Religions sans Frontières": Present and Future Trends of Migration, Culture, and Communication*, edited by Roberto Cipriani (Rome: Presidenza del Consiglio dei Ministri Dipartimento per L'Informazione e L'Editoria, 1994), p. 182; Colin Campbell, *The Romantic Ethic and the Spirit of Capitalism* (Oxford: Blackwell, 1987).

13. *Heritage & Renewal*, pp. 136–137. Though now dated (1994), *Heritage & Renewal* represents an important source for both statistical and historical information on English cathedral life. While its statistics are certainly not without flaws, they nevertheless provide one lens through which to examine the role of tourism in historically religious settings and vice versa. Regrettably, although the report mentions pilgrimage in passing at a few points, the commission seems only minimally to have considered the potential religious motivations of tourists—that is, tourists were categorized generally as a body without religious motivations to which the (putatively religious) cathedral staff was to respond.

14. Personal communication, Cipriani to Swatos, 15 September 1999.

15. Data supplied by the Washington D.C. Visitor and Convention Bureau, 10 September 1999.

16. A useful historical example, quite different in character from the present time but accurate in its reflection of the place of the abbey pulpit is Hal W. French, "The Victorian Broad Church, Seedbed of Twentieth-Century Religious Pluralism and Implicit Religion: An Historical Perspective," *Implicit Religion* 1 (1998), pp. 55–67. (A dean is the most senior member of the clergy staff of a cathedral. Under the dean come canons and then lesser clergy.)

17. Data supplied by Association of Leading Visitor Attractions (ALVA), 9 November 1999.

18. It is difficult to estimate what proportion of the participants are Anglican. The Report of The Archbishops' Commission's research (*Heritage and Renewal*, p. 141) unfortunately used only a relatively small sample (ca. 800), gathered at the moderately distant cathedrals of Coventry, Ely, Lichfield, and Wells. This showed about 40 percent Anglican, a little over 10 percent Roman Catholic, and about a quarter unchurched. In terms of patterns of attendance at religious services in their ordinary practice, the sample was about equally divided among those who attended weekly or more, attended somewhere between annually and less than weekly, and did not attend. Inasmuch as St. Paul's, however, shows over 70 percent from overseas, whereas these others average about 20 percent, it would seem likely that the London churches see a far higher proportion of non-Anglicans than the report's survey suggests.

19. See Victor Turner and Edith Turner, *Image and Pilgrimage in Christian Culture: Anthropological Perspectives* (New York: Columbia University Press, 1978).

20. The psalters are made available for persons who choose to read the psalm texts silently while they are sung by the choir.

21. Henry Hely-Hutchinson, "To Love and Linger: Priests Departed," in *Streets of Heaven: 125 Years in the Parish of St. Mary's Bourne Street*, edited by Neville Price (London: St. Mary the Virgin, 1999), pp. 44–51.

22. Brian Brindley, quoted in Roderick Gradidge, "A Very Ordinary Church: An Architectural History of St. Mary's," in Price, *Streets of Heaven*, pp. 67–68. St. Mary's Web site homepage quotes a more recent review from London's *Time Out* magazine: "A Concealed Treasure . . . Pure Balm for the Mind and Spirit."

23. Shane Fletcher, "The Servant of the Liturgy: Plainsong and Polyphony," in Price, *Streets of Heaven*, p. 90; cf. Timothy Ashurst, "Garments of Salvation: St. Mary's Vestments," in Price, *Streets of Heaven*, pp. 104–113.

24. John W. Meyer, "The World Polity and the Authority of the Nation State," in *Studies of the Modern World-System*, edited by Albert Bergesen (New York: Academic Press, 1980), p. 117.

25. *Heritage and Renewal*, p. 35.

26. See William H. Swatos, Jr., "Revisiting the Sacred," *Implicit Religion* 2 (1999), pp. 33–38.

27. *Heritage and Renewal*, p. 36.

Chapter 6

Popular Religion and Pilgrimages in Western Europe

Liliane Voyé

Pilgrimages come within the province of "popular" religion, which is very important in Catholicism. Many of its manifestations are not only accepted by the institutional authorities but are very often stimulated and encouraged by them (particularly by the present pope). To speak of "popular" religion is not to prejudge its significance. Various studies have shown that neither social class nor educational level is radically discriminant in this field.[1] If differences exist, they concern only the modalities of expression of this kind of religion—some places of pilgrimage, St. James of Compostela and Chartres for instance, have a more elitist and intellectual image than others, say, Lourdes or Medjugorje). If popular religion appears sometimes to be naive, this is because it generally refers to concrete situations of everyday life and addresses feelings rather that intellect. What, then, are the main features of popular religion in general and of pilgrimages in particular? To answer this question, I review two main aspects of actual pilgrimages in Western Europe: the evolution of their polysemic character and their corporeal and material dimension.

A POLYSEMOUS WAY OF ACTING

In various forms of popular religion, and in pilgrimages specifically, people seek to enter into the most direct possible contact with the divine and the sacred, and to create with it a relationship the meanings of which may be multiple but are not necessarily exclusive. If today most European pilgrims come first to ask for protection and personal assistance and so tend to partic- ipate in a relationship of gift exchange, nonetheless the pilgrimage contin- ues, with variable intensity, to encompass other meanings.

A Return to the Origins of the Faith

Turner notes that pilgrimages in Palestine—and we can add Rome—do not have, and never had, as their principal purpose the soliciting of graces, favors, or even miracles.[2] The object of pilgrimage to these places, he maintains, is for pilgrims to revitalize the sense of their own Christianity, immersing themselves in the geographic places of its origins, and to revive the landscapes in which Christ, his mother, and his followers lived—a message that would otherwise come to them only by means of books and preaching.

To be sure, it is not only in Palestine or Rome that we may find pilgrims essentially motivated by this search. All places of pilgrimage share it, if less intensely than Rome and Palestine. They are what Turner calls "prototype pilgrimages," that is, places designated by the founders of a historic religion or by early disciples, which more than other places, re-awaken remem- brance of fundamental principles—in the case of Christianity of the Bible and the Church.[3] Returning to the theories of Van Gennep, Turner adds that Rome is essentially a "liminal" place, a place that goes beyond the normal order of life and that places the person who is there in a transitional state— the "communitas"—where he or she is given another view of the world and where new types of relationships between men and women and ideas seem to become possible and desirable. "Rome differs so from the political orga- nization of the world," he says, "and represents an ordained and legal way— the one of God and the 'communitas'—against the power and the political authority of the Caesar."[4] For this reason this "liminal" character of Rome may be put in relation with the declarations of the present pope about the po- litical scene: he talks of "another place" and so he hopes and presumes that his word will be listened to as a proposal of something transcending worldly organization, its conflicts and its priorities. Many of his speeches delivered during the Jubilee Year were clearly in this direction.

Other places get pilgrims who come, first of all, to confirm and revive their faith. This is particularly the case with national and diocesan pilgrim- ages, organized from a pastoral perspective. It seems to me that it is also the case of persons who, in the name of their faith, individually or in a group, gather in some pilgrimage places to serve the sick: the specific services they seek to offer are prayers, testimony, spiritual expression and manifestation of religious belief.

A Penitential Activity

If, in past times, many pilgrimages reflected a penitential aspect, sometimes requested or ordered by the ecclesiastical authorities, today, they very rarely fulfill this function. Therefore, we should not be surprised to learn from various pieces of research that in Europe the sense of guilt has greatly diminished—as responsibility for "fault" has been transferred from individuals to social structures.

The 1999 survey whose object was to outline "European values" shows, in this sense, a reduction of belief in sin, principally in the devil and hell, as well as an increase in situational ethics that coincides with diminished acceptance of the disciplinary authority of the Church.[5] This general trend is dominant but does not preclude the possibility that some pilgrims may perform in this way a penitential rite.

There are, however, some exceptions particularly linked to specific pilgrimage places and/or to characteristic moments. The most famous of these exceptions is without doubt the Irish pilgrimage to St. Patrick's Purgatory where every year more than ten thousand pilgrims (a number that seems to be more or less triple that of the first half of the nineteenth century) inflict on themselves severe mortification as punishment and expiation.[6] Disputation about such matters arose out of the political division of Ireland and changes in its Celtic culture.

Certainly, the penitential aspect does not need either immediate explanation or external evidences, such as occur at Lough Derg. But all the research reveals that it is not this that today moves most of the pilgrims. I have also suggested some reasons for the decline of the penitence pilgrimage, which are fully recorded in existing cultural models.

Nevertheless, it is worth noting that when one arrives at a pilgrimage site, one is often struck by something now relatively unusual in many churches: confessionals, in greater or lesser numbers according to the importance of the place or the season, are in permanent use. Some pilgrims wait their turn while others, already out, concentrate in silence. Thus even when the demonstrated expression of penitence has almost disappeared from pilgrimage sites, it seems that they create an environment that is, for some, favorable to the spirit of penitence and that promotes this confessional step toward reconciliation.

An Affirmation of Identity

Although urbanization and mobility have contributed profoundly to modifying feelings of territorial belonging, territorial identity has not decreased in importance and, as in the past, its persistence is manifested particularly through pilgrimages. Certainly, many times the territorial unit of reference has changed: this sense of identity is seldom confined to the closest village or group of villages. Even if specific, essentially rural, areas have retained the tradition of the local pilgrimage, it is often regions and nations that search to affirm themselves in a particular place of spirituality. Lourdes—and this is not well known—develops this role for Bigorre, as does Einsielden for the Catholics in Switzerland, where, Campiche writes, "the Catholic culture appears very much linked to a popular religiosity."[7]

If, in the cases we just mentioned, the meanings associated with the pilgrimage do not go beyond the religious field, this is not always the case for other places. Some, in effect, become polyvalent symbols of an affirmation of identity that alternates ambiguous religious fervor with political claims. This especially seems to be the case for pilgrimage places situated in countries where there are (or were) claims for independence or political autonomy and in which religion is (or was) a discriminating factor. In this way, Czestochowa has played a key role in the political changes that Poland has experienced. Has not Lech Walesa always carried an image of the "Queen of Poland?" Besides his religious belief, he indicated the help he hoped to receive from her, and he placed under the protection of the Black Madonna the actions of his movement and his reaction to the atheist authorities guided by Moscow. In the same sense, it is a political claim for reunification of Ireland and a lack of trust in the Protestant supremacy in Ulster, associated with religious causes, which explains the masses that each year invade the little village of Knock, lost in the midst of the peat bogs of the west (but it already has an international airport). In 1879, the Virgin reputedly appeared here, and each year many hundreds of thousands of pilgrims come here to express a faith exacerbated by the political and social struggle of which it fully constitutes a part.

As regions and nations sometimes express their identity in pilgrimage places that are for them "totemic" places, in the Durkheimian sense of the term, Pope John Paul II seems, in the same way, to desire to give Europe a place for its own identity. To this end, in the summer of 1989, he gathered hundreds of thousands of young people at Santiago de Compostela, the same place where he had launched this call in 1982:

The whole of Europe has again met around the memorial of Santiago in those centuries during which it was being built, becoming an homogeneous and spiritually united continent. . . . The pilgrimage of Santiago constituted one of its strong points which encouraged the mutual understanding of the European peoples, as diverse as they are: Latin, German, Celtic, Anglo-Saxon or Slovak. The pilgrimage in fact brought them in closer contact and linked to them all these peoples which, during the centuries, touched by the preaching of the witnesses of Christ, accepted the Gospel, and were born as peoples and nations.[8]

This message is clearly at the heart of the two main concerns of the pope: we should do everything possible to attempt to "re-christianize a secularized Europe," and we should try also in this project to think about Europe "from the Atlantic Ocean to the Ural mountains"—for as the West helps the East to gain freedom, the East contributes to helping the West again to believe.[9]

At the international level, some people also see in this another symbol: to express such a message in Compostela where the patron saint of the Reconquesta rests in the face of the menaces of the "infidels" would also be understood as an affirmation of the Christian identity of Europe at a moment when this continent is being invaded by many people coming from non-Christian parts of the world. Whatever may be said of this comment, Santiago de Compostela is undoubtedly one of the major places at which, for centuries, many of Europe's pathways have coincided.

Fatima offers another complex view of the pilgrimage, looked at as an expression of a specific identity. In addition to the expressed feeling of national belonging, this sanctuary attracts pilgrims from various European countries, many of whom go there for a certain view of the Church and the faith that—without involving any value judgment—can be classified as "conservative." Even if not all the pilgrims of Fatima necessarily agree with this view, it seems clear that it finds a privileged place of expression there. But Fatima also performs another role. Lopes has shown how this pilgrimage place is occupied by Portuguese emigrants who, when returning for holidays to their country, look for that type of mood that will allow them to obtain an equilibrium between the urban and industrial environment that they have just left and the rural and agricultural culture that they find again in their families that remained in Portugal.[10] So, Fatima would be for them a place in the transition between modernity and tradition, and would perform a role similar to an *échangeur de sens* ("exchange of sense").

Another example brings out still further the polysemous relationships of identity that pilgrims maintain with these sacred places that they visit. The place is Banneux, a little town in Belgium, close to the German and Dutch borders, in the center of a region that, at many periods in history, was unified and that today is searching for a common identity at the heart of the new Europe. After World War II, Catholics from various Belgian and Dutch dioceses undertook an action of solidarity with the German Catholics of the neighboring dioceses, particularly to help the Germans "free themselves from guilt feelings." In this spirit, there were some joint pilgrimages to Banneux, and still today, even if this sentiment is no longer so fresh in the memory of many, Banneux remains a gathering place for Catholics of these three countries, who regularly go there together.

When we look at pilgrimages as an expression of an identity, we can advance a final reflection. If we follow Roland Robertson, we see that the process of globalization—which concerns not only the economy but is also a cultural phenomenon—stimulates the rediscovery of different kinds of particularism and of localism. These appear as ways of expressing the need "to find a place within the world as a whole." So, Robertson avers, we may frequently see "struggles for recognition," for identity and its symbolic expression "involving the display of material resources."[11] We may then suspect that, as part of these "material resources," pilgrimages may be used to reaffirm various kinds and levels of particular identities that constitute a basic aspect and a kind of request of globalization.[12] And the fact that increasing numbers of people become more and more mobile does not contradict this quest for localized and rooted identities: on the contrary, some authors insist that even mobile people—even people of high social status, and not only those who are currently called "the migrant workers"—have a "lived experience" linked with specific places, and that they often try to maintain a relationship with them, going back there not only for private circumstances but often also for manifestations of collective identity, such as carnivals or pilgrimages.[13] Some of them appear also to be specifically the ones who try to reintroduce the manifestations that have been gradually deserted by those who are less mobile and who, therefore, are sometimes less sensitive to the significance of a specific place for defining one's identity.

The Logic of a Request

Returning to religious origins and to the immersion of penitential acts in the history of faith, in the process of searching for an entity sometimes full of political and social connotations, the European pilgrimage today, is, above all, part of a logic of request, of gift exchange.

Much recent research, in fact, demonstrates—without excluding the present concomitance of other motivations—that what pilgrims most frequently express is supplicatory prayer. As an example, we can examine the research undertaken in Beauraing, a Marian pilgrimage site situated in Belgium, most often frequented by Belgian and French people.[14] The analysis of the motivation of more than a thousand pilgrims has shown that while 4 percent of them went for praise and adoration, 91 percent went to ask for "a

Photo 7. Pilgrims at Banneux, Belgium, Site of Marian Apparitions in the 1930s. *Lilane Voyé.*

grace." An in-depth study of these results (multiple responses were simultaneously admitted, which explains why totals may be more than 100 percent)
reveals, on the other hand, that these supplications referred, first, to health
problems (48 percent), either to poor personal health, or because supplicants were afraid that it would become so; 35 percent went in order to pray
for the continuity or reestablishment of familial or friendship relationships;
while success in exams, in finding a job, in solving a financial problem, and
the like represented 22 percent of the answers. We should note that 20 percent of these pilgrims made religious requests: the request of eternal rest for
a friend, a request for the conversion or return to the Church of a spouse, a
prayer that grandchildren be baptized—but requests for forgiveness of sin
or for sharing of the faith were very rare. The research also points out that
there was no significant difference between men and women, even though
the latter made more composite prayers. Regarding age, there were significant differences, which may be readily explained by the period of life of
each category: youths prayed more for success in exams, in love, or for the
healing of sickness or injury; older persons had more concern with financial
or job problems, difficulties of family life, and health.

Besides the content of prayers, this research also provided interesting information regarding the designated beneficiaries. The answers were again
cumulative and indicated that 67 percent of prayers were said for family
(spouses, children, relatives) or friends and that 41 percent of them expressed a personal request; furthermore, 11 percent prayed for peace in the
world or the struggle against injustice or famine. The differences shown
were minimal: men prayed a little bit more for themselves than women; old
persons prayed more for acquaintances than young people, who were more
concerned with themselves.

Certainly, we could review other research, but the results mostly point
in the same direction. In addition, the inquiry of 1999 into European values would fully confirm the importance of the "familiar," that is, family
members and friends, in the life of Western European people. In effect,
this reveals that, in the various countries of Western Europe, the family de-
cisively occupies first place in people's concerns, followed very closely
by jobs, friends, and spare time, which are situated at approximately the
same level.

The fact that the family, jobs, friends, and spare time are the first concerns of European people is not a surprise when one reviews the recent literature that analyzes ways of life and contemporary cultural patterns. It
illustrates the increasing importance that "daily life" has in the value range
of Western people. Actual interaction with others "here and now" is what
concentrates attention and concern. It is from specific situations of every-

day life that they seek solutions for their problems, and not from general and abstract rules, enunciated by impersonal agencies unacquainted with the realities of specific situations.

To try to understand this value range of everyday life, many hypotheses may be projected. There is the new regard for science. It is increasingly pointed out that science is far from solving all problems, nor does it seem to be on the way of doing so; its detrimental (or perverse) effects and the grievous risks that are brought by the increasing power of technology are evident day by day; finally, science is in the order of what is general and long term, and leaves people unprotected, confronted by exigencies of sickness and accident, by loneliness and drugs, by violence and hunger. Politics is also very disappointing: it does not respond to the hopes that it evoked. The great political utopias have often led to exasperation with bureaucracy, to all-seeing control, and to totalitarianism, or to laissez-faire societies, which hurt the weak and increase inequalities. Even when it fails to reach these extremes—and this is generally the case in the countries of Western Europe—the politician suffers a serious crisis of image: he or she is seen as less and less credible, and the citizen very often has the feeling that he or she is badly represented by a political class that is detached from reality and seems to act by and for itself. All these criticisms are indicated both by electoral absenteeism and by "white votes" (blank ballots), which increase at every election.

Confronted with this loss of confidence in science as well as in the state (communist in the East, "welfare" in the West)—what Lyotard calls "the grand narratives" of modernity—people search for reasons for life and security within themselves, in their closest affections (which makes us talk about "cocooning").[15] In this way they search to be themselves, to be givers of sense, ritualizing what is daily and private.[16] Thus, the European research into values shows that in Belgium, for example, almost everybody gives an immanent sense to their lives and not primarily a sense derived from belief in God. When a religious dimension is involved in this search, it seems that it is not in reference to the institutional and hierarchical, or to its legislative and disciplinary application. The search is oriented to the construction of a personal meaning for life and for comprehension, support, and hope, in the face of the difficulties and problems of everyday life.

It is in these terms that request pilgrimages make sense. Undoubtedly, it allows us to understand why many of these pilgrimages are Marian pilgrimages or even pilgrimages in the name of saints. Turner shows that Mary is the personification of the Church in its nonlegislative aspect; she is the tenderness and compassion of the mother; she is also the vulnerability to suffering; she is the emotion that appears to contrast with the pretention of the instrumental rationality of modern society.[17] The saints, with their very often "specialized" competencies, are bearers of events and acts from their earthly life that convey a feeling of closeness and create a sense of possible complicity that leads the pilgrim to see them as privileged intermediary persons. Mary and the saints speak—and this is a great quality for supplicatory prayer—to the wholeness of the person and not only to the intelligence; furthermore, neither she nor they impose the inflexibility of the law, the abstraction of science, or the indifference of politicians.[18]

The Quest for Oneself in an Uncertain and Insecure World

The results of the European Values Study show clearly that in their evaluation of what is good or bad, Europeans increasingly adopt what we may call a model of conviction to the detriment of a model of authority but do so—and this is a difference from ten years before—with an increasing feeling of insecurity. People believe less and less that a legitimate authority exists that possesses clear criteria to differentiate the good from the bad, and, that being the case, they are not obliged to follow it. They claim the right to decide by and for themselves what they have to do or not to do, but at the same time, they believe that simple and clear criteria by which to make those decisions do not exist. They are confronted with uncertainty and with the recurrent necessity to reconsider their choices. Nothing is given once and for all, and for many actual circumstances and problems of everyday life, pre-elaborated and pretested models no longer apply.

In this circumstance, pilgrimages appear to some people as a means by which to find themselves: the journey forward that pilgrimage implies is considered to reflect the pilgrim's spiritual progress, the progressive discovery of the self. As Hervieu-Léger says, the pilgrim realizes a work of "biographic construction" in reference to his or her own experience far from any "preconstituted discourse of meaning."[19] Pilgrimage thus becomes a materialization of the efforts the individual has to make to give himself or herself meaning and direction for personal existence through the various situations he or she is experiencing and not in reference to an institutional "program."

An indication of this new significance of pilgrimages may be found in the fact that very often pilgrimages are now embarked upon by personal choice and as a personal quest of one's identity, as is indicated in these findings: if, in Europe, there are more and more "pilgrimages," the agencies of the Church that traditionally undertook their organization have to note that fewer and fewer people participate in "institutionalized" pilgrimages. More and more people visit these sacred places independently (which is naturally facilitated by the development of means of transport, by touristic activities, and by the habit of traveling that many people have developed). Certainly, this is a simultaneous expression of individual autonomy and of the distance from the institutional Church. It indicates that the human being is no longer so much moved by an "external Truth" enunciated by ecclesiastical authority, but he or she is in search of himself or herself and of a personal meaning that he or she progressively constructs through everyday experiences. Meaning appears to be no longer given by God or by the institution that claims to be its interpreter. It is no longer considered to exist on a timeless, universal, and theoretic basis. It has to be constructed by everyone, here and now, and through particular ordinary practices.[20] The authenticity of the personal spiritual process transcends the conformity required by the institution. Pilgrimage materializes this personal quest and appears to be a time of reflexivity and self-discovery.

This quest for oneself is the more urgent now that we live in a "cognitive" mode: for many people, life escapes norms, which appear less and less able to give an appropriate answer to the problems that people have to face; hence they have regularly to invent original responses to novel situations for which no pre-elaborated answers exist. Furthermore, identity seems no longer something that is constructed definitively at a certain moment of life. It changes, more or less often, depending on various experiences and relationships. "Roles" appear less and less ascriptive. So, to travel, to meet other people, to see another environment for a while are conditions that are supposed to help one to discover oneself at a certain moment. It is not in this sense that tourist operators sometimes use slogans like these: "Take your time to discover yourself." "Discover your own hidden talents." Pilgrimage centers may also enter into this perspective, all the more so since they are considered as having a special relation with the transcendental—even by people who have little or no faith.

A COMPLEX OF CONCRETE ACTIONS AND MATERIAL DIMENSIONS

Popular religion refers first of all to practices and to concrete actions, and is not primarily concerned with words or the Book. This is probably one characteristic that explains its qualification and the criticism it induces. It is not centered on a comprehensive attitude or on intellectual reflection. It is not generated by the clergy or the clerks, and it sometimes escapes the rules and their control. The significance of pilgrimage refers to its concrete dimensions, which are intrinsically associated with its meaning.

Corporeal Practices

If the pilgrimage is no exception to this characteristic of popular religion either today or yesterday, undoubtedly many acts formerly found in the pilgrimage have almost disappeared. This happens, for example, in different obligatory ritual mortifications, which certainly are found in a generalized way only in the Irish pilgrimage of St. Patrick's Purgatory in Donegal—and even this one is also changing and becomes less constraining. There, from the twelfth century, between Pentecost and the Assumption only pilgrims were admitted to Station Island. They were expected to devote themselves for at least three days and three nights to a certain number of corporeal mortifying exercises that were difficult and strictly codified.

But other acts are perpetuated elsewhere. This is verified particularly by acts such as taking food and drink and of ablution. To drink water from the sacred fountain in Lourdes (France) or in Banneux (Belgium), to bathe in it or sprinkle it on the parts of the body that are sick or hurt is fully part of the pilgrimage. Now, as in the past, hands clutch the rock of the central pillar of the porch of the Gloria of St. James of Compostela's cathedral, hollowing it out more each day, as millions of pilgrims have done for more than a thousand years. The only difference is that now everyone wants to get a picture with fingers stuck in the traces left by other fingers in this rock, to feel in their own flesh as well as in their own hearts and spirits that they have arrived. It is important to take into account this "rite" of the picture, with the lines of people waiting, the strong light of the flashes, all without pause. This rite participates in the act and memory of the pilgrimage; it is a new kind of appropriation and self-conviction. Bourdieu has shown very well that to take pictures of oneself close to monuments and famous places seeks to preserve "the proof" of an effective personal presence that cannot be effected by buying a postcard.[21] Trivial in the eyes of some people, this picture has, for others, the sense of an accomplishment and so enters the rite itself.

Drinking, immersion, and touching are not the only acts found in the pilgrimages of our times. To light a candle equally constitutes an almost obligatory action. For this purpose, there are two interesting things to notice, which research makes evident. First, electric candles are not appreciated; they do not seem to be able to evoke the same role as "real" candles because we do not feel that we are the ones who light them; even more, the flame fails to come out in the same way, and there is no smell or smoke. Moreover, with electric candles, we cannot choose where we put them. And this is the second thing that has been demonstrated: those who light a candle very often desire to choose where it should be placed. This place should be as close as possible to the "sacred object." We may even sometimes see persons trying to move other candles already placed to put their own candles in a better site. All this might make one smile if it were not known, as Castoriadis has shown, that in what is symbolic there is nothing insignificant, given that all the details have an importance and are simultaneous; and if it were not known that—as Castoriadis emphasizes—"what is symbolic almost always includes a rational-real part: that which represents the real things, or that which is indispensable for the thinking or for the action."[22] These details are in part defined in accordance with reality. To light a candle by oneself and to choose the place certainly derive from the symbolic order, but effectively translate a certain mastery, the idea of acting and of a personal election that is not evoked in the same way by the electric candle, lit in a programmed place as soon as a coin falls in a slot.

So it is that the symbolic develops its own logic independently of the functional and becomes irreducible, but it is not lacking links to this functional logic. For this purpose, the example of the candles shows well that the act in its own materiality is not insignificant or trivial—I myself light that candle without a mechanical mediator. It emphasizes also the importance of the sensual feelings—to touch the wax, to hear the crackling of the wick burning, to see the uncertain movement of the flame and of the smoke, to sniff the smell. All the senses are involved in such simple and repetitive acts that characterize so-called popular religion. This sensual dimension is properly an essential trait of popular religion, and it is these traits that sometimes have been rejected in Europe in the name of the centrality of the spoken and written language, a centrality that a positivist rationalism came to aggravate. If Thomas Aquinas had for so long emphasized that humans understand what is intelligible through what is sensible, anthropology and ethnology indicate the same tendency.[23] They show always more clearly that the sense is impressed in the body and that corporeal practices are in themselves of a spoken nature. The act participates in the memory. It is practice of memory and of recognition.[24] The pilgrims know it intuitively, and the acts that they perform, sometimes with apparent ease, are aimed at communication.

A Temporal Dimension

The importance of the moment in which many pilgrimages were born was demonstrated very well by Turner; this periodization gives them, he says, a certain color.[25] He emphasizes the character of personal prayer and devotion that European pilgrims developed at the end of the nineteenth and beginning of the twentieth centuries. Among them many Marian pilgrimages were particularly promoted, he continues, as a reaction against the progress of secularization as it extended to all fields of life, not excluding the functioning of the Church.[26] Here we will concentrate on formulating some reflections concerning the meaning of the temporal variable for contemporary pilgrimages.

On the one hand, like other expressions of popular religion, the pilgrimage, over time, now lacks that kind of close relationship that it was able to sustain in a society centered on agriculture. Indeed, agriculture ritually associated the moments of the cycle of its own economic activity with diverse practices of popular religion. When the economy passed from agriculture to industry, each ramification of this sector was gifted with a patron saint and he was honored on his feast days: mass, pilgrimage and thanksgiving often emphasized the event and many workers—whether Catholic or otherwise—who prided themselves on their occupation and who sought protection gathered around the celebration. Such a rite has not yet totally disappeared, but we should recognize that today it is an occasion for a feast more than a collective celebration. One may also see that some "modern" occupations have revived pilgrimage events by themselves in another way: thus, each year a sportsmen's pilgrimage maintains the custom of going to Chèvremont Abbey, in the Liège region of Belgium, ascending a steep mountain on foot and stopping at every station of the cross before assisting at a eucharistic celebration.

Present-day society has equally maintained a certain number of pilgrimages in conjunction with the big moments of family life, with rites of passage, and particularly with the pronouncing of vows. But whereas in the past they were collective and almost "obligatory," now they are left to the initiative of the families, who very often organize them by and for themselves. Family life, on the other hand, is at the center of most pilgrimages since, as we have seen, pilgrims always have as a goal the expression of a request for themselves or for their beloved kin. We do not conclude from this that pilgrimages are undertaken only when there is a problem: many pilgrimages serve as "preventatives" and therefore are not—even if circumstances intensify them—systematically associated with an existing problem. Even if family life is organized on the basis of episodic pilgrimages to places more or less distant, it is also, more than anything else, the starting point for short repeated pilgrimages, to places closer to home, with which people have a certain familiarity and which are visited more or less regularly, with or without a precise request, but in a sort of intimate relationship or a maintained mutual acquaintance. An example would be relationships with a relative whom one would like to visit from time to time, without a reason other than affection and particular trust.

Other pilgrimages have a proper temporality: this is so for Marian pilgrimages, which often increase in May, the "month of Mary." Generally, the date of the feast of the honored saint is a moment of revitalization of piety in relation to him. Louvain (Belgium) in this way sees the arrival of trains and buses full of pilgrims on 19 March. They come to pray to Saint Joseph in a church of the city consecrated to him.

But it is indisputable that a relatively recent situation threw the pilgrimage cycle into confusion. This is the development of tourism, which now imposes its own rhythm. For this industry, whatever its determinants, pilgrimage places constitute a "product" that, as such, is "sold" alone or together with other products. Lourdes may be the only purpose of the trip (some tourist operators sell a same-day return airline ticket) or, alternatively, it may be integrated in a more complete program with other places to visit. In any case, tourism helps people visit pilgrimage places far away or unknown beyond their region or their spontaneous "customers." It gathers masses and develops diverse parallel activities of service. Certainly there is a question about just how religious these practices are. If there is no direct answer to this question, it is possible to point out that pilgrimage places, and particularly some of them, continue to attract the masses, and it would be much too simple to see it as only a matter of curiosity. This way of behaving may in itself already deny this reductive kind of interpretation, since it seems clear that there are many persons who search in such ways to expose themselves personally and as directly as possible to the beneficial presence, particularly of the Virgin, and to immerse themselves in an environment that is heavily charged with symbols.

A Spatial Relationship

Tourism has become a decisive factor in the temporal dimension of pilgrimages, and also has greater influence over its spatial dimension. We have already mentioned that it tends to multiply visits to these places and always to lead people toward distant places. Besides all that we have recalled about the motivations of these "tourist pilgrims," it is necessary to recognize that the pilgrimage of our day is very different in its spatial aspect from what it was in the past. If we think about the stories of the pilgrims to Compostela who arrived on foot at the city of Santiago, by routes full of danger: hostility and distrust, rapine and sickness, even death, were always in evidence; shelter and food were seldom found; and if pilgrims escaped all these dangers, most were exhausted by the time they reached their goal.

Those who today initiate such an undertaking are thought "strange," and those who make it are immediately in better condition (even if they are not "sponsored" as some of them are). The greater part travel in relative comfort and no longer experience one dimension that was part of the past pilgrimages: walking the route. It is true that for some people the time of the trip as well as the preparation for it is already a prayer. But for many, the pilgrimage seems to start at the place, and is not a terminus for a trip with diverse and varied atmospheres.

If spiritual practice is in fact not very evident in the greater number of pilgrimages, particularly in those linked to tourism, we should in this connection put more emphasis on the journey for two reasons. First, concerning again the latest research, many Christians now insist that they are not receptive to a dogmatic religion, "a faith already prepared which has fallen from on high," as they sometimes say. In opposition to this, they put forth the personal search, feeling their way in a faith that they say they must construct from experiences of their daily life and from contact with others with whom they exchange these experiences.[27] However short and "inserted" between other activities, the moments that they experience in these pilgrimage places may, for some of these "tourists," contribute toward this personal journey. The social interaction that is experienced in these places confirms and makes evident the belonging to a religious system concurrently international and specific.[28] On the other hand, this interaction takes part in an emotional and symbolic environment, the "contagious" effects of which were long ago studied by Durkheim.[29] Turner says that such an environment is invested with a supernatural effectiveness, which in the Catholic religion will not be reduced without other research to a simple magical dimension: "the place of the apparition," he emphasizes while talking about Lourdes "continues to vibrate with a supernatural effectiveness. And it is not only a magic thinking: this leads again to a theological and ethical doctrine, by which salvation, passing from the sin to grace, is linked to the Communion of the Saints and to the circulation of blessing, soul by soul."[30] The pilgrimage place, even when associated with tourist activity, may in this sense be a privileged place of "contagious" grace and a starting point, surely sometimes purely interior and not at the same time material, as it was in the past in the pilgrimages to Compostela and other places.

The symbolism of pilgrimage places is multiform. We have already pointed out different elements. We should like to add the importance of the territorial organization of the place, with rituals belonging to it. In fact, each pilgrimage place offers a significant methodical organization in relation to space itself. In its organization, for example, we have seen the specific meaning of Compostela at the margins of Christianity. Pirotte notes, on the other hand, that the pilgrimage place is often "cosmically marked (top of a mountain, grotto, extremity)."[31] It will also be noticed that many of the greatest pilgrimage places, which emerged in the nineteenth and twentieth centuries, are found in rural places (even if, as in Lourdes, they brought the later development of a city). It is not surprising that nature is an important constitutive element. These pilgrimage places have in effect arisen in the period in which secularization progressed quickly and appeared to come about particularly from industrialization and urbanization. The peripheral location of these places acquires sense in the conflict between nature and city, agriculture and industry, which has long been a structural dichotomy of Western thinking.

There is perhaps an additional aspect: the criticisms against global economic development, which cared little or nothing for the environment, may occasionally contribute toward making certain pilgrimages particularly relevant now. For example, diverse ecological groups want to be identified with St. Francis of Assisi, the friend of flowers and animals, which he called his brothers. At the same time, consideration of the monopoly of academic medicine brings as a consequence the re-evaluation of so-called alternative medicine, and in this movement causes the reevaluation of pilgrimages for the "sufferings of Saints," or even of the drinking of water from a sacred fountain and the ablutions associated with it.

Besides this often-maintained link with nature, the pilgrimage place offers in itself an "itinerary" for which the pilgrim's observation shows respect, even though there may be variation. For example, in Lourdes, the pilgrim should go to the grotto and to the basilica, to take water and light a candle; often he or she will take flowers that he or she will put in precise places; he or she will participate in the procession or will be present at, and wait for, the blessing. Everything happens in a more or less structured sequence of time and space as if the pilgrim "should" go to different places to receive fully the graces for which he or she waits. Today, as in the past, this long journey is important, and no detail is without sense.

A Festive and Aesthetic Appearance

Each form of popular religion supposes a festive and aesthetic expression. Its aesthetic aspect is indisputable in the tradition of European pilgrimages. For example, some consider that the ways to Santiago were privileged places for diffusing Roman art. But aesthetics are not limited to such "noble" aspects: pilgrimages are always associated with an image trade that, far from being a parasitic derivation, participates fully in the movement that it represents. In fact, words and talk are not alone in conferring depth to human beings; they have to be accompanied by feelings that pass into acts but also through objects that can be touched and seen. Furthermore, people very often try to take home, for themselves or as presents, some images or miniatures of such objects.

The desire for these "souvenirs"—which are largely considered "kitsch" and very ugly by those who believe in aestheticism and by at least a part of the "clergy"—leads to a huge commercial activity around pilgrimage places. This phenomenon is surely sometimes excessive, and is severely criticized. But as Duvignaud observes, the law of supply and demand is not the only prevailing influence: there is also the inner strength of the gift exchange.[32] Additionally there is the desire to perpetuate the visit made to a sacred place and to preserve a daily touchable sign. Certainly, this situation may lend itself to purely commercial exploitation and an industry may develop. There may be also some deviations in the use of these objects, which become fetishes and participate in a magic relationship. But this is not necessarily the case, and to reduce the whole practice in this way would be "to close oneself in the subtle trap of a rationalist anthropology."[33] The object bought, taken, exposed, or given may make sense in a symbolic logic that expresses an emotional relationship or makes it touchable. Does not the picture of someone beloved displayed in our home or carried with us in our wallet perform the same function? As Simmel notes, the object (or picture) plays a role of distance/absence: it escapes from the immediate reality to being close to a "next world."[34] The rationalist effort of European thinking has not voided this dimension of relationship that man searches for with sacred objects: that relationship with his fellows. Despite the abuses that lead to the invasion of some pilgrimage places by trade in souvenirs, these appear as intrinsic elements of the proper movement of many pilgrims.

The false alternative between a profound devotion that avoids everything that is not the Word and an ingenuous and superficial devotion marked by acts and objects is found in the opinion of some who feel uncomfortable with the "festive" dimension of the pilgrimage. But Turner insists that there were always and everywhere "secular intervals in the religious activities."[35] To visit the region, eat, and have fun are part of the pilgrimage, he continues. This leisure component is also, for him, an important element of the affirmation of a feeling of common belonging and of an identity that, in a transitory way, surpasses the differences that characterize daily life. So, in a banal way, some of the major purposes of the feast are met: in finding oneself; in putting aside daily life, physically and symbolically; in gaining new strength and renewed hope from the pilgrimage.[36]

TOWARD THE FUTURE

As has occurred all around the world, Europe—more precisely Catholic Europe—has not renounced its pilgrimages. Some aspects of present, advanced modernity seem immediately to contribute to increasing the vigor of at least some pilgrimages. The same is true for mobility, often proposed as a vehicle of self-knowledge and of openness to the acquaintance of others. The development of the tourism phenomenon has amplified the effects of this mobility and pointed to pilgrimage places as the destinations of some trips or as stopping places on a journey. Criticism of the modern world some years ago also had a role in developing the success of these places. The same development occurs with advanced ecology and its concern to preserve the architectural heritage, the importance of linking territory and its history. The questions that arise from the sciences help in one way to retain confidence in them, but on the other hand they make people search elsewhere for guarantees. The dissatisfaction arising from the nonresults of political utopias directs attention toward places filled with meaning. People whom modernity wanted to be fully rational now rediscover the importance of emotion.

Catholic sanctuaries have many points in common with these features. We have seen that frequenting them may assume different meanings and that each one of them is a bearer of a particular connotation linked to the historical moment of its emergence, to its location, to the political and social context of the place, and to the kind of pilgrims who made the shrine a symbol and a place for the affirmation of their identity. We have equally pointed out that some acts and objects are associated with each pilgrimage, as are certain routes and moments.

With all these characteristics, the pilgrimage discovers man and woman in his or her fullness—body and spirit, emotions, feelings, and thought. As such, it is fully in accordance with today's sensitivity, and it is expressed in many fields. It is also registered in most of the concerns of daily life of the family and friendship relations, and we have seen the importance that Europeans attribute to it. But it is not necessary to hide it: "the return of religion" of which people often talk today does not erase the advance of secularization, understood as a decrease of the power of the Church to impose and to control behavior and the significance people attach to rites that the Church has generated. These are considered an available resource, one that everyone may use according to his or her need, hope, or choice.

NOTES

1. Enzo Pace, "Pilgrimage as Spiritual Journey: An Analysis of Pilgrimage Using the Theory of Turner and the Resource Mobilization Approach," *Social Compass* 36 (1989), pp. 239–240.

2. Victor Turner and Edith Turner, *Image and Pilgrimage in Christian Culture: Anthropological Perspectives* (New York: Columbia University Press, 1978), p. 163.

3. Ibid., p. 18.

4. Ibid., p. 168.

5. Karel Dobbelaere and Liliane Voyé, "De la religion: Ambivalences et distancements," in *Les Valeurs des Belges en l'an 2000*, edited by B. Bawin-Legros, Karel Dobbelaere, and M. Elchardus (Brussels: De Boeck-Université, 2000), pp. 143–176.

6. Turner and Turner, *Image*, p. 132.

7. Roland Campiche, *Pluraité confessionelle, religion diffuse, identité culturelle en Suisse* (Lausanne: IES, 1991), p. 17.

8. *Documentation Catholique*, no. 1841, pp. 1128–1130.

9. R. Luneau, *Le rêve de Compostelle* (Paris: Centurion, 1989).

10. P. Lopes, "Le Pèlerinage à Fatima: Processus de transaction entre tradition et modernité, à partir d'une situation migratoire," *Social Compass* 33 (1986), pp. 93–94; P. Lopes, "Le Pèlerinage à Fatima: Une expression mystique du sacré populaire," *Social Compass* 36 (1989), pp. 187–199.

11. Roland Robertson, *Globalization* (London: Sage, 1992), p. 166.

12. Ibid., p. 172.

13. M. Castells, *La société en réseaux* (Paris: Fayard, 1996), p. 480.

14. B. Van Wunsberghe, "Approche psychologique de la religiosité populaire: Expressions de la prière dans un lieu de Pèlerinage" (Ph.D. diss., Catholic University of Louvain, 1991).

15. Jean-François Lyotard, *La condition post-moderne* (Paris: de Minuit, 1979), p. .7; Dobbelaere and Voyé, "De la religion."

16. G. Balandier, *Le détour* (Paris: Fayard, 1985), p. 40.

17. Turner and Turner, *Image*, p. 171; see François Champion and Danièle Hervieu-Léger, *De l'émotion en religion* (Paris: Centurion, 1990).

18. François Laplantine, *Les trois voix de l'imaginaire* (Paris: Universitaires, 1974).

19. Danièle Hervieu-Léger, *Le pèlerin et le converti: La religion en mouvement* (Paris: Flammarion, 1999), p. 102.

20. See L. Ferry, *L'homme-dieu ou le sens de la vie* (Paris: Grasset, 1986).

21. Pierre Bourdieu, *Un art moyen: Les usages sociaux de la photographie* (Paris: de Minuit, 1962).

22. C. Castoriadis, *Institution imaginaire de la société* (Paris: du Seuil, 1975), p. 178.

23. See M. Jousse, *Anthropologie du geste* (Paris: Gallimard, 1974); M. Leroi-Gourhan, *Le geste et la parole* (Paris: Albin-Michel, 1964).

24. See Liliane Voyé, *Sociologie du geste religieux* (Brussels: EVO, 1973).

25. Turner and Turner, *Image*, pp. 17–20.

26. See Karel Dobbelaere, *Secularization: A Multi-dimensional Concept* (London: Sage, 1981).

27. Dobbelaere and Voyé, "De la religion."

28. Turner and Turner, *Image*, p. 9.

29. Émile Durkheim, *Les formes élémentaires de la vie religieuse* (Paris: PUF, 1960), p. 316.

30. Turner and Turner, *Image*, p. 206.

31. J. Pirotte, "Les Pèlerinages en Wallonie," in *La Belgique et ses Dieux*, edited by Liliane Voyé, Karel Dobbelaere, Jean Remy, and Jacques Billiet (Louvain-la-Neuve: Cabay, 1985), p. 266.

32. J. Duvignaud, *Fêtes et civilisations* (Geneva: Weber, 1973), p. 33.

33. J. Baudrillard, *Pour une critique de l'économie politique du signe* (Paris: Gallimard, 1972), p. 97.

34. Georg Simmel, *La tragédie de la culture* (Paris: Petite Bibliothèque Rivages, 1988), p. 145.

35. Turner and Turner, *Image*, p. 37.

36. A. Villadary, *Fête et vie auotidienne* (Paris: Ouvrières, 1968).

Photo 8. Collage of Images, Stonehenge. *Richard Lee Switzler.*

Chapter 7

Contemporary Pagan Pilgrimages

Michael York

Within the Western religious world today, contemporary Paganism is often cited among the fastest growing spiritual orientations.[1] This development is found in particular among Euro-American and Euro-Oceanic youth. The spirituality involved places a strong emphasis on sacralization of place and in this respect shares the same intense sensitivity to geographic contour that we saw in traditional pre-classical paganism in the Greco-Roman world. Contemporary Western Paganism involves itself with localizing the sacred as well as honoring the sacred in a specific locality. In this respect, ancient and contemporary paganism has strong affinities with the dynamics of pilgrimage—especially ecclesiastical practices during the medieval ages. While the time-honored practice of visiting sacred places for purposes of holiness or healing has persisted into the present, a modern transformation has occurred, which we can term religious tourism as opposed to traditional pilgrimage per se. The question this chapter wishes to address concerns the ways in which religious tourism differs from medieval pilgrimage and how the use of and/or visitation to sacred place by contemporary Pagans relates to the pilgrimage-religious tourism continuum and differentiation.

PILGRIMAGE

A general purpose of pilgrimage is the acquisition of merit. It is most often thought to consist in the movement of focused people to a revered place. This is understood as "exterior pilgrimage." It may also comprise metaphorical movement to a particular condition of holiness or healing. In contrast to exterior pilgrimage, consisting of journeying to a physical place, this is an "interior pilgrimage." This latter type describes an individual's transformation from a spiritless or degrading position to one held in relatively high esteem according to the religious framework involved. The established Christian version of interior pilgrimage is John Bunyan's *The Pilgrim's Progress*. But each of the major religions (e.g., Islam, Hinduism, Sikhism, etc.) describes the possibilities and parameters for revelatory experience and spiritual awareness becoming purely internal or mental journeys. In such contexts, the nonliteral but metaphysical world of pilgrimage becomes a spiritual metaphor.

On the other hand, in contrast to the purely metaphorical or psychological, exterior pilgrimage—in terms of journeying to a physical place—is a tangible and overt process. It is associated with a particular religion's goals or the location of venerated objects believed to assist the religious seeker. Whether these are relics of a Christian saint or the bathing facilities of a sanctified Hindu religious center, the idea of being physically present in a particular aura of holiness is paramount. It is in this sense of the literal pilgrimage that I address the issues that follow in this chapter.

In an overall sense, the entire pilgrimage undertaking approximates a rite of passage in which the aspirant seeks absolution, healing, holiness, special knowledge, or enlightenment. A pilgrim may journey to a sacred site in response to a vow, to undergo penance, or to celebrate an event associated with the location. The Christian retraces the steps of Jesus along the Via Dolorosa in Jerusalem; the Muslim performs the *Hajj* to the Ka'ba in Mecca during the month of Dhû'l-Hijja in commemoration of Mohammed's last visit; and the Hindu bathes in the Ganges on the day of Makar Sankrantî when the sacred river was first believed to descend to earth. This reenacting of events of the past suggests the inevitable link between the religious festival and the religious pilgrimage center. The celebration of holy days may, in fact, be seen as the temporal equivalent of the geographic sacrality of the pilgrimage site. So while each major religion has its particular timetable, which is expressed in a religious calendar, each also provides a topographic orientation through a mapping of physical territory in terms of the sacred. Pilgrimage refers to the physical counterpart of commemorating auspicious moments—whether birth dates or death dates of religious leaders, various saints or divine incarnations, or holy days dedicated to a particular deity or one celebrating the anniversary of a collective rite of passage. Literal or external pilgrimage involves the physical half of a religion's worldview that encompasses the dual dimensions of both sacred place and sacred time.

As with the festival, everyday life and its values are suspended during a pilgrimage and at the pilgrimage center. The holiday character becomes emblematic of the value and status inversion described as liminality. In identifying three key elements in passage rites, Van Gennep located marginality in between the separation and temporary removal of an individual from ordinary life and the person's subsequent re-incorporation into society.[2] In the *rite de passage*, the liminal phase is the most precarious in terms of psychic and spiritual vulnerability: it represents the position between social roles after the subject's preparation for change but before the affirmation of new status. In Van Gennep's sequential understanding of transition comprising rites of separation, rites of marginality, and rites of aggregation, the actual moment of initiation, the middle moment of liminality, is a time in which the individual is subject to restrictions and taboo.

The holiday atmosphere of pilgrimage, however, often places it closer to the proverbial carnival as a time-in-between-time, a *tempus interregnum*, than to the initiatory transition involved with circumcision, mortuary ceremonies, and other *rites de passage*. Certainly this carnivalesque festivity is closer to the feeling associated with modern religious tourism in contrast to the ordeals often involved with Hindu pilgrimage—fasting and hardships—or medieval Christian pilgrimages of penance and vow fulfillment. Perhaps one of the greatest differences between traditional pilgrimage and religious tourism is the absence in the latter of liminality in the sense of initiatory danger. While there may be risks involved with both travel to—and movement in—unfamiliar places, whatever change in perception and status that occurs for the tourist is not something that is deliberately and formally undertaken in explicit accordance with religious rules and procedures.

It is perhaps this very risk of danger that distinguishes the pilgrim's sacred journey from that of the twentieth-century tourist. The pilgrim accepts the fact that he or she might not return the same person he or she was before the journey. A true pilgrimage entails transformation. There is also anticipation that the pilgrimage experience might become one of intense rapture. In other words, there is a greater range of emotional extremes that the pilgrim is willing to tolerate than is the modern-day tourist. While ecstatic passion is one thing, hardship is another. It is something the pilgrim expects and accepts. By contrast, difficulties, inconvenience, and ordeal are not things the average tourist either expects or is willing to accept.

Conventional pilgrimage is virtually ubiquitous—appearing the world over. The annual *hajj* to Mecca is perhaps the most well known, and since Islam enjoins all Muslims who are able to visit Mecca once in their lifetimes, it involves the greatest numbers. But apart from Mecca, the holy cities of Jerusalem, Rome, and Benares, the sacred mountains of T'ai Shan, Fuji, Sinai,

Kailasa, Abu, Athos, and Croagh Patrick, the Roman Catholic site of Santiago de Compostela, the shrines of Our Lady of Guadalupe in Mexico, Fatima in Portugal, Medjugorje in Bosnia, and Lourdes in the Pyrénées, and the Church of Santa Maria degli Angeli in Assisi all draw countless numbers of devotees annually. These attest to the universality and perdurable popularity of pilgrimage throughout the world. In Britain alone, revered places include Walsingham, Canterbury, Winchester, and even Glastonbury. Hindu India is itself a massive circuit of pilgrimage destinations. The country appears to be meticulously divided and parceled between sacred temples and shrines, holy cities, mountains and rivers, and places associated with particular saints or deities. Each of these can attract huge numbers of worshipers from far or near at the time of the annual feast associated with the locality. Other places to which pilgrims journey every year include the Camargue in France, the island of Shikoku in Japan, Saint Catherine's Monastery in the Sinai, the Sikh Gurudwara of Harmandir Sahib (the Golden Temple) in Amritsar, and the places associated with the key events in Gautama Buddha's life: Lumbini, Bodh Gaya, Sarnath, and Kusinara.

But while pilgrimage is intimately associated with every major religion, whether the Jewish 'aliyah to Jerusalem—now centered on the Wailing Wall; or Mount Abu in India for the Jains; or even, despite Guru Nânak's emphasis on interior rather than exterior pilgrimage, the Golden Temple and the baoli or bathing place at Goindval for Sikhs, it is also traditionally a part of paganism. Pausanias, for instance, describes the sacred topography of ancient Greece in the second century C.E. Paganism possessed the same associations of sacrality with place as we find now with the thriving world religions: sacred mountains, springs, rocks, trees, shrines and temples. Because, however, of its eclipse through Christianity, Islam, Hinduism, and Buddhism and relative marginalization in world consciousness even where it does survive, it is a religious orientation that remains largely unknown. Before I am able to compare pagan pilgrimage and the modern pagan use of sacred sites with either medieval pilgrimage or twentieth-century religious tourism, I must first present a brief understanding of paganism as a coherent theology and spiritual practice.

PAGANISM

In reconstructing an understanding of paganism as a non-Abrahamic and non-Dharmic world religion, it is necessary to examine various indigenous as well as global practices. The religions I have in mind include the tribal spiritualities of Africa, Asia, Oceania, and the Americas, Japanese Shinto, the classical folk religion of China as well as Confucianism and, to a lesser extent, Taoism, and the Afro-Latin spiritist religions of Santería (La Regla de Ocha, Lucumí), Candomblé, Macumba, Umbanda, and so forth. Each of these exhibits an intense locality in its respective perception of and encounter with deity. They are primarily this-worldly orientations, and while they have absorbed or at least been influenced by other traditions, there is little fundamental interest in soteriology or afterlife affairs. Most important, however, is the realization that even when interest occurs in what we might consider the "purely spiritual," this does not occur in rejection of or by degrading the physical.

While pagan practice is local, indigenous, often ethnic, and always highly varied, its underlying theological apprehension remains remarkably consistent. It understands the godhead as immanent within the world rather than as something radically and transcendentally other. The godhead is, in addition, both personal and impersonal as well as male and female. Moreover, traditional paganism by and large understands the godhead as comprising a plurality of gods and goddesses. In other words, we can say that the pagan godhead comprises an understanding of a pantheistic, polytheistic, and immanent reality that is identified with or at least includes the natural and tangible realms of being.

The dichotomy expanded by Catherine Albanese (1990) concerning nature as real versus nature as illusion is perhaps helpful here.[3] When the world is taken as *mâyâ*, an illusory veil to be penetrated, we have what we could broadly consider the gnostic religions of Hinduism, Pythagoreanism, Neo-Platonism, and Gnostic Christianity. If the world instead is seen to be real, in fact, as divine, we have the pagan understanding of godhead and reality. Christianity and Theravada Buddhism occupy to a large degree a more intermediate position. In Christianity, the world is real as the creation and gift of God, though still as something separate from God. In Theravada, while the world may be real, it is of little or no value. It remains something from which to escape. Pagan religions, by contrast, do not posit the world as something to reject or to escape from or even of secondary importance vis-à-vis any transcendental godhead.

Consequently, paganism, like Christianity, considers the world, humanity, and the supernatural as all real—at least in some sense. But beyond this common stance toward this equivalent acceptance, the two religions take radically different stands on the identity and relationship between these three components of reality. Christianity, in fact, gives its God an absolute monopoly on the supernatural in a binary or dualistic interpretation: whatever is not strictly of God (e.g., astrology, tarot, magical practice, spiritism, etc.) becomes by default "of the devil." In other words, Christianity dichotomizes the supernatural into a black-and-white duality.

Paganism, by contrast, allows a greater spectrum of color within its god-head and the approaches to it. As magic itself may be "white," "black," or "neutral," supernatural reality is considered neither good nor evil but potentially a mixture of the positive and negative—perhaps in some kind of hierarchical understanding, or perhaps as a plethora of intermingling tendencies. The key distinction between Christianity and paganism with regard to the supernatural is that Christianity takes an exclusivist attitude, whereas paganism is perhaps infinitely more inclusive in navigating whatever is deemed to be the supernatural. In Christianity, therefore, the "salvational" agenda is much more clearly defined and pursued. For paganism, on the other hand, the cosmogonic program remains more open to individual and community interpretation.

Consequently, as magical practice is not automatically under the authority of an antithetical principle, it finds a more conducive home within the diversified range of what we can accept as pagan practice. While the two are certainly not synonymous, there is a recognizable overlap between magic and paganism. Christian magic, if it does exist, is more likely to be found in prayer as well as the doctrine of transubstantiation. While Christianity might be said to involve a hierarchy of sanctification of physical reality, and the entire world is itself the creation of the Genesis God, the world may be sanctified by God but is still not to be identified with "Him." Only in the magical transformation of bread and wine through the Eucharist do they then become the body and blood of God himself. The complex interaction between God and the world as achieved through the Incarnation relates to the possibility of matter transcending even sanctification into pure divinity. But this intersection of the divine and tangible reality is really a "once only" instance in Christianity. For paganism, by contrast, the world itself is the godhead—perhaps, although speaking in a Christian context, what Grace Jantzen identifies as the "body of God."[4]

This different attitude toward the world and its relationship with the divine suggests important differences between Christian and pagan notions of pilgrimage and the reason for undertaking a sacred journey. For the Christian and any transcendent spiritist, the pilgrimage must ultimately imply a metaphorical event—one that simply augments the internal or spiritual transformation of the individual who visits a holy place. For the pagan, on the other hand, it is the magical act of contact with a sacred site or object that is crucial and leads to the acquisition of fortune, power, or healing usually, though perhaps not invariably, in tangible terms.

While there are many contrasts to be made between paganism and Christianity, it is enough for present purposes to recognize that a pagan theology does exist, albeit one that has been historically marginalized and largely ignored. Drawing from the figures edited and projected by David Barrett in the *World Christian Encyclopedia*, the adherents to global paganism represent approximately 5 to 6 percent of the world's population. By contrast, the largest spiritual following would be Christianity with approximately one-third of the world's inhabitants. A fifth of the world's citizenry are each represented by Islam, by the combined number of Hindus and Buddhists, and by those who are non-religious—including agnostics and atheists. The new, syncretistic mass religions of Asia appeal to essentially 2 percent of the world's population, while all other religions together—including Judaism, Sikhism, Jainism, and Baha'i—would be identified by less than one percent of the people on the planet. In other words, despite its global invisibility, paganism ranks with the fourth largest number of adherents after the Abrahamic, non-religious, and Dharmic religious coalitions.[5]

PAGAN PILGRIMAGE

As Jennifer Westwood explains, "In conventional pilgrimages a physical shrine or other holy place, having acquired a reputation for sanctity, exerts a spiritual magnetism that draws pilgrims to some fixed geographical location in the quest for the divine."[6] In this sense, pilgrimage is as much a part of paganism as it is of Islam, Christianity, Hinduism, or Buddhism. A place is considered sacred because it encapsulates in some way proximity between the divine and the mundane. The Sanskrit term is *tirtha*, which refers, literally, to a "ford" (of a river). The *tirtha* or sacred shrine is supposedly where the veil between this world and the other world is the thinnest—allowing for easier passage from one to the other. In this way, the *tirtha* becomes a place of inspiration, revelation, and encounter with the divine. It is a "spiritual ford"—a place of crossing.

Paganism is no exception in presenting the *tirtha* or pilgrimage center as a revered place where merit, healing, and communion with the godhead are considered to be optimally possible. Its shrines include the Saut d'Eau waterfalls near the Haitian town of Bonheur, the Externsteine or Dragon Stones of the Teutoburger Forest of northern Germany, the Navajo Prophecy Rock in northeast Arizona, the Arthurian woods of Brocéliande, west of the French city Rennes, Mount Fuji in Japan, and the Hong Kong temple of the oracular and healing god Wong Tai Sin. Pilgrimage was also a major activity for pagans of the Classical world during, as well as before, the Roman empire.[7] In Greece, pilgrimages included traveling home to attend one's civic festivals, but they also involved various pan-Hellenic sanctuaries. The example *par excellence* of the latter is the great festival of Zeus in Olympia every four years in which the Olympic Games were celebrated as part of the worship. Other significant sacred pilgrimage foci included centers famous for divination, prophecy, or healing such as Delphi, Dodona, Epidaurus, Abae, Amphiaraus, Branchidae, Trophonious, and even farther afield, the shrine of Ammon in Libya. Apart from these, we also have such centers for initiation mysteries as Eleusis and Naxos.

The diversity of ancient pilgrimages most clearly resembles not only the practices of Hinduism but also those of the pagan religions that survive today. For instance, apart from the Sodo or pilgrimage on 17 July in honor of the goddess Elizi and the Vierj Mirak, Haiti also hosts the annual pilgrimage of Ogou, chief of the Vodou pantheon, syncretized with St. James, in its Plaine du Nord. Here, pilgrims anoint themselves with mud mixed with the blood of bulls and drawn from a series of potholes near the Church of St. James. Some will even lie face down in the rain-produced sludge pits and then engage in frenzied dancing. The three-day festival is accompanied by the rhythmic beat of sacred drums. People have come for blessing, healing, vow fulfillment, and to honor the god at his most important shrine.

If Vodou and other Afro-Latin pilgrimage expressions are seemingly more frenzied and ecstatic than Christian and Islamic equivalents, the difference is only a matter of degree. Many spiritual sites of Christianity, in fact, were formerly homes of pagan temples and shrines: for example, the Cathedral of Chartres, Aix-la-Chapelle, Notre Dame in Paris, the Church of Aracoeli in Rome, St. Paul's in London, the cathedrals of Mexico City and Peru's Cuzco, and Old Uppsala Church in Sweden. Whatever the reasons behind these transformations, the continuity of many pilgrimage sites has been long and uninterrupted, and the passion we often detect in pagan as well as Hindu pilgrimage seems equally similar to that found in many popular Christian sacred places. In fact, pagan pilgrimage then and now may consist of arduous experiences: fasting, long travel, walking barefoot, absence of creature comforts, sexual abstinence, general inconvenience, over-crowded venues, and so on—and for these reasons it is often more similar to pilgrimage in the contexts of Christianity and other world religions than it is to twentieth-century spiritual tourism.

CONTEMPORARY WESTERN PAGANISM

A modern spiritual resurgence calls itself "Paganism." This is often referred to as Neo-paganism by sociologists and other scholars of the day—a term that is generally rejected by contemporary Pagans themselves. But in designating themselves as "pagans," "witches," and/or "Wiccans," we must consider the degree that the modern development represents a continuation of pre-Christian paganism or the degree to which it is simply a new religious movement.

Contemporary Western Paganism may be said to include most broadly Neo-paganism, reco-paganism, and geo-paganism. The predominant form of contemporary Western Paganism is clearly the Wicca-inspired Goddess Spirituality new religious movement we can identify as Neo-paganism. Neo-paganism is certainly a religion in itself—one which is identifiable by its congregational structures, its calendar of eight sabbats, and its bi-theistic understanding of the divine as God and Goddess. Margaret Murray hypothesized that those persecuted by the Church as witches during the Middle Ages were the descendants of pre-Christian pagans. This theory has now been largely discredited, and most Pagans themselves no longer accept it. Instead, modern witchcraft or Wicca is recognized as a new religious movement founded by Gerald Gardner (1884–1964). In most respects, Wicca has been the informing or seminal influence behind Neo-paganism as a predominant form of Goddess Spirituality. In speaking of contemporary Western Paganism, it is essentially Neo-paganism to which we are referring.

Contemporary Western Paganism, however, is not totally subsumed by Neo-paganism. There are also several current attempts to recreate or reconstruct particular pagan traditions such as the Egyptian and Greek mysteries, the Ódinist or Ásatru Northern traditions, Druidry and other Celtic-inspired developments, and so forth. These "reco-paganisms," however, need not be only attempts to revive ancient traditions but include in principle even such new formations as Feraferia, the Church of All Worlds, and perhaps the Discordian and Erisian movements.

On the other hand, geo-paganism is a convenient label for the more unstructured earth worship celebrated in general by individuals or small communities. Folk practices would be included here as well. For the geo-pagan there is little articulated theology per se but more of a general and spontaneous orientation to the natural, to nature, and to whatever are considered haphazard eruptions of the divine. Geo-paganism consists of subliminal practice and may be expressed in earth-based or quasi-earth-based rites that are automatic and largely unconsciously performed. Even when geo-pagan ceremony is done deliberately and consciously, its rituals are simple and without elaboration.

In referring to traditional paganism, Margo Adler describes it as animistic, pantheistic, and polytheistic.[8] The Greek, Roman, Egyptian and Nordic pantheons we encounter in reco-paganism are obviously polytheistic. To a lesser extent, the spontaneous tendency of geo-paganism is also polytheistic, though perhaps less clearly articulated or formulated. With Neo-paganism, however, the many gods and goddesses that are encountered or invoked are generally thought of as simply different names for either the Goddess or the God. Consequently, contemporary Western Paganism is largely less polytheistic per se than traditional paganism. Its pluralism as such is erected upon a gender dualism and is often directed as a contrast and critique of the patriarchal position of the Abrahamic monotheisms. In other words, the polytheism of Neo-paganism is more nominal than actual, and this constitutes its chief contrast with the indigenous and traditional paganisms found more universally. In some sense, then, the term "Neo-pagan" as a pagan religion is a misnomer.

The pantheism said by Adler to delineate contemporary paganism is also in part an inaccurate attribution. Pantheism in itself describes the theological position in which the all is God. Or, vice versa, God is all. The thrust of Adler's understanding, however, is that whether or not the all includes "everything," it does at least include the physical, tangible universe. Once again, it is this material bias that constitutes the *sine qua non* of paganism. The earth is seen as sacred. Materiality is divine. It may also be the source, matrix, or mother of all existence, but it is the inherent, immanent divinity of the physical that comprises paganism's unique stance vis-à-vis the theological perspectives of the world's other major religions. On this front, Neo-paganism, contemporary Western Paganism, and traditional paganism all share an outlook that is fundamentally the same.

Whether the state or tribe, paganism has always been concerned with its immediate society and culture. Contemporary Western Paganism has stretched this concern to include both the community of the individual and the community of collective humanity. Its ethical declaration, known as "The Pagan Ethic," fully endorses this position: "An [if] it harm none, do as thou will." What this means for the contemporary Western Pagan is that, as long as no one is reduced or harmed against his or her will, whatever a person wishes to do is permissible. Contemporary Western Paganism more often than not includes nature as one who is also not to be detrimentally aggrieved through the proper actions of both individual and community. As the primal reservoir for both physical and spiritual sustenance, nature as a reified construct is perceived to be under threat by modern industrial and technological advance. Consequently, the ethical focus for contemporary Western Paganism is primarily ecological.

But apart from its emphasis on nature as the chief locus of spirituality and chief source of religious metaphor and its predilection or incorporation of magic, another way in which contemporary Western Paganism in general relates to classical paganism is through its pluralistic understanding of the godhead. It draws its inspiration to understand deity through three cherished sources: the natural, the human, and the exotic. For the worshiper of a pagan persuasion, the "other" invokes fascination and the desire to honor or venerate it. To the degree that the other becomes personified, the supernatural becomes understood either bi-theistically *à la* Wicca or as a range or plethora of gods and goddesses. But whether these deities remain exotic or in some sense "foreign," pagan worship attempts to connect them with the natural and human worlds of activity. It is the Abrahamic religions, especially Christianity, that seek to understand the other as the "wholly other"— rendering its God as totally transcendent to the worlds of time and space.

Neo-paganism and traditional paganism differ, however, in the issue of idolatry. We find this last throughout much of the indigenous paganisms— including Shinto as well as classical Greco-Roman paganism. Contemporary Western Paganism in general is, or seems to be, much less overtly idolatrous than traditional paganism. But while there may not be a pantheon of foci, as in traditional paganism, there is also no single theological focus, as in Christianity, Judaism, and Islam. If there is a resistance to biblical condemnation of idolatry, paganism goes one step further and exalts the tangible expression of divinity in graphic, representational form. As with the ritual phallus or Hindu lingam, however, the idol is simply an instance of translating a universal idea or constellation of ideas into a tangible object of the here and now. It is this very transformation of the *idolon* into something corporeal that represents, in part at least, paganism's attempt to make the other intimate and accessible.

As paganism continues to move beyond its tribal and ethnic origins into a position commensurate with a modern or postmodern world, the other is not excluded through either outright rejection or assimilation to the Hegelian logic of the same, but becomes instead incorporated into the base community of identity. Paganism's pluralistic/polytheistic foundation, which not only recognizes but also endorses variety of choice, exemplifies the spiritual consumerism of new religious movements in the West. The concrete idol is not only an affirmation of the divine in physicality but also one more attraction within the range of competitive goods in the spiritual market that has increasingly come to signify our times.

Consequently, paganism in both its contemporary and traditional forms finds nature, humanity, and the spiritually exotic as divine embodiments with which to transact. The assistance of the sacred is what is sought for both worldly concerns and transpersonal exploration. Paganism is, of course, not at all immune to approaching the divine in tangible form. If the whole, ultimate point of a god is to become manifest, paganism takes this one stage further and manifests its gods in corporeal existence—whether "man-made" idols, natural phenomena, or nature as a reified construct in itself. But the location of the sacred in the physical is also the ultimate justification for the notion and practice of pilgrimage—the "going to" a sacred geographic place or object. Pilgrimage and paganism, in fact, are the most natural of allies.

PILGRIMAGE, SPIRITUAL TOURISM, AND THE CONTEMPORARY PAGAN USE OF SACRED SPACE

For contemporary Pagans in the West, pilgrimage is still an important undertaking. In the current "scene," Great Britain and sometimes Ireland are high on the lists of places to be visited by Neo-pagans from the United States, Canada, and Australia, if not elsewhere as well. In line with my own research, I have offered to be a contact source in England through Circle Sanctuary, the former Pagan Spirit Alliance, and the Covenant of Unitarian Universalist Pagans. I also frequently receive requests and subsequent visitors through the New Age and Pagan Studies Programme that is sponsored by the Department for the Study of Religions at Bath Spa University College. As in ancient Greece, where much pilgrimage involved returning to one's native habitat for civic festivals, modern Pagans often feel an umbilical pull to what they consider their mythic and ancestral "homeland."

Pagans who come to the British Isles, however, come in the capacity of both pilgrim and tourist. The prime purpose of their journey is to visit the "holy places" of Britain, but they will also frequently include such tourist destinations as the Crown Jewels in the Tower of London, Westminster Abbey, Buckingham Palace, the British Museum, and the West End. They usually come as individuals on these journeys, sometimes as couples. There are occasions, however, when Pagan pilgrims travel to Europe in small groups—generally ranging between seven and twenty people. I once viewed sunrise in Stonehenge with a group of approximately twenty-five Neo-shamans who had arrived from the United States with this purpose as the highlight of their visit.

Indeed, the foremost pilgrimage destinations for Pagans who come to Britain are Stonehenge and Glastonbury. Many will also visit the stone circle of Avebury. Those who have the means and time to travel further might include the stone circle of Callanish on the Isle of Lewis in the Hebrides, those in the Orkneys, the tumuli of Newgrange, Knowth, and Dowth in Ireland's Boyne Valley, or the Irish coronation center of Tara. Another popular destination is Sherwood Forest of Robin Hood fame in the English midlands. Druids would include the Island of Iona off the west coast of Scotland. In fact, throughout the British Isles, there are more tumuli, passage graves, and stone circles per capita than virtually anywhere else in the world.

Pagans will undertake a sacred journey to as many of these ancient sites as is feasible or possible.

In the United States, on the other hand, local pilgrimage sites for Pagans include Mt. Shasta in California, Chaco Canyon in New Mexico, even the Grand Canyon in Arizona, Ohio's Great Serpent Mound and other Indian sites along the Great Miami River, and for some, Niagara Falls. Australian Pagans will consider a visit to Ayer's Rock (Uluru) as a sacred quest journey. More regional sacred places include Flinders Ranges in South Australia, the Three Sisters in the Blue Mountains outside Sidney, and Mt. Franklin in Victoria. All these as well as the other sacred sites in Australia have strong Aboriginal associations. In continental Europe, pilgrimage centers appropriate for Pagans include Germany's Black Forest and Herz Mountain, the island of Gotland, the former Druid center of Chartres, the megalithic sites of Bretagne, the Old Prussian site of Romuva, and the classical ruins of Italy and Greece (e.g., Delphi, Delos, Olympia, the Acropolis, the Capitol, the Roman Forum, the Pantheon, Paestum, Agrigento's Valle dei Templi, etc.).

One frequent characteristic of the traditional pilgrimage is the dress code: the white dress of the Muslim *hajj* and the Buddhist Kôbô Daishi circumambulation of the Japanese island of Shikoku; the penitential dress of medieval Christian pilgrimage such as that of Santiago de Compostela; and the black clothes worn by Hindus for pilgrimage to the Sabarimala shrine of Sri Ayyappa. For the feast of St. James focused on Haiti's Plaine du Nord, pilgrims arrive in either blue suits and red scarves or in the multi-striped garb of a penitent. While contemporary Pagans may be indistinguishable from ordinary tourists when they are traveling, they will often wear special amulets, cloaks, and/or robes when visiting a sacred site such as Stonehenge, Chalice Well, or the Glastonbury Tor. Black is a favorite color. Otherwise Pagan pilgrims might wear greens and browns, emulating organic earth hues. Others will dress as shamans, witches, or Druids. As with traditional Hindu, Buddhist, and Christian pilgrims, many modern-day Pagans will walk barefoot. Few, however, would countenance sexual abstinence as a prerequisite for pilgrimage or ritual.

But if contemporary Pagan practice, through its theology of immanency, encourages visiting sacred places as part of a vision quest and to absorb a local aura of divinity, it also uses such places for the performance of its rituals. In fact, the chief contemporary Western Pagan ceremony consists in the creation *of* a sacred space in which to conduct its rites and celebration. If this creation can occur *within* a revered place, so much the better, and often for the solstices and other key moments, one can find Druidic or Pagan circles performing various rites at Avebury, Stanton Drew, or—depending on weather, governmental permission, and crowd management—even Stonehenge. Otherwise, for more local and daily purposes, the Pagan sacred circle of space is constructed in a nearby woods or field, at a beach or municipal park, in a member's garden, a rented university hall or, for security reasons, within the privacy of an individual participant's home.

The standard procedure today is to invoke the ruling powers of the four cardinal directions—beginning with the east. Each direction has a particular element associated with it, and one of the differences between traditional paganism and contemporary Western Paganism is the more universal association of the east with fire by the former and with air by the latter.[9] But once the spirits of the four directions are called forth, the magic circle is believed to come into existence—removing its participants from ordinary, mundane time. It is then, within the ad hoc sacred space and time, that contemporary Pagans perform their various rites for both collective and individual healing and for political and social change. Within the confines of this liminal space, Wiccans and/or witches will raise what is called a "cone of power" to effect their declared wishes. Another ceremony is the Drawing Down of the Moon or the power of other deific entities. The sacred circle is also used for handfastings (marriages) as well as naming and initiation ceremonies. The Pagan sacred circle, in short, is where Pagan rites of passage are conducted and sanctified, but it is also primarily where all rites are performed.[10]

The ceremonies conducted within a sacred circle will usually conclude with what is called a "spiral dance." The participants in the circle have generally been holding hands. One person then lets go of the person before him or her and leads the others in a spontaneously meandering human chain—often until everyone forms one great knot of adrenalin-charged people. This is the peak moment for the Pagan circle and the time in which its "cone of power" is raised and sent forth. Then, reforming the original circle, the spirits of the four directions are thanked with the words, "Hail and farewell!" After this, the presiding officiant declares that the "circle is open but never broken!" Each participant will kiss the person to his or her right and left and say, "Merry meet, merry part, and merry meet again!" Consequently, the ritual circle and the ceremonies involved with it constitute all together what we may consider to be a "micro-pilgrimage" in and of itself.

The ceremony of the Neo-pagan sacred circle is fairly standardized and recognizable throughout by its Western world practices. Its primary purpose is the establishment of liminal space and time in which to work magic and effect change. In this sense, it differs little from the objective of pilgrimage, which includes the stage of liminality and endeavors to remove the pilgrim from ordinary life and return him or her as a transformed person. Both pilgrimage and the ceremonial creation of sacred or magical space seek to achieve personal—if not also collective—change in a spiritual context. The single most prominent difference between pilgrimage movement and circle performance, on the one hand, and religious tourism, on the other, is intent. The former is far more dependent on singlemindedness of purpose; the latter is more akin to the American idea of vacation as a "chance to get away from it all."

TOURISM, SPIRITUALITY, AND DEMOGRAPHY

"Pilgrimage is a pan-human religious behavior, practiced by all cultures in much the same manner and for similar reasons—boons, expiation of sins, healing, nearness to God and enlightenment."[11] For Pagans in particular, a pilgrimage site usually allows a closeness to nature as well as to a location sanctified by their pagan predecessors. It becomes also a place in which to augment personal power, to feel or connect with the numinous, and to perform magic. But unlike their pagan "ancestors," there is little consciousness of "seeing" the divine, that is, of having a direct encounter with the sacred in the Hindu sense of *darshan*. Traditional pagans wish to see their deity's image housed in its revered sanctum. He or she wants to see the holy rock, holy spring, or holy tree associated with the pilgrimage shrine. The pagan pilgrim wishes to be close to the divine in the same way that the Hindu considers the *tirtha* the fording place between this world and the other. And in this sense, the modern Pagan seeks the same interpenetration between the two worlds: that of nature and that of supernature. The modern Pagan quests for identity or inspiration or both.

But in his or her willingness to encounter both enchantment and personal enhancement, the modern Pagan is willing to undergo the discomforts and hardships of pilgrimage. In this way, the Pagan pilgrim follows a course that is comparable to that of the medieval Christian pilgrim. Details vary, but the essentials remain the same. We might note that the sacred bath and the shedding of refinement or even shaving of the head, which is found with traditional paganism both past and present, as well as in pilgrimage more generally, are not major concerns for late twentieth-century witches, Wiccans, Druids, and followers of the Northern Path (whether Ásatru, Ódinism, or Vanirism). But, all the same, while the Neo-pagan of today is less concerned with ritual purity and spiritual regeneration as such, he or she nevertheless still surrenders to inclement weather, long journey, and other sacrifices in order to experience the awesome.

By contrast, the modern religious tourist, like virtually all tourists, is reluctant to tolerate discomfort and inconvenience. This and the lack of devout intent are what distinguish the twentieth-century spiritual tourist from the pilgrim—whether Hindu, Muslim, Buddhist, Jain, Sikh, Shinto, medieval Christian, modern Christian, traditional pagan, or contemporary Western Pagan. In general, the tourist is not as willing to risk personal peril as is the pilgrim. The religious tourist's visit to spiritual places is part of a fuller agenda of sightseeing. It is more casual and superficial. There is no deliberate intent for transformation and no framework in which to rationalize whatever hardships arise.

Of course, this difference is often only one of degree. Fifty-two pilgrims died in January 1999 when a hill collapsed during the annual Makar Sankrantî pilgrimage to Sabarimala in India. But tourists too can die while traveling—as exemplified by a bus disaster involving 26 elderly English travelers in South Africa in September 1999. If, by contrast, a pilgrim expires during a pilgrimage, this is often considered to be a fortuitous transition in an opportune and exalted state of grace. But even without death, the hardships frequently persist. In more traditional sites, especially in the Third World, the logistics involved with attempting to expedite the convergence of large numbers of people into small shrines can make the sacred journey and the moment of *darshan* a tortuous ordeal. The pilgrim, however, unlike the religious tourist, is motivated by a single purpose: the desire to experience deity *in situ*. He or she tends to have a motivation that the tourist does not, and this motivation is what allows the pilgrim to put up with what the tourist will not.

Moreover, the pilgrim is usually not cluttered with secondary purposes such as visiting with relatives, handling business, or meeting professional concerns. Here we can see that for the modern Pagan pilgrim, the going away from worldly life toward holiness is not necessarily the agenda. First, for most Neo-pagans, there is no separation between the secular and the sacred. If a dichotomy does occur, it is one between nature and civilization. But, second, most Pagans I have met who have made a sacred journey to Britain are also interested in meeting other Pagans. Sometimes they are even collecting data for a research or academic project. So in this sense, the line that distinguishes the pilgrim from the tourist becomes blurred and less clear. Consequently, the "true" pilgrim and the religious tourist are increasingly ideal types at best. They represent polar extremes along a single continuum. If the pilgrim has a spiritual intent and the tourist instead is concerned with pleasure, the dynamics of modern travel and a much more complicated lifestyle may make the distinction between the two much less definitive. For paganism in general and the contemporary Pagan in particular, spirituality and pleasure are no longer separate and distinguishable concerns.

But there is more: the dynamics between traditional paganism and twenty-first-century religious tourism are increasingly determined by the steady augmentation of global population. At the turn of the millennium, the countries of China, India, the United States, and Brazil each had populations greater than a hundred million. The nations with the highest urban population growth after these are Russia, Japan, Indonesia, Mexico and Nigeria. While New York has increased from twelve million in 1950 to an estimated 16.5 in 2000 and a projected 17.6 million for 2015, the figures for the years 1950, 2000, and 2015 in some of the other cities of the world are truly staggering: Mexico City reads 3.5, 17.6, and 19 million for these years; São Paulo, 2.3, 17.3, and 20.8 million; Lagos, 1.0, 12.2, and 24.4 million; Cairo, 2.1, 10.5, and 14.4 million; Karachi, 1.1, 11, and 20.6 million; Mumbai, 2.8, 16.9, and 27.4 million; Calcutta, 4.45, 12.5, and 17.3 million; Dhaka, 0.4, 16, and 19 million; Beijing 1.7, 11.7, and 19.4 million; and Shanghai, 4.3, 13.9, and 23.4 million. The cities of Los Angeles, Buenos Aires, Tokyo, and Jakarta show similar increases.

While the mid-point of the twentieth century saw six of the ten largest cities of the world in Europe and the United States, by the year 2015, the ten largest cities will be found in Asia, Africa, and South America. In 1950, 30 percent of the world's population lived in urban areas. By the year 2005, the United Nations projects that half the world's population will live in cities. Meanwhile, population figures for the world as a whole expand comparably. United States Census Bureau figures indicate that the number of world inhabitants had reached one billion by 1804. That figure doubled by 1927. The figure again doubled by 1974 to four billion. Five billion was attained in 1987; six billion by 1999. The Census Bureau's *World Population Profile: 1998* (1999) expects the number to become seven billion by 2012, eight billion by 2026, and nine billion by 2043.[12]

The implications of this prodigious expansion of human numbers on the global scale present an incontestable physical threat to the very possibility of pilgrimage. The physical viability of the traditional shrine is increasingly endangered. Whatever the ratio between population figures and numbers of pilgrims, the exponential increase of the former translates into an exponential increase of the latter. The ultimate suggestion is that pilgrimage itself must become, at least relatively, a decreasing phenomenon. In this light, present-day tourism may be viewed as a spontaneous attempt for a palatable alternative to an increase in pilgrimage traffic. It represents a containment of numbers as well as a compromise between virtual/vicarious reality and "hands-on" pilgrimage contact.

The Travel Industry Association of America distinguishes "historical and cultural travelers" from travelers as a whole. These are people who journey to historical sites, museums, cultural events, and festivals. The key difference is the reason for traveling; historic and cultural travelers are twice as likely to travel for entertainment. They tend in general to be older and more likely to be retired. However, cultural travelers can be distinguished from historical travelers as well. The former are more likely to visit family and friends.

Cultural travelers drive their own cars more than historic travelers who fly more frequently. Cultural travelers take more trips by themselves; historic travelers journey more often with children. On average, cultural travelers take more daytrips and stay a shorter time than historic travelers. Historic travelers take longer trips and more often spend the night in hotels, while private homes are used by more cultural travelers. Historic travelers participated more often in virtually every activity, particularly visits to national and state parks.[13]

It is within the category of historic/cultural traveler that the contemporary spiritual tourist is to be placed.

The constraints of touristic travel and the wear and tear on spiritual and quasi-spiritual sites must be seen against the tourist industry's impetus to increase and expand its business volume. For instance, in the United States alone, travel and tourism are touted as having an annual economic impact—both direct and indirect—exceeding $526 billion. They are held to be responsible for more than 17.5 million jobs, and they generate the largest trade balance of any industry. In 1998, this reached nearly $25 billion.[14] Consequently, in response to predictions that international tourism will nearly triple in volume during the first two decades of the twenty-first century, a summit meeting of the World Tourism Organization (WTO), held in Santiago, Chile, on 1 October 1999, drafted a Global Code of Ethics for Tourism: "The tenth article involves the redress of grievances through the creation of a World Committee on Tourism Ethics. . . . Investors and public authorities are required to carry out environmental impact studies before beginning tourism development projects and to involve local residents."[15] Article 3 of the Global Code stresses the need of tourism to maintain sustainable development and respect "the carrying capacity of the sites."[16]

In this respect, a shifting emphasis is seen to be developing upon "nature tourism"—the visiting of nature preserves, wildlife sanctuaries, and the like—and "eco-tourism," that is, "tourism with ecologically high ethical standards . . . that minimizes environmental impact and benefits local people and businesses."[17] Twenty-first-century spiritual tourism and modern pilgrimage along with tourist travel in general will be increasingly constrained by the ethical parameters suggested by nature tourism and eco-tourism. The motivation, of course, differs between the tourist and pilgrim—that of the tourist being adventure or recreation; that of the pilgrim, to have a life-changing spiritual encounter.[18] Nevertheless, both the pilgrim and the spiritual tourist are advised in the context of visiting sacred places not "to barge into a site," to "[b]e open to the energies of the place," to "leave no trace" of one's visit—such as "offerings," and to take nothing tangible from the site.[19]

For the contemporary Western Pagan, the sacred sites of the British Isles include Stonehenge, Avebury, Glastonbury, the West Kennet Long Barrow, the stone circles of Boscawen-un, Rollright Stones, Hurlers, Cheesewring, and Duloe, the dolmens of Lanyon Quoit and Trethevy Quoit, and the holy well of Madron. Northern England boasts Long Meg and Her Daughters and Castlerigg Circle. In the Scottish mainland, there are the Clava Cairns, the holy island of Iona, Callanish on the Isle of Lewis, and the Stones of Stenness, Maes Howe, and the Ring of Brodgar on the Orkneys. Ireland hosts Newgrange, Knowth, Tara, and Loughcrew (County Meath), Lough Gur (County Limerick), Dun Aengus (County Galway), and Carrowmore and Carrowkeel (County Sligo). For the contemporary Pagan, these sites may be organized into pilgrimage excursions such as the Mists of Avalon Sacred Journey to England or the Sheela na Gig Sacred Journey to Ireland—both being in this case sacred journeys designed exclusively for women.[20] Others might choose to visit Greece and such ancient sites as Athens, Corinth, Delphi, Delos, Rhodes, and Ephesus. With the increasing interest in nature religion, however, such places as Amerindian reservations and national parks in the United States (e.g., Arizona, Utah, New Mexico) or India's wildlife sanctuaries of Ranthanbore, Bandhavgarh, and Kanha and the Baharatpur Birds Sanctuary/Keoladeo National Park are also popular destinations. Alternatively, SpiritQuest sponsors ethno-botanical workshop retreats and explorations of ayahuasca shamanism in the Upper Amazon.

Meanwhile, according to the Redondo Beach Tourist Bureau in California, of the four million visitors to the spiritual center of Sedona, Arizona, 7 percent are on a spiritual quest, while El Pocito ("Room of Miracles") at the Santuario Chimayo in New Mexico currently attracts 300,000 visitors a year—two thousand pilgrims on Good Friday alone. Once again, however, these steadily increasing numbers suggest difficulties and problems for future tourism on a global scale. One solution is the creation of new sites such as Disney World for the general tourist or, for the pagan pilgrim/modern spiritual tourist, the Geo Group's recently constructed Mutiny Bay Stone Circle in Medina, Washington.[21] However, the carrying capacity of sacred sites—new and old—and sustainable development of indigenous areas remain limited. The increasing numbers of potential visitors represent a real and dangerous threat to the physical and cultural viability of the targeted destinations.

Nevertheless, the world's shrinkage into a global village is accompanied and, in fact, augmented by vast telecommunications networks. Perhaps the actuality of globalization and the recognition of the emerging virtual community reached its apogee during the Millennial 2000 celebrations watched on television around the world as each individual time zone entered the new millennium. One by one, mass media viewers joined into the New Year's Eve festivities in Sydney, Tokyo, Delhi, Moscow, Cairo, Rome, Paris, London, New York, and Los Angeles as midnight successively occurred locally. This suggests that future pilgrimage and spiritual tourism might become more virtual as video documentaries on special places and the medium of the Internet continue to offer contact and encounter without involving the physical transport of large numbers of people. For the contemporary Western Pagan, virtual access will be balanced by an increasing awareness of and satisfaction with the local shrine. As Elaine V. Emeth explains, "A pilgrimage need not involve a long journey, great expense, or a lot of time."[22] The "mini-pilgrimage" involving worship and inner and outer exploration can occur at a nearby sacred site—perhaps involving a day trip or something even less time consuming. It is within the orbit of contemporary Western Paganism to develop a keen awareness of the sacred geography of immediate locality. This, combined with cybertravel and the advantage and freedom provided by the electronic information network, may encourage the cultural and spiritual "soft tourism" and "soft pilgrimage" of the future.

NOTES

1. While there has been as of yet no empirical study to ascertain whether Neo-paganism is expanding more rapidly than other religions, the cover blurb of Anodea Judith's book *The Truth about Neo-Paganism* (St. Paul, MN: Lewellyn, 1994) asserts: "The facts about the world's fastest growing religion!" The first paragraph of the book itself qualifies that claim by stating that "Neo-Paganism is the fastest growing religion in America." The consensus among other colleagues in the field and my own observations on new religious movements and contemporary Western Paganism is that it is currently at least a rapidly growing religion.

2. Arnold van Gennep, *The Rites of Passage* (London: Routledge, 1965 [1908]); see Victor W. Turner, *Dramas, Fields and Metaphors: Symbolic Action in Human Society* (Ithaca, NY: Cornell University Press, 1974) and Victor Turner and Edith Turner, *Image and Pilgrimage in Christian Culture: Anthropological Perspectives* (New York: Columbia University Press, 1978).

3. Catherine L. Albanese, *Nature Religion in America from the Algonkian Indians to the New Age* (Chicago: University of Chicago Press, 1990).

4. See John Macquarie, *Twentieth-Century Religious Thought* (London: SCM Press, 1988).

5. David B. Barrett (ed.), *World Christian Encyclopedia* (Oxford: Oxford University Press, 1982).

6. Jennifer Westwood, *Sacred Journeys: Paths for the New Pilgrim* (London: Gaia Books, 1997), p. 28.

7. In classical pilgrimage temples, one found "a world of preliminary rites, of sacrifices, of dreams and purifications which frequently involved fasting or abstinence from certain foods. . . . Visiting a temple such as that at Epidaurus offered access to the supernatural through dreams and visions, through miracles and cures, and through inscriptions which recounted histories of previous encounters with the god" (Simon Coleman and John Elsner, *Pilgrimage Past and Present: Sacred Travel and Sacred Space in the World Religions* [London: British Museum Press, 1995], p. 21).

8. Margot Adler, *Drawing Down the Moon: Witches, Druids, Goddess-Worshippers, and Other Pagans in America Today* (Boston: Beacon Press, 1986), p. 25.

9. The full association between the directions and elements for traditional paganism is east (fire), south (earth), west (water) and north (air). For contemporary Western Paganism or Neo-paganism the associations are: east (air), south (fire), west (water) and north (earth). As far as is determinable, this latter grouping is derived from the practice of Freemasonry associations, which Aleister Crowley bequeathed to Gerald Gardner, the "founder" of modern Wicca.

10. By contrast, unlike contemporary Western Paganism, which has focused on the creation of sacred space within the confines of the ceremonial circle, traditional paganism is more processional in orientation and centered on the altar, shrine and temple. In this sense, the activities of traditional paganism entail more the movement of people: from shrine to shrine or from home to pilgrimage center. Twentieth-century Western Paganism is instead more concerned with centering on the immediate presence of an ad hoc time and location. There is less "going to"—at least on a daily basis. The traditional pagan has "sacred rounds" within his or her home environment. In contemporary urban environments, the modern Pagan has "venues" to reach in which sacred space is created and rituals are performed.

11. "Sacred Pilgrimage," *Hinduism Today* (May 1997), p. 30.

12. John W. Wright (ed.), *The New York Times Almanac* (New York: Penguin Books, 1999), p. 483.

13. Travel Industry Association of America, "Profile of Travelers Who Participate in Historical and Cultural Activities," <http://www.tia.org/research/summculture.asp> (11 January 2000).

14. "Travel & Tourism—A White Paper," <http://www.wttc.org/reports/wttc-tbrreport.htm> (11 January 2000).

15. World Tourism Organization, "Tourism Sector Takes Steps to Ensure Future Growth: Global Code of Ethics Adopted at WTO Summit," <http://www.world-tourism.org/pressrel/99_10_01.htm> (11 January 2000).

16. World Tourism Organization, "Global Code of Ethics for Tourism," <http://www.world-tourism.org/pressrel/codeofe.htm> (11 January 2000).

17. Sacred Earth—Eco-Travel Adventures Unlimited, "Eco-Travel," <http://www.sacredearth.com/travel.htm> (11 January 2000).

18. Elaine V. Emeth, "Visiting Sacred Places as a Modern Pilgrim." *Village Life Travel: Parish Holiday*, <http://www.villagelife.org/carousel/travel/modernpilgrim.htm> (11 January 2000).

19. NewAge Travel.com, "Sacred Sites of the British Isles," <http://www.newagentravel.com/robert/britisls.htm> (11 January 2000).

20. Sacred Journeys for Women, "The Mists of Avalon Sacred Journey to England," <http://www.sacredjourneys.com/avalon_overview.html> (11 January 2000); Sacred Journeys for Women. "Sheela na Gig Sacred Journey to Ireland," <http://www.sacredjourneys.com/sheila_overview.html> (11 January 2000).

21. The Geo Group, "The Mutiny Bay Stone Circle," <http://www.geo.org/mutiny1.htm> (11 January 2000).

22. Emeth, "Visiting."

Chapter 8 _____

Visitation to Disaster Sites

Anthony J. Blasi

The purpose of this chapter is to examine cases of one kind of pilgrimage and conceptualize it in order to develop a framework for sociological research. The kind of pilgrimage in question is visiting places where public disasters have occurred. By "pilgrimage" in general, it is meant simply that one or more people travel with the purpose in whole or part of visiting, seeing, or touching a physical place or thing that is in some manner associated with ultimate or nearly ultimate concerns.[1] For example, Muslims visit Mecca and Christians visit Bethlehem, Nazareth, and Jerusalem. Islamic practice has a religious norm behind it, while the Christian practice is entirely voluntary. Barbara Myerhoff describes another example, an annual ritual pilgrimage into a wilderness area by the Huichol people of Mexico, wherein the participants' orientation toward the physical and social worlds is reversed.[2] Not all pilgrimages are religious; the objective in the ancient world was sometimes a healing or an oracle—something supernaturalist to be sure, but not corresponding to the modern concept of religion so much as to magic. Luigi Tomasi broadens the general concept by distinguishing pilgrimage per se from what he terms "religious tourism"; the latter refers to the inclusion of religious sites in leisure-time travel.[3] Since leisure interludes presuppose an industrial world with scheduled employment, religious tourism in a strict sense would be a relatively modern phenomenon. Also in the modern setting, wherein since the nineteenth century the state has become the object of a surrogate religiosity, pilgrimages may involve visits to public buildings in national capitals, the graves of national heroes, and travels to sites of battles that figure importantly in national histories.

It may be instructive at the outset to consider both the medieval penitential pilgrimage and contemporary religious tourism. Medieval pilgrimages began with an individual state of *anomia*. An early meaning of *anomia* was being at odds with traditional normativity.[4] It was not a matter of lacking norms (a meaning that has emerged from the reading of Durkheim's famous study of suicide rates) but of finding oneself deserving condemnation because of the norms.[5] In the medieval setting, the penitent needed to abandon the social situation in which a non-normative identity had been established and return at a future date as a changed person. This involved entry into a liminal state, not unlike that associated with puberty rites in some tribal societies.[6] The penitential pilgrimage itself would be an extended circumstance of liminality in which the individual would undergo a transformation of self, realigning the self with the norms of society prior to a reentry into normalcy.

Contemporary religious tourism presupposes a privatized religiosity. There is less concern with public norms per se, though that does not mean that individuals are no less sensitive to values. Their values, however, need to be cultivated personally. Firsthand experiences with some of the referents of religious symbols can enter into this kind of cultivation of personal values. Religious tour groups may even maintain a mobile worship service in the course of their travels as a part of the desired experience.[7] This differs from the medieval phenomenon largely in that, rather than striving for a state of liminality beyond the usual worship service, it is a quest for the meaningful entry of religious culture into everyday life. The traveler does not return as a different person but rather is strengthened as a personality already established.

What the cases of medieval penitential pilgrimage and modern religious tourism exemplify for us is a dialectical tension between experiences, which are particular, and the placement of the individual self in the wider general scheme of the cosmos. In the penitential pilgrimage, the experience of the sinful self leads the individual into a sequence of countervailing experiences that, taken together and recapitulated in a remapped biography, constitute a new cosmos for the individual. In the modern religious tour, the feeling for a greater cosmos leads the individual into a serial schedule of experiences that individualize the person's place in the world. Because of the importance of individual experience in this tension, we can speak of pilgrimages and pilgrimage-like activity entailing multiple discourses—that is, it is not necessary to assume that all participants share in a symbolic monolith.[8] Nevertheless there are shared aspects of pilgrimage phenomena; the very ritualization of the visits ensures that.[9]

All of us who have lived long enough have experienced personal tragedies, and we may even return to a place where a tragedy occurred or has
been memorialized. Some of us develop personal rituals—visiting a grave
on a routine basis, for example. One thinks of Japanese widows who bring
fresh flowers to the home altar daily in commemoration of their deceased
husbands. These practices bear some resemblance to visiting disaster sites
but are not quite the same thing. A disaster is a public event, not a private
one. A disaster pertains to a collectivity, such as a local community or a nation, not specifically to an individual or family. The public meaning is typically borne by a semiclosed symbol system that requires a native's inside
knowledge to comprehend adequately. Thus I will limit myself to examples
from my own nation. This is simply to accommodate my own limitations,
not to suggest any fundamental differences among the memorialized disasters of the various nations.

The United States does not have a long tradition of pilgrimage to serve as
a paradigm for the establishment of new sites. Founded as a predominantly
Protestant nation in the eighteenth century, it had no heritage of shrines
from the past comparable to the great shrines and holy places of Europe and
the Middle East. Two sites from the nineteenth century appear to have
served as the principal models for later commemorative disaster sites—the
Gettysburg battlefield and the site of the Johnstown Flood. The fact that the
second half of the nineteenth century rather than the revolutionary period
provided the paradigms is understandable. It was in the nineteenth century
that truly national transportation routes and communications media were
established, and it was with the American Civil War that American politics
became truly national. It is in this sense that the Civil War had the ironic effect of uniting the nation.[10] We shall examine these two sites and the disasters behind them and then proceed with considerations of some sites that
have been established more recently. These seem to fit the public paradigm
established by Gettysburg for military disasters and Johnstown for natural
disasters.

GETTYSBURG CEMETERY AND MEMORIAL, PENNSYLVANIA

Every year some 1.5 million people visit the Gettysburg battlefield,
where the characterization of modern war as disastrous was unalterably established in the American public consciousness. Other Civil War battle-
fields are significant in military terms or in terms of the loss of life, but it
was from Gettysburg that one nation, as opposed to one of the two sides in
the war, marked a loss. The Battle of Gettysburg was fought in the first three

days of July 1863, in south-central Pennsylvania, some fifty miles north-west of Baltimore, Maryland. The battle concluded with a daring and disastrous uphill charge by the Confederate Army, against which Union forces held their ground under the concerted pressure. The result was a victory for the Union's Army of the Potomac, turning back the second invasion of the North by Robert E. Lee's Army of Northern Virginia. There were over fifty-one thousand casualties in the encounter.

Within three months a Gettysburg Memorial Association was formed to organize commemorations of the fallen soldiers of the Union Army. President Lincoln's address of 19 November 1863 at the dedication of the cemetery at Gettysburg has become a historical event itself; in the speech he eloquently summarized the democratic ideal so seriously threatened by the war and pondered the sacrifice of soldiers who gave their lives to preserve the nation. Some thirty-five hundred Union soldiers were buried in Soldiers' National Cemetery, and an equal number of military graves were added in later years. In the 1870s further monuments, in addition to those in the cemetery, were erected on the battlefield. Postwar ceremonials at Gettysburg expressed a sentiment of conciliation rather than a renewed partisan spirit. In the postwar years, some fifty-five thousand veterans gathered annually to participate in reenactments of the battle. The federal government purchased a section of the battlefield in 1895, and in the space of six square miles there are some thirteen hundred memorials, including two hundred for fallen Confederates. The last reunion of some two thousand surviving veterans was held in 1938, on the seventy-fifth anniversary of the battle; President Franklin Roosevelt delivered a speech on the occasion that was broadcast to the nation. Reenactments are organized to this day, with great attention to detail. At the centennial in 1963 some forty thousand spectators watched such a reenactment.[11] Annual commemorations occur on Memorial Day in the cemetery, with special activities on the battle anniversary (1–3 July), and ceremonies on the anniversary of Lincoln's Gettysburg Address (19 November) and Remembrance Day (closest Saturday to 19 November). After the Gettysburg battle, a new American civil war became unthinkable; an American would not identify another American as a military enemy. Gettysburg was a disaster that has played and still plays a role in the national consciousness. By its civic nature, the Gettysburg site highlights the difference between disaster, as that term is used here, and personal tragedy.

THE JOHNSTOWN FLOOD NATIONAL MEMORIAL, PENNSYLVANIA

The reference to the Johnstown Flood is to the "Great Flood" of 30 May 1889, though significant Johnstown floods on 17 March 1936 and 19–20

July 1977 also qualify as disasters. The National Park Service maintains a Johnstown Flood National Memorial and an accompanying museum. The 1889 flood is generally considered one of the worst in the nation's history because there were over twenty-two hundred victims and a general devastation of the local infrastructure. Only the hurricane and storm tide in Galveston, Texas, among the natural disasters in America, resulted in a greater number of deaths. The Great Flood was well publicized in the newspaper medium, with graphic photographs suggesting the violence of the destruction and President Benjamin Harrison urging the raising of funds for relief and reconstruction. Interest in the disaster still appears to be great; the late-twentieth-century Johnstown Redevelopment Authority, having set up a Web site, was deluged with requests for information. The agency saw fit to post maps and other information to satisfy the public demand. The Pennsylvania Railroad posts the nineteenth-century history of the disaster on the Web.[12] The noted historian David McCullough, intrigued by photographic negatives he found in the Library of Congress depicting the flood's destruction, began writing a history of the disaster in his off hours while working for the United States Information Agency, and the resultant book launched his career as a public figure.[13]

One of the notable features of the Johnstown tragedy is that it was not entirely a natural disaster. Neglect, incompetence, and arguably a degree of indifference on the part of the upper-class members of the South Fork Fishing and Hunting Club led to the loss of life, mostly of working-class residents of Johnstown, Pennsylvania. A small natural lake, Conemaugh Lake, had been enlarged by means of a dam decades before the disaster to supply water to a portion of the Pennsylvania Canal System. A second but entirely artificial lake was also created for the same purpose, but after the canal fell into disuse because of the development of the railroad, its dam was torn down upon the insistence of local farmers, who feared it would break if neglected. The Pennsylvania Railroad acquired the still extant Conemaugh Lake site.

A club called the South fork Fishing and Hunting Club was organized some years ago, and got the use of the lake from the Pennsylvania Company. Most of the members of the club live in Pittsburgh, and are prominent iron and coal men. Besides them there are some of the officials of the Pennsylvania [rail] road among the members. They increased the size of the dam until it was not [far] from a hundred feet in height, and its entire length . . . was not far from nine hundred feet. . . . Some of the people of Johnstown had thought for years that the dam might break.[14]

On the fatal day, water sprayed through leaks in the dam, flowed under the structure, and poured over the top. Then the dam simply moved and disintegrated. Many people in Johnstown failed to heed warnings because they had heard such warnings in past years only to find that nothing happened. Even as the water began flooding the city, many seemed to have no idea of the height that the flood waters would reach.

FORD'S THEATRE, WASHINGTON, D.C.

The assassination of President Abraham Lincoln at Ford's Theatre, 14 April 1865, took place two dozen years before the Johnstown Flood, but considerable time passed before it drew much attention. It became a destination of visitors only after the development of the Gettysburg and Johnstown memorials. The site of Ford's Theatre had first been occupied by a church that was built in 1833, but the congregation vacated the building in 1859 when it merged with the Fourth Baptist Church. The entrepreneur John T. Ford leased the church building for use as a theater late in 1861, but a December 1862 fire gutted it. Ford built a new theater in its place, which opened 27 August 1863.

John Wilkes Booth assassinated Lincoln there two years later. Booth was a popular actor from Maryland who abandoned his career in 1864 to devote his energies to the Confederacy. He had been plotting to capture President Lincoln on 17 March 1965 and exchange him for Confederate prisoners of war. That plan failed, and within a month Confederate general Robert E. Lee surrendered his army to the Union general Ulysses Grant, thereby ending the Civil War. Booth then plotted with others to assassinate President Lincoln, Secretary of State William H. Seward, and Vice President Andrew Johnson, with the intent of plunging the nation into political confusion. Only the Lincoln murder succeeded, though the presidency of Andrew Johnson did occasion considerable tumult in the nation. Booth escaped for a time, exiting the theater through an actors' passageway. A young physician, Charles Leale, attended to Lincoln, and military officers pressed back the crowd of people so that the mortally wounded Lincoln could be brought out onto the street. Henry Safford, a resident of the nearby Petersen boarding house, saw the officers and physician with Lincoln out on the street and beckoned them to use the Petersen house. Lincoln lay unconscious on a bed in the house until he died the following morning.

Ford hoped to reopen his theater after a decent interval, but there were threats of arson. In July 1865 Secretary of War Edwin Stanton stationed troops outside the building, after which the War Department leased the building from Ford, converting it into a three-story office building. In December 1865 the surgeon general authorized the use of a floor of the structure as an Army Medical Museum, and the following April Congress voted to purchase the building. In 1887 the medical museum was relocated, and the entire building was used for offices. The interior of the structure collapsed in June 1893, killing twenty-two clerks. After that the War Department used the former theater as a warehouse. Thus, while public opinion prevented the site from being used for entertainment in the post–Civil War period, no effort was made to make it a memorial or site of visitation. It was not until 1928 that the War Department vacated the site, and the Lincoln Museum was opened there in 1932. Congress eventually voted to restore the building as a theater, and President Dwight Eisenhower signed the act to do so in 1954. After an extensive study, the restoration was carried out from 1965 to 1967. A dedication took place, followed by a gala reopening ceremony, in January 1968, and the first theatrical performance in the hall since 1865 began 5 February 1969. In 1970 Congress established the theater and the Petersen House as a national historical site. A museum and the Petersen House are open during normal business hours for self-guided tours, as is the theater when rehearsals are not taking place. Fifteen-minute talks are provided in the theater six times a day.[15] Thus, through the course of a century the site changed from a place where entertainment should not occur to a site of visitation. One is tempted to believe that the Gettysburg site served as a general model for the development at the Ford Theatre site.

LITTLE BIGHORN BATTLEFIELD NATIONAL MONUMENT, CROW AGENCY, MONTANA

Little Bighorn Battlefield National Monument is the site of the defeat of the United States Army's Seventh Cavalry at the hands of a force of Lakota Sioux, Cheyenne, and Arapaho on 25 June 1876. The event has entered into legend as "Custer's Last Stand." The battlefield was designated a War Department cemetery in 1879, and in 1881 a memorial was erected on Last Stand Hill over the mass grave of the cavalry soldiers. The National Park Service maintains two parts of the battlefield—the site of Custer's stand and the "Reno-Benteen" site where a part of the cavalry force commanded by Major Marcus A. Reno and Captain Frederick W. Benteen engaged the Native American forces. The Custer Battlefield Preservation Committee raises money to purchase and preserve other portions of the battlefield. Visitations at the monument maintained by the National Park Service average twenty-five hundred people per day, with four thousand visiting during the anniversaries of the battle.[16] For more than a century the significance of the monument was quite ambivalent; the legends narrating the event featured the deeds of the colorful but irresponsible commander "General" George Armstrong Custer. At the end of the twentieth century the National Park Foundation is raising funds to construct an Indian Memorial at the monument site. Rather than featuring "General" Custer, the focus is on the clash in a "life or death struggle" of two peoples having divergent cultures. "The essential irony of the Battle of the Little Bighorn is that the victors lost their nomadic way of life after their victory."[17] At the time of the battle in 1876, the slaughter of the cavalry and Custer shocked the nation.

Continuing interest in the site stems in part from the colorful characters of George Armstrong Custer and Sitting Bull. Custer graduated at the bottom of his class at the United States Military Academy in 1861 and saw action in the Union Army in the Civil War. He was eventually appointed brigadier general over a force of volunteers. After the war he served in the West and the South with the rank of lieutenant colonel in the regular cavalry. He managed to run afoul of the Army's authorities, at one point being arrested and suspended from pay and rank. He made himself a public figure as a writer, authoring *My Life on the Plains*, among other things. Sitting Bull had been a warrior in his youth and military leader in the 1860s. He refused to make peace when Red Cloud signed a treaty with the Americans and managed to gather leading warriors to his cause. When gold was discovered in the Black Hills, the military sought in vain to keep miners out of Indian areas and to keep the bands Sitting Bull inspired on the reservations. At the time of the fall of Custer and 267 of his men, Sitting Bull did not participate as a warrior but was only a spiritual leader. He fled to Canada, but was forced to return to the United States, where he turned himself in. He served eighteen months in confinement. In 1885 he joined the Buffalo Bill Wild West Show, traveling around the United States. After retiring from that, he and his teenage son were killed in an attempt to arrest them at the time of the Ghost Dance craze, which the U.S. government feared would turn into a major rebellion.

USS *ARIZONA* MEMORIAL, PEARL HARBOR, HAWAII

The *Arizona* memorial at Pearl Harbor in Hawaii marks an event that united the nation after it had undergone considerable internal stress arising from the Great Depression of the 1930s. The *Arizona* was a battleship sunk by war planes from the empire of Japan on 7 December 1941. Because it was damaged beyond salvage, it not only became a tomb for the sailors whose remains could not be recovered from the wreckage, but it also serves as an obdurate reminder of the unprovoked attack that destroyed much of the Pacific Fleet of the United States Navy and forced the United States into World War II. The attack forever changed the place of Americans in the wider world, thrusting their nation into international affairs. Because of the Pearl Harbor attack, there is an enduring "foreign policy" of the modern

American populace that is suspicious of overseas authoritarian regimes and militarily proactive in the defense of democracy; this popular foreign policy—hardly comprehensible from outside the American borders—often contradicts and sometimes overrules the official foreign policy formulated by the American State Department. Thus, while the State Department pursued what its professionals deemed a coherent policy of opposing the regimes of both Cuba and Nicaragua in the 1980s, popular sympathy distinguished the authoritarian regime of Castro in Cuba from the elected Ortega government in Nicaragua. Visits to the *Arizona* memorial are part of the symbolic complex of Americans' national consciousness that explains this popular foreign policy sentiment.

The USS *Arizona* Memorial, dedicated in 1962, stands over the sunken hull of the *Arizona* in Pearl Harbor itself. Some million Americans and an additional half-million people from other nations visit the site annually.[18] It is a particular focus of ritual events and attention on the 7 December anniversary.

DEALEY PLAZA, DALLAS, TEXAS

Dealey Plaza marks more than the killing of a personally popular politician on 22 November 1963. Indeed, history will probably describe John F. Kennedy as a minor twentieth-century president, and his assassination will likely be deemed comparable to that of another progressive president, James A. Garfield, in 1881. Dealey Plaza marks a disaster; presidents had moderated progress rather than promoted it since the early years of the Franklin Roosevelt administration. There was an important social agenda in America of including all nationalities and races in the public life; as a member of an immigrant nationality willing to make common cause with the African American civil rights movement (however reluctantly behind the scenes), Kennedy represented a long-awaited leadership on social issues. Kennedy's successor, Lyndon Johnson, was a far more serious advocate of the civil-rights movement, but as a white Anglo-Saxon Protestant he represented an acceptance of a minority by a majority rather than a leader who could unite the "ethnics" and African Americans. Kennedy's assassination was a national disaster, cutting short a development that many felt was needed.

Little appears to have been done to commemorate the assassination, even though many people still mark it in their memories. There is a museum on the sixth floor of the Texas School Book Depository building where the assassin, Lee Harvey Oswald, fired his rifle, but there are no city-sponsored ceremonials on the anniversary. About thirty people per day lead themselves through a tour of the museum. Even for November 1988, the twenty-fifth anniversary of the assassination, the city of Dallas planned no commemoration. Some three thousand people showed up anyway and roamed about. Some visitors use the site to express protests against the U.S. government, which adherents of various conspiracy theories maintain is suppressing a "truth" about the assassination. Some people bring old news photographs of the scene and compare them with the real place. When asked, the visitors speak of an era of hope and idealism that ended at the spot.[19]

VIETNAM WAR MEMORIAL, WASHINGTON, D.C.

The Vietnam War Memorial marks many personal tragedies, but it also marks the disaster of a democratic government that had broken faith with its people. The Vietnam War—at least the American phase of it—emerged from an arrogant bureaucracy pursuing geopolitical tactics rather than from any evident national need or popular sentiment. The memorial marks the pervasive distrust of government that is found among Americans to this day. Congress authorized the memorial in 1980, in hopes of separating the commemoration of the sacrifices made by the fallen military servicemen from the controversial nature of the war itself. A wall inscribed with the names of the fallen, designed by Maya Ying Lin of Athens, Ohio, was intended to do just that and was set up in 1982, but veterans groups were dissatisfied with the absence of some kind of artistic endorsement of the war. According to the Web site maintained by the National Park Service, "Rather than allow the memorial to the veterans of a controversial war to itself become divisive and controversial, it was decided to add Frederick Hart's *Statue of the Three Servicemen* to the overall design."[20] The addition was made in 1984. It occurred to the National Park Service to add a Vietnam Women's Memorial in 1993. The Vietnam Veterans Memorial is today the most visited National Park Service site in Washington, D.C.

KENT STATE UNIVERSITY, KENT, OHIO

An incident at Kent State University in Ohio that occurred on 4 May 1970 touched the consciousness of many Americans and set in motion a generalized desire among them to consecrate a memorial site. There was widespread support for the construction of a memorial, and many people in fact commemorated the event spontaneously. However, the state government of Ohio found the event itself embarrassing and blocked any formal or official memorialization for years. At a popular level, many local inhabitants of northeast Ohio resented what a Kent State memorial would represent and supported the state's effort to resist establishing any official memorial.

At the time of the incident in 1970, controversy over the Vietnam War had divided American society.[21] In northeast Ohio many middle-aged inhabitants had found a seemingly secure place in American society as members of the stable working class. Many were the children of immigrants from the less industrialized parts of Europe; they assimilated successfully into American society through hard work, conventional lifestyles, and ardent American patriotism. It was their dream that their children would attend a college or university and enter a profession. Kent State University was, in fact, an institution of higher education that represented the dreamed-of opportunity for the working class of northeast Ohio. Yet there was widespread ambivalence over what went on at Kent State and other universities. The students often discarded the conventional beliefs and lifestyles of their elders. Student demonstrations against the Vietnam War came to symbolize all the misgivings their elders harbored over the conduct of the younger generation.

The American president, Richard M. Nixon, assumed office in 1969, having narrowly won an election with a campaign that was ambiguous about the war. He seemed to promise peace by referring to a plan he claimed to have for ending the conflict. He also appealed to the pro-war sentiment of many by emphasizing "law and order" and overt American patriotism. His own very conventional public image had symbolic value in the eyes of people such as the solid working class of northeast Ohio. On Sunday 3 May 1970, Nixon announced that he had ordered the American military to invade Cambodia in a maneuver to capture transportation routes that the North Vietnamese forces were using. This was seen as a broken commitment on Nixon's part by opponents of the war. Nixon was overtly expanding the conflict rather than ending or withdrawing from it. Spontaneous protests occurred throughout the nation, especially on university campuses. A protest on the Kent State University campus spilled out into the downtown area of the city of Kent. Broken windows and damage to some downtown businesses led the city's mayor to seek assistance from Governor John Rhodes of Ohio. On the morning of 4 May student volunteers helped clean up and repair damage in the city.

Governor Rhodes, a conservative politician who shared the widespread apprehension over the unconventionality and apparent rebelliousness of university students in general, activated the Ohio National Guard and sent it to the Kent State University campus. The guard units carried loaded weapons, of a kind that would be used in combat. In the early afternoon, after a student demonstration refused to disperse, a contingent of twenty-eight guardsmen fired on the students for thirteen seconds, leaving four students dead, one permanently paralyzed, and eight others wounded. Some of the victims were not even involved in the demonstration. Local news organizations were present for the tragedy, capturing aspects of it in pictures and videotape.

The impact of media reports of soldiers in American uniforms firing rifles at young Americans engaging in the constitutionally protected right to assembly cannot be underestimated.[22] The fact that neither President Nixon nor Governor Rhodes criticized the guardsmen's behavior, but rather criticized the demonstrators, was not lost on the public. Despite inquiries and hearings and trials over the next several years, error was never admitted. The government could not admit to error. In the following years, when people sought to memorialize the tragedy, it was this arrogance on the part of government that outraged them and helped make them all the more insistent that a memorial be constructed. Frozen in its apprehension over the younger generation, much of the northeast Ohio public agreed with the state government's prohibition of the construction of any memorial.

Spontaneous commemorative visits appear to have begun in 1973.[23] Every 4 May, individuals showed up, sometimes joining organized memorial services. In May 1974 there was a rally at the site. In 1975 there were some minor memorial markers in place, but a memorial service did not attract many people. There was a widely felt need for a meaningful memorial, however, and in 1976 many students boycotted classes for a day in support of the demand for one. The next year the university announced plans to build a gymnasium near the site of the shooting, and a series of protest demonstrations against the plans began. A number of court cases, confrontations with unarmed police, and arrests marked the controversy into the summer months of 1977. Seeking compromise, the university president proposed incorporating a marker into the gymnasium design; the protesters were not satisfied and, contrary to court orders, occupied the site. While members of Congress proposed the construction of some kind of memorial, the university trustees voted to proceed with the construction of the gymnasium. A federal judge delayed the gymnasium construction to give Congress time to act; Congress did not act. Protests, confrontations, and vandalism at the site continued into the fall of 1977.

While the university eventually built its gymnasium, the desire for a memorial to visit did not die out. In 1978 the Mildred Andrews Fund of Cleveland commissioned the sculptor George Segal to create a memorial. Meanwhile, people continued to visit the site on 3 May every year. Segal captured the intergenerational ambivalence that resides behind the passionate feelings over the 1970 incident in a sculpture of Abraham about to sacrifice Isaac. As Abraham wields the sacrificial knife with his right hand, he nervously digs the fingers of his left hand into his thigh, betraying an underlying state of doubt. The sculpture simply portrayed more truth than the northeast Ohio public could bear. The university rejected the $100,000 monument, even when offered it as a gift. George Segal's *Abraham and Isaac: In Memory of May 4, 1970*, was accepted by Princeton University in October 1979, since Kent State would not take it. The following May, some fifteen hundred people attended the annual memorial service at Kent State.

At century's end people still visit Kent State University every May, often participating in an annual 3 May candlelight walk and vigil. They also comprise an audience for the annual scholarly symposium on the event and on the place of protests in democracies. The university now, belatedly, appoints a commemoration committee and offers 4 May commemoration grants for commemoration program entries. Revealingly, the theme for the year 2000 commemorative program is "Experiencing Democracy: Inquire, Learn, Reflect." The academicians, a few of whom were present for the fateful event thirty years before, visit intellectually rather than by pilgrimage, when they endeavor to come to terms with the case in a spirit of objectivity and balance. No doubt the lone visitors setting their candles down on the ground at the site, in vigil, are doing the same. There is a memorial now—not George Segal's sculpture: "A granite plaza, measuring 70 feet wide, rests on the crest of the wooded hillside adjacent to Taylor Hall overlooking the Commons. Bound by a granite sidewalk and bench to the east; to the north, a series of four black granite disks lead from the plaza into the wooded area where four free-standing pylons are aligned on the hill."[24] A plaque with the names of the victims has been placed near the sidewalk north of the memorial. The decision to authorize this modest memorial was not made until 1984, fourteen years after the killings.

In the Kent State instance we have a demonstration of the social necessity of commemorations of public events that occasion deeply felt emotions, commemorations that are not simply calendric markers but physical objects that people can visit and see. As much as the Ohio officials and their sympathizers did not want a physical reminder of the disaster, a significant part of the public seemed to need precisely such a reminder. Meager as the current memorial might be, it occasions the emotional labor of many people still unreconciled to the dominant political and social consensus, emotional labor realizing in a tangible way the right of the dissident to full membership in society.

MURRAH FEDERAL BUILDING SITE, OKLAHOMA CITY

A resident of Indiana drove to Oklahoma City in July 1998 and visited the commemorative site of the bomb explosion that had destroyed the Murrah Federal Building three years before. "As a resident from Indiana,"

Photo 9. American Sculpture, George Segal, 1924–2000. *Abraham and Isaac: In Memory of May 4, 1970, Kent State University,* bronze; H. 205.5; base: 284.5 × 157.5 cm. The John B. Putnam, Jr., Memorial Collection, Princeton University. Partial gift of the Mildred Andrews fund. Photo Credit: Clem Fiori © 1985 Trustees of Princeton University. May not be reproduced without permission in writing from The Art Museum, Princeton University, Princeton, NJ 08544.

he reports, "I felt detached from the bombing . . . , so I didn't expect to be emotionally affected by the site. I was wrong. This was a heavy, sorrowful place."[25] He posted his thoughts on the Internet, along with a photograph of the site, in which a white statue of a woman in a long robe is shown; she buries her face in one hand and presses the other hand, half clenched, onto her breast. Black stone pillars of irregular height appear about her. In the background is a distant fence decked with cut flowers. It is as if a madonna misses her child and stands amidst ashen rubble, with symbols of death in the background.

The Oklahoma City monument marks a disaster of distrust going too far—Vietnam without Gettysburg, as it were. It was the site of an enormous explosion on 19 April 1995 that killed 168 people, set by a young former soldier named Timothy McVeigh. The Murrah Building had not been particularly symbolic in itself. It was completed in March of 1977, an energy-efficient nine-story office building built at $2.5 million under the projected $15.822 million budget. It housed a variety of federal agencies, employing some 724 people—a United States Marshall's Office, offices of the General Services Administration, the Social Security Administration, and the General Accounting Office, a United States Army Recruiting office, and so forth, as well as a day care center for children, a credit union, and a food court area.[26]

Timothy McVeigh entered the United States Army in 1988 and served in the 1990 Gulf War. He left the military after not being admitted to the elite Green Beret unit, becoming something of a wanderer who lived with various friends. Gradually he fell under the influence of the "militia movement," a fringe phenomenon in American society that is often associated with shadowy white racist groups that have a right-wing antigovernment ideology. According to an affidavit presented to a federal magistrate after McVeigh's arrest a

former co-worker of Mr. McVeigh said he was "known to hold extreme right-wing views" and had been "particularly agitated" about the Waco raid, which led to a fire that killed some 80 members of the Branch Davidian sect.

The co-worker . . . said Mr. McVeigh had been so upset about those deaths that he had visited the charred site and later expressed "extreme anger at the federal Government" and said the Government "should never have done what it did."[27]

The fact that McVeigh himself had been a visitor to a disaster site is not mere irony. In a televised interview he acknowledged going to the Waco, Texas, site during the siege, and as noted above, an unnamed former co-worker believed McVeigh had visited the Waco site after the disaster there.[28] Timothy McVeigh's resentment against government had harmlessly inhabited a fi-

nite rhetorical province of meaning, in an unreal realm of right-wing imagination; but after his Waco visit it crossed into the experiential world of
everyday life. Witnessing actual events and their consequences caused
something of a transformation in his mentality.

The date 19 April had taken on a symbolic value in the discourse of the
right-wing fringe movement. It was the anniversary of an incident in which
FBI agents shot the wife and son of Randy Weaver, a white supremacist in
Montana whom they were trying to arrest. On 19 April 1993, the tragic conclusion to the Waco standoff between the Branch Davidians and federal law
enforcement officers occurred. This same date was also on the forged South
Dakota driver's license that McVeigh used to rent the truck that he employed in the bombing of the Murrah Building. On 19 April 1995, the date
of the Oklahoma City explosion, Richard Snell, a white supremacist who
had killed a Jewish businessman and an African American policeman in
Texarkana, Arkansas, was scheduled to be executed, and indeed Snell was
executed that day.[29] One can surmise that McVeigh wanted the coinciding
of the dates to communicate something to adherents of the right-wing fringe
movement. He evidently expected the truck he rented to be traced to the
forged driver's license bearing the 19 April 1993 date; however, he did not
expect it to be traced to himself.

As early as 17 July 1995, the Families/Survivors Liaison Subcommittee
met in Oklahoma City to plan a memorial. The history of its deliberations,
entered upon in an exercise of participatory democracy, has been preserved,
allowing us to see the process of preparing a visitation site.[30] After deliber-
ating for some months, the committee described the feelings of the affected
people with ten themes:

1. Focus on victims and survivors
2. Never forget/always remember
3. Quiet, peaceful, serene, sacred
4. Hope, spiritual
5. Something special for the children
6. Universal symbol
7. Comforting
8. Sense of pride
9. Educational (study of non-violence)
10. Loss of innocence/security[31]

The memorial that was to be erected should, they thought, communicate
these themes to visitors.

THE SOCIAL EXTENSION OF DISASTERS

People who visit such sites as these first know, in some way, about the disasters the sites memorialize. Some will know of a disaster from personal experience; veterans from the two armies at Gettysburg, for example, participated in gatherings and activities there in the late-nineteenth- and early-twentieth-century commemorative ceremonials, and some veterans of the Pearl Harbor attack still visit the *Arizona* Monument. Other people know of disasters through the loss of family or close associates; members of the American generation that came of age in the 1960s, for example, lost friends or family or both in Vietnam. They cannot be unmoved by the Vietnam War Memorial. For most people, however, knowledge of disasters comes through the communications media. People can tell us where they were and what they were doing when they learned about the disaster through the media. Or if the disaster is far enough back in history, they learn about it in history texts in school or perhaps from elders' recollections about where the latter were when the disaster occurred.[32] The media play an important role in making knowledge of a disaster common currency for an entire population.

Knowledge of a disaster is only the first step toward what occurs when people visit a disaster site. The visiting activity comes to represent ramifications that are experienced beyond any knowledge about what had happened. Such ramifications can be taken as indicators of what the visiting activity accomplishes for the individuals. These are not uniform but vary with the circumstances of the visitor.

In cases in which individuals personally experienced the disaster in question, a site visit can become a significant episode in a redefinition of the self. We generally know of our selves on the basis of the responses of other persons toward us. Each of us is the person to whom a parent, sibling, or friend paid attention. Each of us is an individual known by others in the workplace. We carry about a sense of self, originating in childhood and developing thereafter. There is a general continuity, broken by thresholds that demarcate different stages of life; these may be life-cycle events or other significant changes. If we had a personal experience of a disaster, we may be able to locate other events in our lives as occurring *before* or *after* the disaster, in a manner analogous to locating events before or after the more routine threshold events such as graduations and marriages. However, when one comes back to the site of a disaster in which one participated, or when one visits a memorial to such a disaster, one faces a part of one's own life as an "object" that is not mediated by the responses of other individual people but by the mass media in an impersonal way. One experiences a peculiar kind of realism wherein what is a symbolic reality to others is simultaneously a concrete memory for oneself. In visiting the site or memorial, one finds one-self redefined from the vantage point of the mass media as a veteran or a part of history. One finds a part of one's self not open to re-negotiation or development, not open to a living future. One's self has become in part something set in stone, as it were.

There is a liberating aspect to being thus defined as a part of history. The very impersonality of the process in which the new definition of self occurs gives one less of a stake in the defining process. One may not be able to distance one's self emotionally from the family and friends through whose attentions one became a self-conscious individual at the beginning of life; family and friends, and by extension one's subjectivity, should not be mere objects to one's self. Self-respect and respect for others require a sense of attachment and investment of self in family and friends. However, to be a part of impersonal history allows one a critical degree of detachment. From the new perspective as some *other*, as one caught up in the sweep of events in a now-memorialized disaster, one can transcend the biographical limitations of one's private life. After Gettysburg, how could one be either a northerner or a southerner? World War I led to peace between church and state in France; could the memorialization of events in which both chaplains and secular actors were involved be a large part of the reason why? The bombing of the federal building in Oklahoma City involved people of different races in frantic efforts of rescue and resilient attempts to resume everyday life: can the people who were involved see themselves after a memorialization as members of one race or one faction only? Such redefinitions of self contribute to changes in social structures, and visits to memorials of such disasters affirm and cement that kind of change.

A somewhat different process is involved in the victimization, especially the death, of a close associate in a disaster. There is an understandable resistance to making the situation into an object from an impersonal perspective. Rather, changes occur in one's interpersonal involvements; one's social network has been altered. One's self undergoes a change, but that change consists not of a liberation that comes with making one's past self an object from an impersonal perspective but rather a redefinition of the particular other persons through whom one experiences one's self. One finds one's biography partitioned into a period in which the lost one was a part of one's life experience and another period in which that person is no longer present. A visit to the scene or memorial of the disaster heightens the status of a memory *as memory*. The scene comes to be associated in one's thinking with the responsibility of breaking the news to others that some special person had been lost in the disaster, perhaps with the responsibility of handling the lost one's affairs, or with objectifying the lost one's expressed or presumed intentions. The visit evokes one's status as an agent carrying out necessary tasks not of one's own choosing. Both this artificial status and the very real change in one's social involvements are given experienced facticity and renewed reality by the visit. This seems to be the experience the Vietnam War Memorial was meant to evoke with its massive list of the names of the fallen.

Disasters that are known through the communications media give rise to a third set of distinctive dynamics. If the disastrous events are sufficiently remote in time, they may serve a largely cognitive purpose in periodizing history; visiting a memorial may at best join one's personal experience to a widely shared cultural phenomenon. Thus, as noted above, Gettysburg symbolizes an American national identity represented by the word "people" in President Lincoln's triadic reference to government "of the people, by the people, and for the people." Disasters, as noted, also come to represent attendant individual tragedies; the visitor to a war memorial may well have a lost relative or friend principally in mind. The visit creates or cultivates a linkage between the public and private dimensions of a disaster. More often, however, a visitor who knows of a disaster largely through the media or through history lessons individualizes a shared attitudinal change that derived from or was marked by the disaster.[33]

PILGRIMAGE ACTIVITIES AND DISASTER SITES

When the visitor arrives at a grave, war memorial, or some other monument, an empirical experience lends its facticity to a development in the world of symbols. The visit is capable of occasioning a reconfiguration of the visitor's motivational resources. The veteran or other participant in a memorialized event arrives at a new objectivity. The mourner translates loss into responsibility or perhaps recognizes the emergence of a new interactional network. The individual made knowledgeable by the communications media finds an unmediated experience that affords a placement in an otherwise mediated realm; the quasi-reality of images comes to be supplemented by factual experience. It would be incorrect to think of such processes as merely psychological developments; the visitors are placing themselves in reappropriated cultural contexts. Social structure is at work. Even the unfortunate transformation of a Timothy McVeigh from an ideologue into a terrorist is in part a structural phenomenon.

In some instances, a visitor may "come to terms" with a personal tragedy that had been an aspect of a social disaster. The momentary reliving of a sad experience serves as a catharsis not merely by being experienced again but also by being experienced in the context of a continued life. The personal side of the disaster is not necessarily diminished but is repositioned in a new perspective, one that allows for new and renewed life projects. Nothing forces one to move forward from a past event as effectively as that event being appreciated from a new perspective.

Visitors to disaster sites sometimes pray, either with traditional formulas or simply by beholding the scene, as it were, through the eyes of eternity. Prayer is essentially an affirmation of life, a mental insertion of the companion life-form into a comprehension of the world. One reevaluates what is important in life by contemplating it from the perspective of eternity. Even the primitive discourse of a *do ut des* religiosity raises the issue of how one's wishes appear in the eyes of the anthropomorphized deity. The tellingly social form of prayer, often conversational and usually linguistic, indicates that again a social rather than merely psychological development is occurring. The disaster and its aftermath have changed social reality, and the individual is being socialized into the new state of affairs.

Visitors often employ "marks." A mark is less than a sign, having no shared significance in the wider society comparable to a linguistic statement. A mark is more or less individual, meant to have a meaning for the visitor alone.[34] Sometimes a visitor may leave a mark at the disaster site—a ribbon or bouquet of flowers, for example. At other times, a visitor may purchase a souvenir and leave with it, subsequently placing it somewhere in an everyday life-space. Such marks serve as bridges between old and new lives, mementos of lives past retained in lives present. The very existence of such bridges suggests the chasms that have come into the visitors' lives. The practice of visiting disaster sites is ultimately grounded in lives with chasms in them, chasms intruding upon the present, wanted or unwanted, from history or memory or both. It is the inconvenient location and troublesome character of such life chasms that generate the yearning that people have for memorials and their propensity to visit them.

NOTES

1. See Paolo Giuriati and Elio Masferrer Kan, *Pellegrini a Guadalupe* (Padua: Centro Ricerche Socio-Religiose, 1999), p. 14; Maria I. Macioti, *Pellegrinaggi e giubilei: I luoghi del culto* (Rome: Laterza, 2000), p. vii.

2. Barbara G. Meyerhoff, *Peyote Hunt: The Sacred Journey of the Huichol Indians* (Ithaca, NY: Cornell University Press, 1974). Myerhoff's ethnographic material accords with the theoretical framework of Victor Turner; see Victor W. Turner, *The Ritual Process: Structure and Anti-Structure* (Chicago: Aldine, 1969), and idem, *Dramas, Fields and Metaphors: Symbolic Action in Human Society* (Ithaca, NY: Cornell University Press, 1974).

3. Luigi Tomasi, "Pilgrimage/Tourism," in *Encyclopedia of Religion and Society* (Walnut Creek, CA: AltaMira Press, 1998), pp. 362–364.

4. On the use of the term *anomia* by Thucydides, see Donald A. Nielsen, "Pericles and the Plague: Civil Religion, Anomie, and Injustice in Thucydides," *Sociology of Religion* 57: 397–407.

5. See Émile Durkheim, *Suicide: A Study in Sociology* (New York: Free Press, 1951[1897]), pp. 241ff.

6. This was Victor Turner's point of departure, though he did not limit his analysis to penitential settings.

7. I personally observed this in the summer of 1993 while participating in a "tour" of biblical sites in Turkey.

8. See John Eade and Michael J. Sallnow (eds.), *Contesting the Sacred: The Anthropology of Christian Pilgrimage* (London: Routledge, 1991), p. 5.

9. See Juan Eduardo Campo, "American Pilgrimage Landscapes," *Annals of the American Academy of Political and Social Science* 558 (1998): 42.

10. See Anthony J. Blasi, "Fundamental versus Influential Factors in Regional Identities," in *The Local Community: A Sociological Interpretation of European Localism*, edited by Luigi Tomasi (Milan: Franco Angeli, 1996), pp. 66ff.

11. Campo, "Landscapes," pp. 48–49; U.S. National Park Service informational Web site, 16 December 1999, <http://www.nps.gov/jofl/home.htm>.

12. Willis Fletcher Johnson, *History of the Johnstown Flood* (Edgewood Publishing, 1889); Pennsylvania Railroad Web site, 12 March 2000, <http://prr.railfan.net/documents/JohnstownFlood.html>.

13. David McCullough, *The Johnstown Flood* (New York: Simon and Schuster, 1969).

14. Johnson, *History*, ch. 2.

15. U.S. National Park Service, Ford's Theatre National Historic Site Web site, 12 March 2000, <http://www.nps.gov/foth/schedule.htm>.

16. U.S. National Park Service, Little Bighorn Battlefield National Monument Web site, 14 March 2000, <http://www.nps.gov/libi>.

17. U.S. National Park Service, Indian Memorial at Little Bighorn Battlefield National Monument Web site, 14 March 2000, <http://www.nps.gov/libi/indmem.htm>.

18. U.S. National Park Service, USS *Arizona* Memorial Web site, 16 December 1999, <http://www.nps.gov/usar>.

19. Nick Trujillo, "Interpreting November 22: A Critical Ethnography of an Assassination Site," *Quarterly Journal of Speech* 79 (1997): 447–466.

20. U.S. National Park Service, Vietnam Veterans Memorial Web site, 16 December 1999, <http://www.nps.gov/vive/index2.htm>.

21. Kent State University maintains a general account of the incident on its official Web site, <http://www.kent.edu/>, "Events of May 4 1970," 6 September 2000, <http://64.224.189.204/home.asp>.

22. I was an eighth-grade teacher in New Orleans at the time. The children in my classes were beside themselves with anxiety over the incident. They could not concentrate on any lesson for the day, but had to talk through the problem of American soldiers shooting young people "like us." Even conservative colleagues

at the school described local encounters between demonstrators and police with some level of sympathy for the demonstrators.

23. Information reported here is based on *New York Times* reports, 1973–1980.

24. Kent State University Web site, 16 December 1999.

25. "On Hallowed Ground," 13 March 2000, <http://.iufc.indiana.edu/~graham/murrah.htm>, a Web site posted by James Graham, 30 July 1998.

26. Alfred P. Murrah Federal Building History Web site. maintained by the Oklahoma City Fire Department, 13 March 2000, <http://www.fireprograms.okstate.edu/ocfd/htm/hurrhist.htm>.

27. Todd S. Purdum, "Bomb Suspect Is Held, Another Identified," *New York Times* (22 April 1995): 1, 8.

28. CBS "60 Minutes," 12 March 2000, broadcast interview with Timothy McVeigh.

29. Robert D. McFadden, "Links in Blast: Armed 'Militia' and a Key Date," *New York Times* (22 April 1995): 1, 8.

30. Oklahoma City Memorial Foundation History Web site, <http://collections.oklahoman.net/memorial/history.html>

31. Oklahoma City Memorial Foundation History Web site, Appendix A: "Final Report of the Families/Survivors Liaison Subcommittee," 1 March 1996, p. 3.

32. In my childhood, an elderly woman told me about an "Indian raid" in Crescent City, California, that she knew about from her elders; she wanted me to visit a particular old building there on a trip northward and report back to her on its condition. Several elderly people told me about the San Francisco earthquake of 1906, and they would note damage still evident in some buildings. People of my parents' generation would talk about where they were when news of the Pearl Harbor attack was "flashed," associating particular places with news of the event. I can relate where I was when President Kennedy was shot, and should I ever return to the place where I heard the news, the event would come to mind.

33. The 1966 shooting spree from the University of Texas library tower, perpetrated by Charles Whitman, led to Americans' first acceptance of antiterrorism measures. Whitman's victims have been memorialized since 1999. I was present in Austin at the time of the incident, and I had acquaintances whom Whitman tried to kill; however, my awareness of the disaster came from a local radio broadcast. Should I visit the new memorial or even return to the library tower after over three decades, I would have a peculiarly individualized share in the sense of fear and dismay that to this day legitimates in my mind and the minds of many Americans such antiterrorist measures as metal detectors in airports. I wonder, on the other hand, with what frame of mind the students at the University of Texas today regard the memorial; their consciousness must surely be different from mine, though both came through the communications media.

34. Alfred Schutz and Thomas Luckmann, *The Structures of the Life-World* (Evanston, IL: Northwestern University Press, 1973), pp. 274–275.

Chapter 9 _____

Our Lady of Clearwater: Postmodern Traditionalism

William H. Swatos, Jr.

A number of scholars, both in this collection and elsewhere, have noted the increasing popularity of historic pilgrimage sites. Nevertheless, it is also the case that in the process of globalization a pluralism of discourse takes place such that these sites today become contested spaces, arenas "for competing religious and secular discourses," as Eade and Sallnow put it. They go on to observe that "if one can no longer take for granted the meaning of a pilgrimage for its participants, one can no longer take for granted a uniform definition of the phenomenon of 'pilgrimage' either." Not only are their "varied discourses with their multiple meanings and understandings, brought to the shrine by different categories of pilgrims, by residents and by religious specialists," but also "mutual *mis*understandings, as each group attempts to interpret the actions and motives of others in terms of its own specific discourse."[1]

Not all pilgrimage sites, even those that some people might consider "traditional," are in fact particularly old. Lourdes, for example, dates back only a little over a century—Fatima even less. Medjugorje, in the Balkans, is a site whose "miracle" remains in process and has yet to be endorsed by the Vatican. In this chapter, I will describe a pilgrimage site that is in an even more formative state; one that is of particular interest with respect to the intersection of pilgrimage and tourism, because it exists in an area of the United States not only already associated with purely secular tourism, but

Photo 10. Our Lady of Clearwater. *William H. Swatos, Jr.*

also with New Religious Movements. So let me set the stage both for my research and for the site's development.

THE STORY AND THE SITE

On 17 December 1996 an image was noticed on a two-story series of window panels on a building in Clearwater, Florida, at the intersection of Drew and U.S. Highway 19, that was at that time the offices of Seminole Finance Corporation, principally an automobile-financing firm. There was immediate, relatively widespread agreement that the image looked like many contemporary artistic renditions of Jesus's mother—especially of the kind found on more "modernistic" Christmas cards in the United States. News of the sighting was broadcast on radio and television, and within hours, crowds were on hand. During the Christmas season, wherein the image was perceived as a Christmas miracle, thousands of people—Florida already being heavy with tourists at that time—made their way to the site, requiring significant police coordination of traffic at an intersection in which one street carried five lanes of traffic and the other, ten.[2] At times over eight hundred people per hour were attempting to cross this intersection, where normally there is virtually no pedestrian traffic at all. Current estimates are that over a million people have by now visited the site.

Today this image is formally known as Our Lady of Clearwater, Our Lady Clothed with the Sun (see Rev. 12), and it is, in my view, a postmodern pilgrimage site—or a pilgrimage site that reflects the spiritual bricolage that characterizes religiosity in societies dominated by high-technology multinational capitalism. In this chapter, I will try to give some idea of the phenomenon, why it is relatively unique among "sightings" phenomena, and how it has developed into a pilgrimage center.

There is a scholarly literature on apparitions phenomena, which in fact occur quite frequently—or are at least quite frequently reported. As I was preparing the materials for writing an initial draft of this chapter, for example, at least two such phenomena were reported: photographs taken of a statue of the Blessed Virgin in a Roman Catholic school in Streator, Illinois, are purported to show the image of Jesus emerging from the statue as it was carried in a May Crowning procession, and in an Episcopal church in Massachusetts, a wooden door, when stained, was said to reveal a likeness of the bearded face of Jesus.[3] Thomas Duggan has written in the sociological literature about an apparition of the Blessed Virgin on the wall of a Presbyterian church in Michigan; however, interest in that apparition apparently ran its course in four months' time.[4] In other sites apparitional artifacts remain, but devotionalism wanes. A few minutes drive from Our Lady of Clearwater, for example, is the Greek Orthodox Pro-cathedral of St. Nicholas in Tarpon Springs. It has an icon that was said to weep. The icon is on display, but the only time significant crowds come to the church is for the annual Epiphany festival, which is a combination religious and ethnic celebration. A nearby private shrine of St. Michael the Archangel also features an icon to which miraculous cures are ascribed. Individuals do visit sporadically, but not with any pattern. Only in rare cases, in fact, like Lourdes or Fatima, does there seem to be continuing devotion at an apparitional site.

The image of Our Lady of Clearwater is somewhat different from other apparitions in that, first, it has not gone away. The crowds coming to the site have markedly decreased in size, but a series of developments occurred that led to its institutionalization as a devotional center. Second, there is no question of the biophysiochemical origin of the phenomenon. That is, everyone understands that the changes to the windows' coloration were caused by a combination of three factors: large palm trees that stood in front of the window and gave off various particles—and were then cut down, before the apparition was noticed; watering of these palm trees (that also hit the windows); and sunlight. Third, there is no question that the image that has been created looks like that of the Blessed Virgin Mary as she has been portrayed in hundreds, if not thousands, of pictures. No one has to have the image traced out by a guide to see it. The "miracle" of the image is not an unknown cause, but rather that this combination of elements formed itself into this image, rather than, for example, an amorphous series of waves. And it cannot be removed (other than by breaking the glass). Devotees associate the permanence of the image with that of the Virgin of Guadalupe, and also see the image as continuing Mary's work in the Fatima appearance of 1917.[5] Connections are also made to the Infant of Prague, which has Luso-Hispanic associations. Whenever I have visited the site, Hispanic Americans have been disproportionately highly represented among the visitor-pilgrims.[6]

The nonremoval is particularly significant because the image appeared on a commercial building. The crowds completely disrupted the business of the finance company—which had already been sold to, and was being amalgamated into, a nationally franchised used car sales and finance company (ironically, the Ugly Duckling chain). Attempts to have the image removed marred the lower sections but did not succeed. Only removing the panels would have sufficed, and because the building is actually built of these panels, their removal was not feasible. A great victory, and a significant step toward creating an ongoing pilgrimage site thus came in the fall of 1998, when the commercial lessees abandoned the building, and it was rented to Shepherds of Christ Ministries, an independent, largely lay-led, Catholic devotional society. The society is based in Ohio, was founded in 1994, and its primary calling is to pray for priests—particularly that priests will become more holy, hence traditional, and abandon modernist tendencies. Shepherds of Christ circulates a "spirituality newsletter" to all Roman Catholic priests in the United States and several thousand others around the world. Persons affiliated with the movement moved from Ohio to Clearwater to tend the site and conduct its daily public recitations of the rosary. Two years following the initial appearance, a large crucifix was raised alongside the image of the Virgin.

Even before Shepherds of Christ formally assumed lesseeship of the building, however, the practical effects of the image were felt. Pilgrims and tourists made the parking lot virtually unusable. Vigil lamps, flowers, and other paraphernalia were placed all along the edges of the image. People knelt to pray. Others distributed tracts and photographs and spoke of miracles. Like it or not, rational or not, the putative manifestation of Mary in the image on the windows simply made commercial life impossible in that setting. It had become spiritualized, sacred space. Popular devotion ultimately won any contest there might have been for this terrain. This is especially significant: though Shepherds of Christ does have a priest who gives it oversight, it is entirely centered on lay spirituality. The rosary is its practical sacrament. In the liberal democratic culture of "taken for true," there comes a point when the fervent and effective public prayer of righteous men and women avails: Given the physical size of the image and the numbers it attracted, sociomoral pressure rendered impossible the destruction of the image or the forced removal of the devotees from the site.

THE MEDIUM AND THE MESSAGE

But this is not quite the whole story. The pilgrimage site is defined by the messages of Rita Ring, a Catholic lay locutionist affiliated with Shepherds of Christ, who claims to receive daily direct messages from Jesus, Mary, and even God the Father. These messages are attested for theological legitimacy (or "discerned") by Fr. Edward Carter, a Cincinnati Jesuit theology professor, who is the founder of Shepherds of Christ and editor of its newsletter, with whom "miraculous" images of light have been associated and photographed. Fr. Carter also receives messages, but it is those of Ring that most directly affect the present movement. Her daily messages are available in the Message Room at the Mary Image Building (as it is now titled), organized in upright files, for every day of the year. (These may also be obtained via the Internet, <www.sofc.org>.) There, too, are video tapes, and Ring normally comes to the center on the fifth of every month. She has also putatively seen Mary come alive in statues. Beginning in 2000—the year of the Jubilee—"Mary" (the image) has appeared to turn completely gold on the fifth of many months. (Pictures of the image, including the golden apparition, are available on the Web site.)

Ring had been receiving messages (known as "private revelations" in Catholic theology) for several years prior to the Clearwater apparition, but on December 19, 1996 (i.e., two days *after* the Clearwater image was noticed), Mary specifically authenticated her Clearwater apparition to Rita and told Rita to begin the work in Florida.

I appear to you, my children, on a bank in Florida. You have made money your god! Do you know how cold are your hearts? You turn away from my Son, Jesus, for your money. Your money is your God. . . .

I am Mary your Mother. From my site in Florida, I want you to teach my world to pray. I stood beneath the cross and I cried. I wish you to play the *Mary Message* now and continually from this site. I wish you to tell the children I cried beneath the cross, tears of sorrow and great joy for my children. Tears of sorrow for the little ones that would lose their souls despite all my Son did for them. Despite His love, they lost their souls. And tears of joy for all that would go to heaven forever and be with God for all eternity.

I appear without any eyes, for you are my eyes. It is through your eyes, I will reach my children [cf. Rev. 12:1–6]. . . .

I appear my children on this former bank building in Florida, *Our Lady Clothed with the Sun*. I ask you to circulate my *Mary Message* tape made on the feast of Our Lady of Guadalupe, Dec. 12, 1996. . . . I appeared on the building five days later, looking as Our Lady of Guadalupe.

You wish a sign, my sinful world. I Mary your mother and my Son Jesus give you a sign. He gave Himself on the cross. I tell you today the Heavenly Father gave the sign at Guadalupe and He gives this sign today and you ignore the sign. . . .

This is a great Christmas gift for the world. Please be grateful and thank God for these revelations that I give you. These are insights to take you into Our Hearts. . . .

I give to you My Son Jesus born in a stable in Bethlehem on Christmas morn. He is the Almighty God, the Light of the World.

I am the *Lady Clothed with the Sun*. I am the handmaid of the Lord. I wail aloud bringing forth my children of the earth and you my children that will help me create a garden in Florida.

I am the New Eve. In this garden in Florida, I wish to bring forth good fruit, children loving God who have given their lives in consecration to the Hearts of Jesus and Mary.[7]

A related message of 23 January 1997 added the following:

I appear on the building to draw men to the messages given in *God's Blue Book*, *Rosaries From the Hearts of Jesus and Mary*, and *Tell My People* [books that are published by Shepherds of Christ Ministries, containing messages Ring has received]. These books are the messages we give from our hearts to draw men to our hearts. They are the messages my Son gives to bring about the reign of His Most Sacred Heart.

I ask you to circulate *Mary's Message* [an audiotape] in Florida and the rosaries [meditations/messages] of December 13, 1996 and January 13, 1997. These messages were given to reveal insights into His Most Intimate Love. My appearance in Florida and the Shepherds of Christ Movement must be connected. Please work with great fervor to spread my messages and the message of my Son from this location. Do not be afraid. You will make great advances in helping with the completion of the Fatima Message there.

I am Mary your Mother. Please obey me and help me spread these materials there.[8]

ANALYSIS

Lying behind Our Lady of Clearwater is what might be called a non-neopentecostal Catholic charismatic leader. Ring, who has no ordination or theological training, brings direct messages from heaven. It might be objected that since she claims no originality for her messages she should properly be considered a virtuoso, rather than a charismatic figure. But, in fact, in a comparative perspective both what she delivers and how she is received by her followers argue that she should be placed at the charismatic end of the continuum.

What makes the movement distinctive is the lay spirituality it engenders. Virtually all of its public devotional life is in the hands of lay people, and Ring herself is a lay person. This is consistent with a larger shift in postmodernity, in which the religious individual becomes the arbiter of religious genuineness—or "spirituality." The devotionalism that surrounds Our Lady of Clearwater begins with individual visionaries. Jesus, Mary, God the Father give specific individuals specific messages. Although the Shepherds openly express in their publications their willingness to submit to "the Holy See," it is clearly not the Holy See's teachings about Catholic faith and practice at the turn of the millennium that are uppermost in Shepherd publications. Although Shepherds pray for holy priests, the mass itself is not the core of their spirituality: it is the rosary and individual devotion before the tabernacle (where the Blessed Sacrament [consecrated bread] is reserved). This might be called the "unstructured Church." On the one hand, the piety is clearly Catholic in style—evangelicals certainly do not say the rosary or pray before the tabernacle, nor is their devotional expression characterized by the degree of flatness that occurs in the worship at the site—but it is not corporate in the communal sense of the mass. And it is not directed by an official, professionally trained leadership cadre. Other than the messages, there is nothing that corresponds to preaching. The core images are the Sacred Heart of Jesus and the Immaculate Heart of Mary, both relatively recent devotional elaborations in the Roman church.

In addition, when Shepherds of Christ Ministries began "acquisition of the Mary Image Building in Clearwater, Florida for use as a center of spiritual renewal," they also stated:

We want to make this site available to people of all faiths for quiet prayer and reflection. Do we not all pray to the same Heavenly Father? Satan and his fallen angels (Rev. 12:17) fuel the division between men. We do not want to be instruments in their war against God by giving into feelings of hatred or division. We want this site to be a witness to God's love and a catalyst for conversion to God. We want to pray for peace! We want to help bring the Mother Mary's Fatima Mission to completion.[9]

Two things separate the attitude displayed here from that of traditionalism. First, the use of the phrase "spiritual renewal" rather than "renewal of the church" or "religious renewal" associates the movement with postmodern sensibilities—that is, "spirituality," rather than "religiosity," is clearly associated with postmodern individuation and the attenuation of structures of authority outside the self. Second, though certainly cast in the language of Catholic expression, the willingness to ask the question, "Do we not all pray to the same Heavenly Father?" implicitly legitimates religious pluralism. Though they clearly avoid saying all religions are equally good or true, they see all spirituality directed toward the same end, and oppose religious divisiveness. Other materials evidence a tolerance of different family styles: "married persons" and those in "intimate relationships" appear on an equal footing.

At the same time, there are three theological tendencies that associate this movement with postmodern religious reactions. First, there is a "dynamic dualism" in God's nature—that is, while God is incredibly loving, he is also angry at the world and will not continue to tolerate those who ignore him. Sins such as greed, corruption, lying, hatefulness, violence, and a lack of awareness of God's authority over creation will be punished, both in this world and the next. Specific historical occurrences (e.g., floods, currently occurring collapse of buildings, fires, etc.) are stated to be direct acts of God to reveal his displeasure. Second, there is a belief in a "living Satan" —that is, the belief that the world's problems are caused by the active, personal work of an empire of evil. Third, there is a belief that the world will end soon. This is particularly consistent with the Fatima manifestation, and also with Medjugorje. These theological themes may serve to create a new atmosphere of what Max Weber would term "salvation anxiety" in the minds of at least some of those who come to see the site, and hence dispose them to ethical reform.

Four important theoretical points about pilgrimage sites are in turn suggested by the Our Lady of Clearwater site:

First, although Victor Turner's analysis of pilgrimage sites—their liminality and the *communitas* that is generated thereby—is often disputed in anthropological analysis of established sites, this process does seem to occur at this site, which is in a formative state. Our Lady of Clearwater is antistructural in that there exists at the shrine "a state of unmediated and egalitarian association between individuals who are temporarily freed of the hierarchical secular roles and statuses which they bear in everyday life."[10] While it is not clear that this acts as the pilgrim's "fundamental motivation" in coming to the site—even less that of the tourist—nevertheless a radical egalitarianism characterizes the participants in the ritual life.

Second, consistent with its postmodern character, the site is relatively unique in the history of pilgrimage centers in that it lacks entirely a "sacred geography." Neither a natural formation (like a grotto) nor a deceased holy person interred in the ground creates "chthonic powers of the terrain."[11] The image is what it is: a functionally designed office building upon which Mary has chosen to appear to her faithful in the midst of high-technology multinational capitalism. Surrounded by a Toyota dealership, a car wash, a shopping area that includes large discount electronics and furniture stores, Our Lady of Clearwater is without connection to nature but arising from nature supernaturally.

Third, the holiness of the place is reinforced by the charisma of Ring. "[M]ythic discourse registers a shift in the notion of sacred centre, from a purely *place*-centered sacredness to one having to do with the inherent sanctity of a holy *person*." Ring is the charismatic cult leader who authenticates the apparition to the faithful. Thus in this site there is "the triad of 'person,' 'place,' and 'text' " that supplies "the co-ordinates" for the task of examining how the site is itself constructed as a "sacred centre."[12] Ring, the apparition, and the messages create an interpretative whole (*gestalt*) that removes the Our Lady of Clearwater site from the merely curious apparitional experience to one that takes on the crucial religious component of "meaning." Ring makes sense of the apparition, not on her own account, but as messenger of the divine. As Eade and Sallnow point out, "The charismatic individuals who are the foci of these cults embody a divine power which is in no way dependent on the church. . . . [A]dvocates of the new shrines have sought legitimation through the claim that it is through these individuals that the divine has chosen to intervene in order to persuade the laity to return

Photo 11. The Extraordinary and Ordinary Mingle in the Secular Commerce that Surrounds Our Lady of Clearwater. *William H. Swatos, Jr.*

to the true, traditional Catholicism."[13] Indeed, here we find laity praying for holy priests, a virtual standing on its head of popular Catholic piety of an earlier era, wherein holy priests were considered to be appropriate intercessors for sinful laity. Basically without priests, the Shepherds' devotees pray for priests—with Fr. Carter serving as a conduit between the movement and the institutional church.

Finally, whenever I have been present for devotional liturgies, three activities take place simultaneously: corporate recitation of the rosary and prescribed prayers, with the singing of hymns, by a group of people who remain for some period of time (though not without coming and going); private devotional acts, principally going to a kneeler before the image for prayer or the lighting of candles, by persons not participating in this activity; tourist photography, wherein people not participating in either corporate or personal devotionalism photograph either the site or specific persons who come with them to the site. All of this takes place in a way that is relatively structurally freewheeling. Site staff do try to provide those who attend the corporate activity with brochures, pamphlets, and inexpensive rosaries—though none of these is forced. A few young women on the staff appear to wear special garb (long white dresses, of soft fabric, more in a "hippie" or neo-Hindu style than a nun's habit). Men, who are fewer in number, appear to have no special dress. Loudspeakers, electronic keyboards, taped materials, and the like all form a part of the public devotionalism. This mixture of motivations and demonstrations, including what might be called "purely secular" tourism ("Here's Susie standing at the Mary Shrine in Clearwater. Now here's Susie at the beach."), along with the gift shop, all form a part of the site experience.

NOTES

1. John Eade and Michael J. Sallnow (eds.), *Contesting the Sacred: The Anthropology of Christian Pilgrimage* (London: Routledge, 1991), pp. 2–3.

2. On the role of Christmas in assisting in similarly providing miraculous contextualization for the "rescue" of the Cuban child Elian Gonzalez, see Thomas Hambrick-Stowe, "Go Down, Elian," *Religion in the News* (Summer 2000), pp. 10–11, 27.

3. See "Is Streator Image of Jesus a Miracle?" *Moline Daily Dispatch*, 12 May 1999, pp. A1–A2; "Image of Christ Appears on Church Door," *The Living Church*, 25 April 1999, p. 6.

4. Thomas Duggan, "Our Lady of Royal Oak: The Natural History of an Expressive Crowd," *Sociological Analysis* 51, pp. 83–89.

5. However, the site took no notice of revelation of the "third secret" of Fatima, in June 2000, which should have had the practical effect of muting much of the Marian apocalypticism associated with Fatima-inspired movements.

6. See Manuel A. Vásquez and Marie F. Marquardt, "Globalizing the Rainbow Madonna: Old Time Religion in the Present Age," *Theory, Culture & Society* 17, no. 4 (2000), pp. 119–143.

7. "Shepherds of Christ—Our Lady Clothed with the Sun," <http://www.sofc.org/marybook.htm> (28 September 1999).

8. "Shepherds of Christ Ministries: Virgin Mary on Former Bank," <http://www.sofc.org/news_1.htm> (28 September 1999).

9. "Mother Mary's Prayer Site,"<http://www.sofc.org/marypress.htm> (28 September 1999).

10. Eade and Sallnow, *Contesting the Sacred*, p. 4.

11. Ibid., pp. 6, 8.

12. Ibid., pp. 6, 9.

13. Ibid., p. 11.

Chapter 10

Kathmandu and Home Again: A Cautionary Tale

Richard Quinney

The year begins with a blizzard. Keeping ahead of the storm, my wife drives me to O'Hare airport for the afternoon flight to London. By evening there will be a foot of snow on the ground and temperatures will fall well below zero.

On the ride to O'Hare, we make joint resolutions for the new year. Something about mindfulness and the appreciation of life. I muse over the reasons for travel, in particular the purpose of this trip to India and Nepal. I say that travel is part of my daily work, rather than being a diversion from my life. I admit that I would welcome new thoughts and insights, that I am ready to have my sensibilities shaken up a bit, to be stimulated by something new. I go outward in order to travel inward. Spiritual renewal—the sense of being alive, the heightening of wonder—is always a blessing whenever and however it might come.

The wings of our airplane—a Boeing 777—are carefully deiced. Soon we are rolling down the runway marked by small blue lights in the snow; the engines roar, and we take to the air. The lights of Chicago flicker below, and we fly into the dark sky over the black waters of Lake Michigan. Airborne, I am on my way to other lands.

I have been to Hindu lands before—in mind and spirit. The Vedic texts have shaped my thought and daily life for the last twenty years. I am not now on a spiritual quest or on a pilgrimage to the Hindu temples. More likely this travel is to see the physical sites where the ancient wisdom is still practiced. I travel now as a tourist.

Over the Atlantic I read about the travels of others to India. Carl Jung, a previous traveler, is quoted in the book—Jeffery Paine's *Father India*—that I am reading on this flight: "I think, if you can afford it, a trip to India is on the whole most edifying and from a psychological point of view, most advisable, although it may give you considerable headaches."[1] Possibly this is a warning of things to come.

A day later I am sitting in the coffee shop of the Centaur Hotel near the Delhi international airport. It is four in the morning and I have had little sleep since leaving home. Already I am into the dust and haze of India, and an allergy that I had almost forgotten about has returned. There is a smell of mold in the room. A roach darts across the night table. I am still confused from the evening chaos at the airport. Yet, I expect very little, so that I might see and know the world as I am living it. And I will not be disappointed if, this time, there is nothing to be found.

Confusion, disorientation, and reorientation would be enough for this traveler. Jeffery Paine makes an observation about another traveler to India, Christopher Isherwood, on his life in Hollywood. "Doubt was his meat and uncertainty was his drink, and he was in a strange land."[2] My life is an experiment, guided by some practice, rather than something certain. Perhaps I have come this far to revive my doubts and my ambiguities. A holy mind is an open mind, a Buddhist master once told me. A small black-and-yellow antlike insect climbs up the edge of my napkin at the early morning table.

POKHARA

In a small airplane operated by Royal Nepal Airlines, we fly from Kathmandu to Pokhara. The great snow-capped Annapurna Himalayan mountains rise to our right as we fly west over the valleys and the foothills. Below are the villages and the terraced fields. My mentor of years ago, and co-author for the last forty years, has convinced me that I should accompany him to the places in Nepal and India that have been important to him all of his adult life. Much is being lost on me, already, as I suffer from jet lag, loss of sleep, and a persistent allergy. My bodily experience is dominating this trip, and I am feeling vulnerable and homesick. Another night comes. I will stay awake and pace the floor of the hotel.

In the morning sky, black kites, spreading wide their wings, soar over the town. White clouds drift across the sharp peak of Machhapuchare, the sacred mountain of Nepal. Facing the mountain, we take our breakfast in the dining room of the New Hotel Crystal. In the afternoon, we walk and photograph in the dusty streets and alleys of Pokhara. I note in my journal that evening that there are some places in the world that we need not visit. Not because of the places or the people, but because of who we are and why we, removed from the life of these places, visit as tourists. The unreality of this trip is becoming obvious to me.

If our lives were not so comfortable, we would not travel to Pokhara. I, myself, do not have a romantic need for the exotic, for the otherness, of the Third World. I have no desire to encounter, as Pico Iyer notes, the refuse of my own civilization dumped elsewhere.[3]

Before dinner, where we are watched over by attentive waiters, or guards, we take a walk along the street that runs west of the airport. This must be the street that Peter Matthiessen walked and described in his book, *The Snow Leopard*, before making his climb into the Himalayas:

These edges of Pokhara might be tropical outskirts anywhere—vacant children, listless adults, bent dogs and thin chickens in a litter of sagging shacks and rubble, mud, weeds, stagnant ditches, bad sweet smells, vivid bright broken plastic bits, and dirty fruit peelings awaiting the carrion pig; for want of better fare, both pigs and dogs consume the human excrement that lies everywhere along the paths.[4]

I decide that I will end my trip as soon as possible. I will make my escape when I return to Kathmandu. India and Nepal will always provide spiritual grounding for my life, but given my allergy, the physical conditions, and the problems of traveling as a tourist, I will worship from afar. I know enough of the world to realize that suffering of one kind or another exists everywhere. And I do not need to view the suffering of others as a tourist. My traveling companion will continue on his own pilgrimage. Properly reoriented and enlightened, I will return to my own borderland.

SACRED TEXTS

Through all the days of another season, I had read the ancient Sanskrit stories and scriptures in preparation for the well-lived life of body and spirit. I will interrupt my tale of travel to India and Nepal in order to convey what I learned from my exploration of these texts. Daily life seemed to be infused with the wisdom from another place.

My wanderings and writings for years have been filled with the search for a place I might call home. A stabilizing force—*a native state*—was found eventually in my study of the the *Bhagavad Gita* and the *Upanishads*. Affirmed in the dialogue between Sri Krishna and Arjuna is the reality that pervades the impermanence of each passing moment, of each passing life. Krishna, the divine within, instructs Arjuna: "Realize *that* which pervades the universe and is indestructible; no power can affect this unchanging, im-

Photo 12. New Hotel Crystal, Pokhara, Nepal. *Richard Quinney.*

Photo 13. A Different View of Pokhara, Nepal. *Richard Quinney.*

perishable reality. The body is mortal, but he who dwells in the body is immortal and immeasurable." And shortly after, Krishna adds: "Death is inevitable for the living; birth is inevitable for the dead. Since these are unavoidable, you should not sorrow. Every creature is unmanifested at first and then attains manifestation. What is to lament in this?"[5] Reality is in the eternal, and I can realize the eternal now, this day.

Secret Teachings

The journal on my desk, opened in the morning light, reminds me to come to attention. It is a bell of awareness, whether or not anything is written on the page. Its mere presence calls me to attention each morning. Looking back to an entry of several years ago, I reread lines from the eighth chapter of the *Bhagavad Gita*, alluding to that which is beyond even the formless and unmanifested: "Beyond this formless state there is another, unmanifested reality, which is *eternal* and is not dissolved when the cosmos is destroyed. Those who realize life's supreme goal know that I am unmanifested and unchanging. Having come *home* to me, they never return to separate existence." And I am reminded that "this supreme Lord who pervades all existence, the true Self of all creatures, may be realized through undivided love."[6]

Contained in my journal is the "secret teaching" revealed by Krishna. When there is love, the love of that which we may call God, there is peace, and we know that we will not perish. The purpose of all life is to realize the divine within, to know the eternal in the union with the unmanifested reality of the universe. This is our *native state*, realized daily in meditative awareness. Krishna speaks: "You can know me, see me, and attain union with me. Whoever makes me the supreme goal of all his work and acts without selfish attachment, who devotes himself to me completely and is free from ill will for any creature, enters into me."[7]

Renunciation

I had read portions of the *Bhagavad Gita* on renouncing the fruits of our actions. Krishna, speaking to Arjuna, advises: "You have the right to work, but never to the fruit of work. You should never engage in action for the sake of reward, nor should you long for inaction. Perform work in this world, Arjuna, as a man established within himself—without selfish attachments, and alike in success and defeat."[8] Our energies are directed to the action, not to the fruits of action. How could we know in advance what fruits our actions deserve? In surrendering attachment to results, we act in selfless service, in a stilling of the mind and an opening of the heart. We become one with all. Krishna says, "When a person has freed himself from attachment to the results of his work, and from desires for the enjoyment of sense objects, he ascends to the unitive state." What remains is to "renounce and enjoy," as one of the *Upanishads* advised long ago.[9]

I have gradually abandoned the desire to know with certainty all that is around me. I experience not so much the desire to know, but the peace of the inevitable mystery of it all. One now lives in wonder, and in the overwhelming compassion that comes from this wonder. Beyond knowing—in awareness—one is united with that which is formless and unchanging in the entire universe.

In answer to the question, "Who are you?" Krishna replies: "I am time, the destroyer of all; I have come to consume the world. Even without your participation, all the warriors gathered here will die." Beyond the duality of existence and nonexistence, there is that which is changeless and everlasting. Arjuna responds, in wonder: "You are the knower and the thing which is known. You are the final home; with your infinite form you pervade the cosmos."[10]

The search for peace in this life continues each day. Years of practice have made me know that home ultimately is to be found beyond the illusion of the self, in the realm of the larger Self, referred to throughout the *Bhagavad Gita*. The teaching is expressed in the Sanskrit words *tat tvam asi* (*Thou art that.*). The traveler is on the way toward oneness with the eternal Self.

Good Days

Every day is a good day when no distinction is made between good and bad. It is thought as much as an event that lights each day. Every day is a perfect day, a day of holiness, when no distinctions are made.

It is the distinction between life and death that I seek to erase in my daily living. We are born out of life, and we die into life. The life we know in our conscious being, while we are "alive," is life in its manifested form. Death is but a part of the continuity of life. As Philip Kapleau notes in his book *The Wheel of Life and Death*, "All life is life after death."[11] Nothing is lost in the universe. And the supreme Reality is the void, the formless, the unmanifested—an emptiness that we sometimes call God. We are, always, the unborn.

My true being, my *native state*, is a realm where death cannot reach. This is the secret teaching of the Hindu scriptures. In the *Katha Upanishad*, death is the teacher, and we learn:

> When all desires that surge in the heart
> Are renounced, the mortal becomes immortal.
> When all the knots that strangle the heart
> Are loosened, the mortal becomes immortal.
> This sums up the teaching of the scriptures.[12]

When death comes, the body is shed—as in taking off a jacket at the end of the day—and unity with life eternal is completed once more.

In the meantime, in our mortal, manifested form, we seek to end the fear of death. I am instructed by the *Taittiriya Upanishad*:

> When one realized the Self, in whom
> All is one, changeless, nameless, formless,
> Then one fears no more. Until we realize
> The unity of life, we live in fear.[13]

There is so much in our mortal life to which we remain attached. We want to hold onto the pleasures we know in our conscious, everyday lives. Beyond all the suffering of being human, brought about by our ego, there is the wondrous sense of being alive. But only as I begin to focus on my true nature—beyond birth and death—do I have some relief from the fear of dying.

To live is to die: that is my true nature. In an essay written near the end of his life, Karlfried Graf Dürckheim asked, and then exclaimed: "The eternal question is: How can we obey the living impulse of the Absolute within us? How can we attain the life that we ourselves are in the depths of our true nature? Only by dying!"[14] And there is assurance in the sacrifice we humans all must make in our oneness with others. "Physical death may be the supreme sacrifice that anyone can make in life's service—and the whole of life itself can be lived as a sacrifice in the service of others."[15] Our true nature is to live for all others, for plants, animals, and stones as well—to be one with all that is.

This mortal, earthly life is increasingly being lived in a relaxation of the tension between my ego nature and my true nature. I know that my ego nature has a beginning and an end. But in my true nature, there is no birth and no death. There is only life, always and eternal, in my native state. Each day of my mortal existence can be lived with an awareness of my true nature. The formless is in the formed, and the formed is in the formless. As the Heart Sutra instructs, "Form is emptiness, emptiness is form, form does not differ from emptiness, emptiness does not differ from form."[16]

Looking down into the gently flowing river, I see delicate bubbles forming on the surface. Each bubble lasts its time, and disappears into the flowing water from which it came. Everything changes, but the river flows on.

Photo 14. Retreat from Kathmandu, Nepal. *Richard Quinney.*

What is there to gain? Where is there to go? Such were the thoughts—such were the beliefs—I had that other season some time ago.

RETREAT

About to make my retreat from Kathmandu, I am told that next time I should read the travel guides more carefully. On the airplane from Pokhara, before riding to the center of Kathmandu in a taxi along the narrow streets, with handkerchief pressed to my face, I have read the description in the Lonely Planet guidebook:

For many people, arriving in Kathmandu is as shocking as stepping out of a time machine—the sights, sounds and smells can lead to sensory overload. There are narrow streets and lanes with carved wooden balconies above tiny hole-in-the-wall shops, town squares packed with extraordinary temples and monuments, markets bright with fruit and vegetables and a constant throng of humanity. Then there's the choking dust and fumes, stinking gutters, concrete monstrosities, touts, Coca-Cola billboards and maimed beggars.[17]

Reaching the Yak and Yeti Hotel for the anticipated days and nights in Kathmandu, I immediately take the taxi back to the airport. With ingenuity and the skill I had forgotten I possessed, I find a flight to Delhi on Indian Airlines. After a night in Delhi, I wait as a standby for the afternoon flight to London.

For ten hours at forty thousand feet on Air Canada, I fly over the deserts and mountains of many countries. Near the end of the flight to London, I am transported by the music video being played on the monitor above me—Natalie Merchant singing "Break Your Heart": "I know that it will break your heart the way things are—and the way they have been. . . . It's enough to make you lose your mind."[18] Arriving in the evening at Heathrow, I am ready for a good night's sleep at the Forte Crest.

The next morning I take the underground to the center of London. I have a full English breakfast at Charing Cross, and spend the morning at the National Gallery where I stand for a long time before Caravaggio's *The Supper at Emmaus*. At noon I go to St. Martin in the Fields to hear a Russian pianist play Rameau, Bach, and Beethoven. At the National Portrait Gallery, later in the afternoon, I see Richard Avedon's photograph of W. H. Auden. Back at the Forte Crest in the evening, I watch the programs on BBC.

The next morning I am on the United flight to Chicago. With nothing to declare, I pass through customs and find my wife waiting to take us home.

HOME AGAIN

The end of the winter month, and we have had several nights of thawing snow and gentle rain. This is the time, as Aldo Leopold described it fifty years ago in *A Sand County Almanac*, "when the tinkle of dripping water is heard in the land."[19] Animals stir from their sleep; I see the opossum scurry under the wooden fence in the backyard. By day, three squirrels climb along the limbs of the maple tree. Chickadees, sparrows, and juncos forage among the wet seeds thrown earlier across the patio. A brown creeper probes the bark of another tree. Yesterday, a pair of robins rested in the hawthorne bush. And this morning, starlings are chirping somewhere in the chimney. The curiosity of this observer stirs with the winter thaw. I am home again.

POSTSCRIPT

Pilgrimage is as much travel in time as it is travel in space. All pilgrimage takes place in the passing of time; the pilgrim grows older in the course of the journey. Wherever the pilgrim may be going geographically, he or she is ultimately a traveler in time.

Our pilgrim of the foregoing tale—the one who studied and practiced the ancient Vedic wisdom, the one who traveled to India and Nepal—began his pilgrimage in search of the mystical realm where all things are one. The quest gradually changed, however, from the desire for things not seen to something that was concrete and already here. The living of everyday life with some degree of attention and awareness replaced the pilgrimage to higher realms. The pilgrim, in other words, ceased being a pilgrim when he became immersed in the details of the daily life he already had.

This is not to say that the earlier pilgrimage—and travel to sacred places—became irrelevant to the life of the pilgrim. Maybe his current life exists because of the pilgrimage. Maybe the earlier consciousness still provides the background of his universe. But any of this searching and traveling, he would tell you now, seems long ago and far away.

There is nothing like illness—the failing of the body—to bring you home again. The esoteric wisdom of the oneness of life and death no longer makes daily sense to our pilgrim, nor does it provide solace in the face of mortality. He had known for many years that the blood disease was growing within his body, and perhaps his earlier travel and pilgrimage had been with hope of preparation for ultimate times. But once the disease progressed and chemical treatments began, other resources more existential in nature were called upon: science and medicine, clinical care, love and friendship, the skill to be alone, and some courage.

Photo 15. South Branch of the Kishwaukee River, DeKalb, Illinois. *Richard Quinney.*

You could call what is happening in the pilgrim's life another kind of pilgrimage. But our pilgrim prefers not to, saying that life itself is enough. He would say, also, not to look for any universal truths in his tale of travel and pilgrimage, that any truth is in the particular life as lived daily. He would say, if he were to use religious terms, that God is in the details.

As in the allegory of ox herding, the end of the search begins where one started from. Gone now are the ox and the ox herder. Confusion has dissipated and there are times of equanimity. Even the idea of holiness—even the Buddha—has vanished. As before the long quest for enlightenment began, mountains are mountains and rivers are rivers. There is no need to strive: entertain an open heart and open mind, know compassion toward all beings, extend a helping hand. One lives an ordinary life—free of pilgrimage.

NOTES

1. Jeffery Paine, *Father India: How Encounters with an Ancient Culture Transformed the West* (New York: HarperCollins, 1998), p. 109.

2. Ibid., p. 206.

3. Pico Iyer, *Video Night in Kathmandu* (New York: Knopf, 1988).

4. Peter Matthiessen, *The Snow Leopard* (New York: Viking, 1978), p. 11.

5. *Bhagavad Gita* (Petaluma, CA: Nilgiri Press, 1985), pp. 63–64.

6. Ibid., p. 126.

7. Ibid., p. 157.

8. Ibid., p. 66.

9. *Upanishads* (Petaluma, CA: Nilgiri Press, 1987), pp. 208–212.

10. *Bhagavad Gita*, pp. 154–155.

11. Philip Kapleau, *The Wheel of Life and Death* (New York: Doubleday, 1989), p. 285.

12. *Upanishads*, p. 97.

13. Ibid., p. 144.

14. Karlfried Graf Dürckheim, "The Voice of the Master," *Parabola* 15 (August 1990), p. 12.

15. Ibid., p. 10.

16. Nhat Thich Hanh, *The Heart of Understanding: Commentaries on the Prajñaparamita Heart Sutra* (Berkeley: Paralla Press, 1988), p. 1.

17. Hugh Finlay, Richard Everist, and Tony Wheeler, *Nepal* (Victoria, Australia: Lonely Planet, 1996), p. 130.

18. Natalie Merchant, "Break My Heart," © 1998 Indian Love Brid / ASCAP.

19. Aldo Leopold, *A Sand County Almanac* (New York: Oxford University Press, 1966 [1949]), p. 3.

Epilogue: Pilgrimage for a New Millennium

William H. Swatos, Jr., and Luigi Tomasi

A pilgrimage is a journey undertaken for religious purposes that culminates in a visit to a "holy place," one considered to be the locus of supernatural forces and where divine intervention may be more easily forthcoming. The usages and rituals associated with the phenomenon of pilgrimage are present in all the ancient religions and in those still professed today in the world, not only in the great religious cycles, but also in so-called primitive cults, on the one hand, and new religions, on the other. Moreover, the pilgrimage lives on, assuming substantially parareligious features, in contemporary political and popular cultural contexts.

From the eighth century onward, pilgrimage for essentially penitential purposes grew increasingly widespread: given its expiatory function, the journey was to be arduous and dangerous, and that to Jerusalem certainly fulfilled these criteria. After the eleventh century, a great new pilgrimage, to Santiago de Compostela in Galicia, assumed prime importance. This was a crucial development as regards the organization of routes, the founding of sanctuaries and markets, and the creation of a common European epic-legendary language, that of the *chansons de geste*. With the Jubilee of 1300, following the decline of Santiago and Jerusalem's return to the Saracens due to the failure of the Crusades, the popes proposed pilgrimage to Rome to Western Christians.

Simultaneously, or a little later, other minor places of pilgrimage sprang up, often along the itineraries linking the larger centers of pilgrimage.

These were usually the sites of relics and celebrated apparitions. Famous in the Middle Ages were the Marian shrines often situated in inaccessible and ancient places of worship and testifying to the persistence of profound beliefs unaffected by the changing nature of official religions. Distinctive of a mass religiosity of remote origin but still vigorously alive, pilgrimages played a social role of prime importance in prompting road building, the opening of hospices, and the creation of markets.

Much has changed from then until now, yet a scanning of travel and tourist literature, popular religious periodicals, and the general press indicates that "pilgrimage" has become renewed as a way of conceptualizing a style of travel experience. The term at once conjoins explicit and implicit religion, and embodies a new spirit of globalization.

Travel has become a pastime. But there is also a new "spirituality" in advanced industrial society (or postmodernity) that values personal *experience* as a key to religious meaningfulness. The visit to a putatively holy site is an experiential way of "touching" the numinous. Yet it does so no longer in a context of authoritative exposition, but rather as subjective encounter, with the interpretation supplied not from outside but from inside. The pilgrim experience and the religious tour blend. They are not historically discontinuous, however, as much as reinterpreted. As we study religions up until modern times, we see that pilgrimage was a major religious "style of life." Looked at across the *longue durée*, it may well be argued that the modern era of rationally organized congregational religiosity is in fact the deviant case. Hence, we should anticipate that the pilgrim tourist and the tourist pilgrim will continue to grow anew into the coming centuries.

Selected Bibliography

Adler, Judith. 1989. "Travel as Performed Art." *American Journal of Sociology* 94: 1366–1391.

Boorstin, Daniel. 1964. *The Image: A Guide to Pseudo Events in America.* New York: Harper & Row.

Brown, Mick. 1998. *The Spiritual Tourist: A Personal Odyssey through the Outer Reaches of Belief.* London: Bloomsbury.

Campo, Juan Eduardo. 1998. "American Pilgrimage Landscapes." *Annals of the American Academy of Political and Social Science* 558: 40–54.

Cohen, Erik. 1984. "The Sociology of Tourism: Approaches, Issues and Findings." *Annual Review of Sociology* 10: 373–392.

Coleman, Simon, and John Elsner. 1995. *Pilgrimage Past and Present: Sacred Travel and Sacred Space in the World Religions.* London: British Museum Press.

Davidson, Linda Kay, and Maryjane Dunn-Wood. 1993. *Pilgrimage in the Middle Ages: A Research Guide.* New York: Garland.

Davie, Grace. 2000. *Religion in Modern Europe: A Memory Mutates.* Oxford: Oxford University Press.

Eade, John, and Michael J. Sallnow (eds.). 1991. *Contesting the Sacred: The Anthropology of Christian Pilgrimage.* London: Routledge.

Ferrarotti, Franco. 1999. *Partire, tornare: Viaggiatori e pellegrini all fine del millennio.* Rome: Laterza.

Frey, Nancy Louise. 1998. *Pilgrim Stories: On and Off the Road to Santiago.* Berkeley: University of California Press.

Grayburn, Nelson H. H. (ed.). 2001. "Relocating the Tourist." *International Sociology* 16: 147–239.

Hervieu-Léger, Danièle. 2000. *Religion as a Chain of Memory*. Cambridge: Polity Press.

MacCannell, Dean. 1976. *The Tourist: A New Theory of the Leisure Class*. New York: Schocken.

———. 1992. *Empty Meeting Grounds: The Tourist Papers*. New York: Routledge.

Macioti, Maria I. 2000. *Pellegrinaggi e giubilei: I lugohi del culto*. Rome: Laterza.

Nolan, Mary Lee, and Sidney Nolan. 1989. *Christian Pilgrimage in Modern Western Europe*. Chapel Hill: University of North Carolina Press.

Nuryanti, Wiendu. 1996. "Heritage and Postmodern Tourism." *Annals of Tourism Research* 23: 249–260.

Ousterhout, Robert (ed.). 1990. *The Blessings of Pilgrimage*. Urbana: University of Illinois Press.

Rinschede, Gisbert. 1992. "Forms of Religious Tourism." *Annals of Tourism Research* 19: 51–67.

Smith, Valene L. (ed.). 1977. *Hosts and Guests: The Anthropology of Tourism*. Philadelphia: University of Pennsylvania Press.

Stoddard, Robert H., and E. Alan Morinis (eds.). 1999. *Sacred Places, Sacred Spaces: The Geography of Pilgrimages*. Baton Rouge, LA: Geoscience Publications.

Sumption, Jonathan. 1975. *Pilgrimage: An Image of Mediaeval Religion*. Totowa, NJ: Rowman & Littlefield.

Swatos, William H., Jr. 1999. "Revisiting the Sacred." *Implicit Religion* 2: 33–38.

Swatos, William H., Jr., and Daniel V. A. Olson. 2000. *The Secularization Debate*. Lanham, MD.: Rowman & Littlefield.

Tomasi, Luigi. 1998. "Pilgrimage/Tourism." In *Encyclopedia of Religion and Society*, edited by William H. Swatos, Jr., pp. 362–364. Walnut Creek, CA: AltaMira.

Turner, Victor W. 1969. *The Ritual Process: Structure and Anti-Structure*. Chicago: Aldine.

———. 1974. *Dramas, Fields and Metaphors: Symbolic Action in Human Society*. Ithaca, NY: Cornell University Press.

Turner, Victor W., and Edith Turner. 1978. *Image and Pilgrimage in Christian Culture: Anthropological Perspectives*. New York: Columbia University Press.

Van Gennep. Arnold van. 1965 [1908]. *The Rites of Passage*. London: Routledge.

Voyé, Liliane. 1973. *Sociologie du geste religieux*. Brussels: EVO.

Webb, Diana. 1999. *Pilgrims and Pilgrimage in the Medieval West*. New York: Taurus.

Westwood, Jennifer. 1997. *Sacred Journeys: Paths for the New Pilgrim*. London: Gaia Books.

Index

About the Contributors

Primarily a sociologist of tourism and art, JUDITH ADLER, who completed her Ph.D. at Brandeis, is an associate professor of sociology at Memorial University, St. John's, Newfoundland. Her publications include *Artists in Offices* (1979), and an *American Journal of Sociology* article, "Travel as Performed Art."

ANTHONY J. BLASI is a member of the sociology faculty at Tennessee State University (Nashville) and has served as president of the Association for the Sociology of Religion. He has published extensively in the sociology of religion. His most recent work focuses on the sociology of the New Testament and early Christianity, as evidenced in the compendium *Early Christianity and the Social Sciences*, which he has co-edited with Paul-André Turcotte and Jean Duhaime (2002).

LUTZ KAELBER is assistant professor of sociology at the University of Vermont. His first book, *Schools of Asceticism: Ideology and Organization in Medieval Religious Communities*, received the American Sociological Association's Sociology of Religion Section's Outstanding Book Award in 1999.

MARIA I. MACIOTI is professor of Sociology at the Third University of Rome. She has written on new religious movements and on the sociology of religion. She has most recently published *Pellegrinaggi e giubilei* (*Pilgrimage and Jubilee* [2000]).

RICHARD QUINNEY is professor of sociology at Northern Illinois University. After a distinguished career in criminology that included the American Criminological Society's Edward Sutherland Award, he turned in the 1980s to work in the sociology of religion, accompanied by photography and autobiographical reflection. This is evidenced in his books *Journey to a Far Place* (1991), *For the Time Being* (1998), and *Borderland* (2001).

WILLIAM H. SWATOS, JR., is executive officer of the Association for the Sociology of Religion and also of the Religious Research Association. He is author or co-author, and/or editor or co-editor, of approximately twenty books, including the *Encyclopedia of Religion and Society* (1998). His most recent book is the co-edited volume *The Secularization Debate* (2000). With Kevin J. Christiano and Peter Kivisto, he has completed a new textbook, *Sociology of Religion: Contemporary Developments* (2002).

LUIGI TOMASI is professor of sociology and president of the Centre for Euroasian Studies at the University of Trento, and has a continuing relationship with the Royal University of Phenom Phen, Cambodia. He has written or edited approximately two dozen books in the history of sociology, the sociology of religion, and the sociology of youth. His most recent edited volume is *New Directions in Sociological Theory and Research: The Frontiers of Sociology at the Beginning of the Twenty-First Century* (2001).

LILIANE VOYÉ has had a distinguished career in the sociology of religion as a member of the faculty of the Université Catholique de Louvain, Belgium, which culminated in her election as president of the International Society for the Sociology of Religion in the late 1990s. Beginning with her *Sociologie du geste religieux* (1973), she has made an ongoing contribution to the sociology of religion in Western Europe.

The author of *The Emerging Network: A Sociology of the New Age and Neo-Pagan Movements* (1995), MICHAEL YORK is research fellow at Bath Spa University College in the United Kingdom. He coordinates the Bath Archive for Contemporary Religious Affairs, housed in Corsham Court, serves as director of the Amsterdam Center for Eurindic Studies in the Netherlands, and as co-director of the Academy for Cultural and Educational Studies in London.